A MAXWELL SROGE REPORT

The United States

Mail Order Industry

BUSINESS ONE IRWIN

Homewood, Illinois 60430

This publication is designed to provide accurate and
authoritative information in regard to the subject matter
covered. It is sold with the understanding that neither the
author nor the publisher is engaged in rendering legal, accounting,
or other professional service. If legal advice or other expert
assistance is required, the services of a competent
professional person should be sought.

*From a Declaration of Principles jointly adopted by a Committee
of the American Bar Association and a Committee of Publishers.*

Sponsoring editor: Cynthia A. Zigmund
Project editor: Karen J. Nelson
Production manager: Ann Cassady
Printer: Arcata Graphics/Kingsport

Library of Congress Cataloging-in-Publication Data

The United States mail order industry / Maxwell
  Sroge Publishing
       p.   cm.
    ISBN 1–55623–486–4
    1. Mail-order business—United States—Statistics.   2. Direct
marketing—United States—Statistics.   I. Maxwell Sroge Publishing
(Firm)
HF5466.U49   1991
381 ' . 142 ' 0973021—dc20   91–428

Printed in the United States of America

1 2 3 4 5 6 7 8 9 0 AGK 8 7 6 5 4 3 2 1

The United States Mail Order Industry

Author:	Maxwell Sroge
Editor:	Ann Keeton
Research Editor:	Alice Kimsey
Editorial Researchers:	Chris Andresen
	Mario Kroll
	Scott Love
Art and Production:	Sherri Munns

In addition to research by our own staff, we would like to express our appreciation to the many people at the following organizations who contributed to the completion of this book:

Advertising Age
Adweek Magazine
AT&T
Australian Direct Marketing Association
British Direct Marketing Association
California State Board of Equalization
Canadian Direct Marketing Association
Consumer Resource Institute
Danish Direct Marketing Association
Deutscher Direktmarketing Verband
Direct Marketing Instituut Nederland
Direct Marketing Services International
Direct Marketing Association
Dow Jones
Equifax Inc.
Fraud & Theft Information Bureau
Hanson Publishing Group
Impact Resources, Inc.
Inbound/Outbound Magazine
JAMI Marketing Services, Inc.
McCann-Erickson
Mill Hollow Corporation
National Consumers League
North Dakota Tax Department
Placewares
Schweitzerischer Verband fuer Diretmarketing
Simmons Market Research Bureau
Spiegel
Standard and Poor's
T. J. Litle & Company
Time Warner Inc.
United States Bureau of Economic Analysis
United States Postal Service
United States Bureau of the Census
United States Government Printing Office
United States Bureau of Labor Statistics

MAXWELL H. SROGE

Maxwell H. Sroge is founder and President of Maxwell Sroge Publishing, a leading source and repository of information on the U.S. mail order industry and catalog marketing. He is also president of Marke/Sroge Communications, the Chicago based subsidiary of a leading catalog development firm specializing in business-to-business and consumer catalogs. As president of Maxwell Sroge Company, he is one of the leading catalog consultants in the country.

Mr. Sroge's business career began in 1950 when he joined Bell & Howell Company as a district salesman. During the 14 years he spent with Bell & Howell, he rose to the positions of director of sales, director of product planning, and president of the mail order subsidiary he established. At the age of twenty-seven, he was the youngest sales manager in Bell & Howell's seventy-year history.

In 1966 he formed his own mail order marketing services firm, but retained his association with Bell & Howell as a marketing consultant. In 1970 he created Maxwell Sroge Company/Consulting Group -- a first for the direct marketing industry -- to conceive and develop new direct marketing businesses into operational activities.

Sroge compiled and published the first statistical report on the mail order business in 1972. This work, now referred to as the U.S. Mail Order Industry Annual Report, has been quoted by every major business publication in the country.

To serve the industry's growing needs for statistical and other information, he founded Maxwell Sroge Publishing in 1977. Headquartered in Colorado Springs, Maxwell Sroge Publishing gathers data and publishes a variety of newsletters, seminars and special reports, all directed to the mail order and direct marketing industry. Other books published include Inside The Leading Mail Order Houses, How To Create Successful Catalogs and 101 Tips for More Profitable Catalogs.

Active in industry affairs, Maxwell Sroge assisted in the development of the Direct Marketing Association's Standards of Practice, has organized seminars in financial planning and analysis, and conducts seminars throughout the country on catalog marketing.

Featured speaker for a wide variety of clubs, universities and association conferences in the United States and abroad, he was voted the most outstanding speaker to have appeared before the Chicago Association of Direct Marketing. His articles and speeches have been reprinted in numerous U.S. and foreign publications.

His firm is the winner of the DMA Gold Mailbox Award for Best Direct Mail Campaign and the Gold Carrier Pigeon International Award.

A mid-westerner since 1950, he was born in New York and attended City College of New York and New York University.

Mr. Sroge is listed in Who's Who in America, Who's Who in Industry, Who's Who in the Midwest and Who's Who in Advertising.

Preface

Every day questions come to us by mail and phone, from investment bankers, newspapers, consultants, associations, investors and researchers of all types.

How big is the mail order business? Who are the leading companies? How much business is done in apparel? How big is the computer supplies and accessories mail order business? Why is mail order growing?

To serve your needs and theirs, this book, "The United States Mail Order Industry" was created.

In 1972, recognizing the need for statistical data on the mail order business, we researched and published the first U.S. Mail Order Industry Annual Report. From that first 4-page effort, it has grown to "The United States Mail Order Industry:" the finest, most complete product of its type we have ever produced.

We are proud that the facts and figures developed by us over the years have become the accepted data on mail order. Not only the business community, but members of Congress, the Postal Service, The U.S. Department of Commerce and government agencies worldwide have come to rely on this information.

No matter what your reason for seeking information on the mail order industry, you will find "The United States Mail Order Industry" a valuable and reliable source.

Our company is uniquely positioned to collect, analyze and report this information to you. As a result of our consulting work and our publication of such books as "Inside the Leading Mail Order Houses" and "How To Create Successful Catalogs", as well as our newsletters "Non-Store Marketing Report" and "The Catalog Marketer," our researchers and editors are in close touch with sources unavailable or unknown to many others. The great care and thought exercised in the preparation and presentation of this information has resulted in these "estimates" becoming reliable reference when seeking information, planning and when used as supportive material.

Whether you are Vice President in charge of Corporate Development for a multi-billion dollar company or an entrepreneur with a dream, we have developed "The United States Mail Order Industry" to be your reliable guide to this fast growing method of distribution -- mail order.

To the hundreds of data sources who contributed to this volume, our "thanks . . ." To the staff of Maxwell Sroge Publishing, Inc., my deep appreciation for this "best ever" report. And to the thousands who will use this data, our hope that it will serve you well.

Maxwell Sroge
Chicago, Illinois

The United States

Mail Order Industry

7. MAJOR FACTORS AFFECTING MAIL ORDER GROWTH 69

8. MAIL ORDER BUSINESSES 95

Chapter 1

Primary

Mail Order

Industry

Statistics

THE GROWTH OF MAIL ORDER

Mail order and direct marketing, including consumer and business-to-business markets, is one of the fastest growing industries in the United States. The decade of the eighties saw mail order evolve, due to both internal and external causes, from an alternative marketing vehicle for retailers and direct sales forces to an important legitimate, profitable marketing medium in its own right. As socioeconomic trends turned towards two-income families and single households, and as discretionary income increased, many consumers turned to the convenience and availability of mail order. Communication channels in the eighties opened new possibilities for direct marketers in reaching consumers and technological advances allowed direct marketers to better target, serve, and sell to consumers. The office place experienced similar transitions; in the eighties, many businesses turned to mail order as a cost effective way to buy supplies, services, and increase efficiency. Mail order proved resilient in the 1982 recession and weathered the stock market storms of 1981 and 1987 as well. Despite its resilience, competition within the industry is increasing and costs are rising, forcing mail order marketers to streamline operations and respond more fully to buyers' needs. Mail order growth in the late eighties has had to overcome rising costs, competition, and its own proportional size. (A company which does $1000 in business can grow at 50 percent, while a company which brings in $100 million may only grow by 10-15 percent annually -- both represent large, healthy growth.) As the nation enters the 1990s, mail order is capturing an increasing share of the retail market with no ceiling in sight.

Consumer and Business-to-Business Mail Order

The late eighties showed steady sales growth in mail order as the industry as a whole continued to grow at the rate of nearly double over-the-counter retail business. During the recession of the early eighties, mail order revenues and growth continued to increase, while profits suffered. The mail order industry experienced a catalog boom in the middle eighties which tapered off by the end of the decade as the national market place cooled and competition and costs rose.

The chart on page 4 shows the volume of mail order sales of consumer and business-to-business goods and services, and their corresponding rates of growth, in the United States over the past ten years. For comparative purposes, the sales and growth rates for general merchandise, total department stores, and retail operations for non-durable goods have been included.

General Merchandise

In the general merchandise category, Maxwell Sroge Publishing has reported "General Merchandise, Apparel, Furnishings" (GAF) totals. These figures include the sales volume of general merchandise, chain and variety stores, plus stores in the following merchandise groups: books, cameras/photography, jewelry, sporting goods, hobbies, gifts, luggage and sewing. By compiling data on total revenues for marketers in these merchandise groups, the Department of Commerce has included a substantial percentage of mail order sales in GAF. This duplicates a portion of revenues attributable to mail order operations (exclusive of in-store sales) which Maxwell Sroge Publishing reports independently as part of "Mail Order" totals.

Department Stores

As in its measurement of the GAF, the Department of Commerce has reported total merchandise sales by department stores. For a number of department stores, this includes revenues from both retail and mail order operations. The mail order segment of total annual department store sales is included independently (exclusive of retail revenues) in "Mail Order" totals.

Non-Durable Goods

Total U.S. retail sales of non-durable goods is an overall retail classification most closely related to the vast, diverse mix of merchandise sold by mail order marketers. The Department of Commerce concurs, as their break-down of non-durable goods sales includes the Standard Industrial Classification labeled "Mail Order". For Department of Commerce purposes, this classification covers companies which market exclusively through mail. Maxwell Sroge Publishing contends that due to the Department of Commerce's reporting of mail order revenues included in retail store aggregates under other merchandise classifications (as indicated above), its "Mail Order" total (currently at $17,115,000,000) is a highly inaccurate measure of the industry.

Participating Companies

It is estimated that more than 19,000 firms and organizations used direct mail promotions and mail order channels for the marketing and distribution of goods and services in the United States in 1989. Of that total, roughly 40 percent, or 8,000 companies, market goods and services through catalogs.

MAIL ORDER VS RETAIL SALES

Sales, Billion $	1979	1980	1981
Consumer Mail Order	$25.78	$28.75	$31.56
Business to Business MO		$17.58	$18.68
General Merchandise (GAF)	$219.09	$232.63	$254.35
Retail Sales	$896.84	$957.35	$1,038.70
Department Stores	$89.24	$93.19	$103.52
Non-Durable Goods	$589.86	$658.13	$713.89

	1982	1983	1984
Consumer Mail Order	$34.07	$37.43	$41.42
Business to Business MO	$19.77	$23.12	$27.50
General Merchandise (GAF)	$261.50	$287.54	$317.79
Retail Sales	$1,069.28	$1,167.93	$1,281.66
Department Stores	$107.16	$116.38	$128.83
Non-Durable Goods	$733.12	$777.05	$827.82

	1985	1986	1987
Consumer Mail Order	$45.30	$49.70	$54.20
Business to Business MO	$31.05	$34.91	$43.09
General Merchandise (GAF)	$341.07	$368.84	$394.30
Retail Sales	$1,365.85	$1,435.95	$1,521.41
Department Stores	$134.89	$142.78	$151.91
Non-Durable Goods	$869.20	$897.62	$948.93

	1988	1989
Consumer Mail Order	$63.50	$73.00
Business to Business MO	$53.22	$64.90
General Merchandise (GAF)	$418.71	$466.36
Retail Sales	$1,629.15	$1,737.73
Department Stores	$158.57	$176.57
Non-Durable Goods	$1,000.61	$1,078.76

Exhibit 1A   Maxwell Sroge Publishing

MAIL ORDER VS RETAIL SALES

Percent of Change	1979-80	1980-81	1981-82
Consumer Mail Order	11.5%	9.8%	8.0%
Business to Business MO	11.6%	6.3%	5.8%
General Merchandise (GAF)	6.2%	9.3%	2.8%
Retail Sales	6.7%	8.5%	2.9%
Department Stores	4.4%	11.1%	3.5%
Non-Durable Goods	11.6%	8.5%	2.7%

	1982-83	1983-84	1984-85
Consumer Mail Order	9.9%	10.7%	9.4%
Business to Business MO	16.9%	18.9%	12.9%
General Merchandise (GAF)	10.0%	10.5%	7.3%
Retail Sales	9.2%	9.7%	6.6%
Department Stores	8.6%	10.7%	4.7%
Non-Durable Goods	6.0%	6.5%	5.0%

	1985-86	1986-87	1987-88
Consumer Mail Order	9.7%	9.1%	17.2%
Business to Business MO	12.4%	23.5%	23.5%
General Merchandise (GAF)	8.1%	6.9%	6.2%
Retail Sales	5.1%	6.0%	7.1%
Department Stores	5.8%	6.4%	4.4%
Non-Durable Goods	3.3%	5.7%	5.4%

	1988-89
Consumer Mail Order	15.0%
Business to Business MO	21.9%
General Merchandise (GAF)	11.4%
Retail Sales	6.7%
Department Stores	11.4%
Non-Durable Goods	7.8%

Exhibit 1A   Maxwell Sroge Publishing

Chapter 2

Direct Marketing

To

Consumers

THE CONSUMER MARKET

The past decade witnessed remarkable growth in consumer direct marketing. As family units moved from traditional to two income households, shopping time decreased and efficiency became necessity. While people had less time to shop in the eighties, discretionary income increased in the middle part of the decade, fueling mail order sales. Later in the decade, a sensitive economy placed greater demands on direct marketers both to fine-tune their operations and respond to tighter consumer budgets. Direct marketers were forced to focus on better targeting strategies rather than on wider exposure.

Today's marketers are able to better manage mailing list databases and are discovering new vehicles to promote products. The eighties saw the advent of video and cable marketing, along with computer marketing through "software catalogs" and networks. As the nation enters the nineties, in-home shopping becomes more attractive to consumers both for browsing and specific purchase needs; the potential for mail order growth in the nineties and beyond is almost unlimited as consumers search for more efficient, responsive shopping avenues.

Projected Growth in Consumer Mail Order Sales

The following chart indicates historic growth and projections for consumer mail order sales, in terms of total volume and per capita expenditures. Consumer mail order revenues are expected to reach $91.5 billion in 1991, and may top $100 billion in 1992.

Projected Consumer Mail Order Growth Chart

(in billion $)	1988	1989	1990	1991	1992	1993
Total Volume	$ 63.5	$ 73.0	$ 81.7	$ 91.5	$102.5	$114.8
Per Capita Sales	$258	$294	$336	$362	$403	$448

Consumer Breakdown by Product Segment

In the consumer marketplace, mail order is becoming a more viable and desireable vehicle for selling and buying. As American social and economic trends change, mail order is increasingly filling the needs of individuals. Mail order has moved from an "alternative" to a need and finally to a preference.

The following chart shows the estimated total volume of consumer goods and services purchased by mail broken down into representative individual product categories. Growth rates and the proportion to total mail order sales are included.

MAIL ORDER SALES TO CONSUMERS

BILLIONS $	1980	%CHANGE
Apparel	1.478	5.1%
Auto Clubs	0.900	3.1%
Automotive	0.198	0.7%
Books	1.531	5.3%
Collectibles	1.015	3.5%
Cosmetics	0.176	0.6%
Crafts	0.577	2.0%
Educational Services	0.430	1.5%
Electronic Goods	0.364	1.3%
Food	0.550	1.9%
Gardening/Horticultural	0.414	1.4%
Gen Mdse/Housewares/Gift	2.978	10.3%
Health/Nutrition	0.469	1.6%
Insurance/Financial	4.412	15.3%
Jewelry	0.121	0.4%
Magazines	2.096	7.3%
Photofinishing	0.400	1.4%
Prescriptions	0.165	0.6%
Records & Tapes	0.459	1.6%
Sporting Goods	0.860	2.3%
Tools/Home Repair	0.331	1.1%
Major Catalog Retailers	5.026	17.5%
Department Stores	2.688	9.4%
Unclassified Mdse	1.108	3.9%
TOTAL CONSUMER SALES	28.746	

          Maxwell Sroge Publishing

MAIL ORDER SALES TO CONSUMERS (continued)

BILLIONS $	1981	%CHANGE	%MO
Apparel	1.729	17.0%	5.5%
Auto Clubs	1.035	15.0%	3.3%
Automotive	0.242	22.2%	0.8%
Books	1.699	11.0%	5.4%
Collectibles	1.167	15.0%	3.7%
Cosmetics	0.204	15.9%	0.6%
Crafts	0.646	12.0%	2.0%
Educational Services	0.469	9.1%	1.5%
Electronic Goods	0.510	40.1%	1.6%
Food	0.594	8.0%	1.9%
Gardening/Horticultural	0.455	9.9%	1.4%
Gen Mdse/Housewares/Gift	3.276	10.0%	10.4%
Health/Nutrition	0.502	7.0%	1.6%
Insurance/Financial	4.853	10.0%	15.4%
Jewelry	0.145	19.8%	0.5%
Magazines	2.285	9.0%	7.2%
Photofinishing	0.449	12.3%	1.4%
Prescriptions	0.180	9.1%	0.6%
Records & Tapes	0.519	13.1%	1.6%
Sporting Goods	0.989	15.0%	3.1%
Tools/Home Repair	0.391	18.1%	1.2%
Major Catalog Retailers	4.772	-5.1%	15.1%
Department Stores	3.145	17.0%	10.0%
Unclassified Mdse	1.307	18.0%	4.1%
TOTAL CONSUMER SALES	31.563	9.8%	

            Maxwell Sroge Publishing

MAIL ORDER SALES TO CONSUMERS (continued)

BILLIONS $	1982	%CHANGE	%MO
Apparel	1.937	12.0%	5.7%
Auto Clubs	1.066	3.0%	3.1%
Automotive	0.286	18.2%	0.8%
Books	1.665	-2.0%	4.9%
Collectibles	1.272	9.0%	3.7%
Cosmetics	0.224	9.8%	0.7%
Crafts	0.730	13.0%	2.1%
Educational Services	0.539	14.9%	1.6%
Electronic Goods	0.592	16.1%	1.7%
Food	0.623	4.9%	1.8%
Gardening/Horticultural	0.428	-5.9%	1.3%
Gen Mdse/Housewares/Gift	3.505	7.0%	10.3%
Health/Nutrition	0.562	12.0%	1.6%
Insurance/Financial	5.435	12.0%	16.0%
Jewelry	0.164	13.1%	0.5%
Magazines	2.536	11.0%	7.4%
Photofinishing	0.530	18.0%	1.6%
Prescriptions	0.203	12.8%	0.6%
Records & Tapes	0.571	10.0%	1.7%
Sporting Goods	1.157	17.0%	3.4%
Tools/Home Repair	0.431	10.2%	1.3%
Major Catalog Retailers	4.734	-0.8%	13.9%
Department Stores	3.428	9.0%	10.1%
Unclassified Mdse	1.451	11.0%	4.3%
TOTAL CONSUMER SALES	34.069	7.9%	

Maxwell Sroge Publishing

MAIL ORDER SALES TO CONSUMERS (continued)

BILLIONS $	1983	%CHANGE	%MO
Apparel	2.150	11.0%	5.7%
Auto Clubs	1.130	6.0%	3.0%
Automotive	0.312	9.1%	0.8%
Books	1.675	0.6%	4.5%
Collectibles	1.348	6.0%	3.6%
Cosmetics	0.237	5.8%	0.6%
Crafts	0.788	7.9%	2.1%
Educational Services	0.604	12.1%	1.6%
Electronic Goods	0.681	15.0%	1.8%
Food	0.654	5.0%	1.7%
Gardening/Horticultural	0.437	2.1%	1.2%
Gen Mdse/Housewares/Gift	3.856	10.0%	10.3%
Health/Nutrition	0.590	5.0%	1.6%
Insurance/Financial	6.142	13.0%	16.4%
Jewelry	0.184	12.2%	0.5%
Magazines	2.815	11.0%	7.5%
Photofinishing	0.609	14.9%	1.6%
Prescriptions	0.238	17.2%	0.6%
Records & Tapes	0.588	3.0%	1.6%
Sporting Goods	1.296	12.0%	3.5%
Tools/Home Repair	0.478	10.9%	1.3%
Major Catalog Retailers	5.039	6.4%	13.5%
Department Stores	3.942	15.0%	10.5%
Unclassified Mdse	1.640	13.0%	4.4%
TOTAL CONSUMER SALES	37.433	9.9%	

    Maxwell Sroge Publishing

MAIL ORDER SALES TO CONSUMERS (continued)

BILLIONS $	1984	%CHANGE	%MO
Apparel	2.473	15.0%	6.0%
Auto Clubs	1.220	8.0%	2.9%
Automotive	0.340	9.0%	0.8%
Books	1.691	1.0%	4.1%
Collectibles	1.428	5.9%	3.4%
Cosmetics	0.258	8.9%	0.6%
Crafts	0.843	7.0%	2.0%
Educational Services	0.682	12.9%	1.6%
Electronic Goods	0.783	15.0%	1.9%
Food	0.674	3.1%	1.6%
Gardening/Horticultural	0.445	1.8%	1.1%
Gen Mdse/Housewares/Gift	4.318	12.0%	10.4%
Health/Nutrition	0.602	2.0%	1.5%
Insurance/Financial	6.940	13.0%	16.8%
Jewelry	0.206	12.0%	0.5%
Magazines	3.125	11.0%	7.5%
Photofinishing	0.670	10.0%	1.6%
Prescriptions	0.268	12.6%	0.6%
Records & Tapes	0.623	6.0%	1.5%
Sporting Goods	1.490	15.0%	3.6%
Tools/Home Repair	0.526	10.0%	1.3%
Major Catalog Retailers	5.433	7.8%	13.1%
Department Stores	4.533	15.0%	10.9%
Unclassified Mdse	1.853	13.0%	4.5%
TOTAL CONSUMER SALES	41.424	10.7%	

                    Maxwell Sroge Publishing

MAIL ORDER SALES TO CONSUMERS (continued)

BILLIONS $	1985	%CHANGE	%MO
Apparel	2.844	15.0%	6.3%
Auto Clubs	1.317	8.0%	2.9%
Automotive	0.367	7.9%	0.8%
Books	1.708	1.0%	3.8%
Collectibles	1.514	6.0%	3.3%
Cosmetics	0.276	7.0%	0.6%
Crafts	0.894	6.0%	2.0%
Educational Services	0.743	8.9%	1.6%
Electronic Goods	0.900	14.9%	2.0%
Food	0.694	3.0%	1.5%
Gardening/Horticultural	0.432	-2.9%	1.0%
Gen Mdse/Housewares/Gift	4.750	10.0%	10.5%
Health/Nutrition	0.614	2.0%	1.4%
Insurance/Financial	7.773	12.0%	17.2%
Jewelry	0.231	12.1%	0.5%
Magazines	3.406	9.0%	7.5%
Photofinishing	0.724	8.1%	1.6%
Prescriptions	0.306	14.2%	0.7%
Records & Tapes	0.673	8.0%	1.5%
Sporting Goods	1.669	12.0%	3.7%
Tools/Home Repair	0.584	11.0%	1.3%
Major Catalog Retailers	5.705	5.0%	12.6%
Department Stores	5.077	12.0%	11.2%
Unclassified Mdse	2.075	12.0%	4.6%
TOTAL CONSUMER SALES	45.276	9.3%	

     Maxwell Sroge Publishing

MAIL ORDER SALES TO CONSUMERS (continued)

BILLIONS $	1986	%CHANGE	%MO
Apparel	3.356	18.0%	6.8%
Auto Clubs	1.410	7.1%	2.8%
Automotive	0.393	7.1%	0.8%
Books	1.725	1.0%	3.5%
Collectibles	1.589	5.0%	3.2%
Cosmetics	0.290	5.1%	0.6%
Crafts	0.929	3.9%	1.9%
Educational Services	0.803	8.1%	1.6%
Electronic Goods	1.054	17.1%	2.1%
Food	0.708	2.0%	1.4%
Gardening/Horticultural	0.458	6.0%	0.9%
Gen Mdse/Housewares/Gift	5.320	12.0%	10.7%
Health/Nutrition	0.639	4.1%	1.3%
Insurance/Financial	8.628	11.0%	17.4%
Jewelry	0.254	10.0%	0.5%
Magazines	3.713	9.0%	7.5%
Photofinishing	0.774	6.9%	1.6%
Prescriptions	0.345	12.7%	0.7%
Records & Tapes	0.747	11.0%	1.5%
Sporting Goods	1.902	14.0%	3.8%
Tools/Home Repair	0.654	12.0%	1.3%
Major Catalog Retailers	5.933	4.0%	11.9%
Department Stores	5.788	14.0%	11.6%
Unclassified Mdse	2.304	11.0%	4.6%
TOTAL CONSUMER SALES	49.716	9.8%	

Maxwell Sroge Publishing

MAIL ORDER SALES TO CONSUMERS (continued)

BILLIONS $	1987	%CHANGE	%MO
Apparel	3.926	17.0%	7.2%
Auto Clubs	1.537	9.0%	2.8%
Automotive	0.416	5.9%	0.8%
Books	1.759	2.0%	3.2%
Collectibles	1.653	4.0%	3.1%
Cosmetics	0.319	10.0%	0.6%
Crafts	1.003	8.0%	1.9%
Educational Services	0.867	8.0%	1.6%
Electronic Goods	1.264	19.9%	2.3%
Food	0.735	3.8%	1.4%
Gardening/Horticultural	0.476	3.9%	0.9%
Gen Mdse/Housewares/Gift	6.171	16.0%	11.4%
Health/Nutrition	0.684	7.0%	1.3%
Insurance/Financial	9.836	14.0%	18.2%
Jewelry	0.287	13.0%	0.5%
Magazines	4.121	11.0%	7.6%
Photofinishing	0.828	7.0%	1.5%
Prescriptions	0.400	15.9%	0.7%
Records & Tapes	0.814	9.0%	1.5%
Sporting Goods	2.130	12.0%	3.9%
Tools/Home Repair	0.732	11.9%	1.4%
Major Catalog Retailers	5.052	-14.8%	9.3%
Department Stores	6.598	14.0%	12.2%
Unclassified Mdse	2.580	12.0%	4.8%
TOTAL CONSUMER SALES	54.188	9.0%	

Maxwell Sroge Publishing

MAIL ORDER SALES TO CONSUMERS (continued)

BILLIONS $	1988	%CHANGE	%MO
Apparel	5.025	28.0%	7.9%
Auto Clubs	1.675	9.0%	2.6%
Automotive	0.462	11.1%	0.7%
Books	1.830	4.0%	2.9%
Collectibles	1.785	8.0%	2.8%
Cosmetics	0.354	11.0%	0.6%
Crafts	1.064	6.1%	1.7%
Educational Services	0.962	11.0%	1.5%
Electronic Goods	1.593	26.0%	2.5%
Food	0.775	5.5%	1.2%
Gardening/Horticultural	0.495	4.0%	0.8%
Gen Mdse/Housewares/Gift	7.221	17.0%	11.4%
Health/Nutrition	0.746	9.1%	1.2%
Insurance/Financial	11.016	12.0%	17.3%
Jewelry	0.330	15.0%	0.5%
Magazines	4.616	12.0%	7.3%
Photofinishing	0.878	6.0%	1.4%
Prescriptions	0.481	20.3%	0.8%
Records & Tapes	0.912	12.0%	1.4%
Sporting Goods	2.513	18.0%	4.0%
Tools/Home Repair	0.820	12.0%	1.3%
Major Catalog Retailers	5.475	8.4%	8.6%
Department Stores	9.248	40.2%	14.6%
Unclassified Mdse	3.225	25.0%	5.1%
TOTAL CONSUMER SALES	63.50	17.2%	

Maxwell Sroge Publishing

MAIL ORDER SALES TO CONSUMERS (continued)

BILLIONS $	1989	%CHANGE	%MO
Apparel	6.533	30.0%	8.9%
Auto Clubs	1.809	8.0%	2.5%
Automotive	0.518	12.1%	0.7%
Books	1.921	5.0%	2.6%
Collectibles	1.946	9.0%	2.7%
Cosmetics	0.386	9.0%	0.5%
Crafts	1.149	8.0%	1.6%
Educational Services	1.106	15.0%	1.5%
Electronic Goods	2.070	30.0%	2.8%
Food	0.826	6.5%	1.1%
Gardening/Horticultural	0.525	6.0%	0.7%
Gen Mdse/Housewares/Gift	8.808	22.0%	12.1%
Health/Nutrition	0.828	11.0%	1.1%
Insurance/Financial	12.008	9.0%	16.4%
Jewelry	0.386	17.0%	0.5%
Magazines	5.196	12.6%	7.1%
Photofinishing	0.931	6.0%	1.3%
Prescriptions	0.567	17.9%	0.8%
Records & Tapes	1.012	11.0%	1.4%
Sporting Goods	2.991	19.0%	4.1%
Tools/Home Repair	0.943	15.0%	1.3%
Major Catalog Retailers	5.804	6.0%	8.0%
Department Stores	10.511	13.7%	14.4%
Unclassified Mdse	4.226	31.0%	5.8%
TOTAL CONSUMER SALES	73.000	15.0%	

Maxwell Sroge Publishing

MAIL ORDER SALES TO CONSUMERS (continued)

BILLIONS $	1990	%CHANGE	%MO
Apparel	8.624	32.0%	10.6%
Auto Clubs	1.954	8.0%	2.4%
Automotive	0.575	11.0%	0.7%
Books	2.017	5.0%	2.5%
Collectibles	2.063	6.0%	2.5%
Cosmetics	0.432	11.9%	0.5%
Crafts	1.240	7.9%	1.5%
Educational Services	1.239	12.0%	1.5%
Electronic Goods	2.650	28.0%	3.2%
Food	0.892	8.0%	1.1%
Gardening/Horticultural	0.561	7.0%	0.7%
Gen Mdse/Housewares/Gift	9.515	8.0%	11.6%
Health/Nutrition	0.902	8.9%	1.1%
Insurance/Financial	13.329	11.0%	16.3%
Jewelry	0.436	13.0%	0.5%
Magazines	5.790	11.4%	7.1%
Photofinishing	0.987	6.0%	1.2%
Prescriptions	0.658	16.0%	0.8%
Records & Tapes	1.143	12.9%	1.4%
Sporting Goods	3.559	19.0%	4.4%
Tools/Home Repair	1.085	15.0%	1.3%
Major Catalog Retailers	6.146	5.9%	7.5%
Department Stores	11.667	11.0%	14.3%
Unclassified Mdse	4.236	0.2%	5.2%
TOTAL CONSUMER SALES	81.700	11.9%	

Maxwell Sroge Publishing

Performance Analysis of Product Segments

The following are descriptions of trends in the major consumer product segments of the mail order industry. Growth patterns for the 1980s and expectations for the nineties have been outlined.

Apparel

The apparel and ready-to-wear mail order segment, the largest single product area, reflects the trends in the mail order industry as a whole. Mail order has become more acceptable to American consumers. Shoppers are looking for convenience and mail order firms are meeting their needs through easy ways to order, with credit cards and 800 telephone numbers and faster delivery of merchandise. Sales growth in the apparel segment continued at a high rate through the early eighties and then tapered off during the mid to late 1980s as the clothing market became soft. Leaders in the industry attribute this slowing to market saturation and the failing strategy of blanket marketing, which didn't target consumers carefully enough. Successful catalogs are now focussing their product mix and specializing and targeting a tighter customer base. Companies are specializing catalogs to specific consumer groups. The growth rate is expected to continue at a higher than average rate.

Auto Clubs

Growth in Auto Clubs segment fluctuated in the mid eighties and began a new upward swing reflecting changes in the industry as more value and services were added to the organizations. The renewed emphasis on mail order marketing resulted in a steady growth pattern which is expected to continue into the 1990s.

Automotive Accessories and Supplies

Mail order sales of auto parts and accessories continued steady growth through the late eighties as dependance on automobiles and required automobile maintenance increased. Segment leaders reported strong international sales in the mid eighties with the rising value of the U.S. dollar and demand for American parts. Through the early nineties, the automotive parts and accessories segment is expected to continue to grow at a steady rate.

Books

Mail order sales of hardbound and paperback books fluctuated in the early eighties as postage and paper costs rose and the economic recession affected the economy as a whole. In the late eighties, the segment experienced slow, steady growth with better customer targeting and higher response rates. Increased across-the-board mail order volume helped with increased sales; segment leaders reported rising response rates as mail order achieved a more legitimate marketing status with consumers. Sales are expected to be slightly below industry average rate.

Collectibles

The increasing number of collectibles marketers suggested a need for more targeted mailings in the nearly saturated catalog market; companies which grew over the past few years at approximately ten to thirteen percent, did so through increased market penetration and discretionary (requests and repeated targeting) mailings. In the mid eighties coins and precious metals were booming as investment items, later low interest rates adversely affected investment in coins and other valuable collectibles. As the market expands, collectibles hold a gradually decreasing share; many marketers assert the growing difficulty in successfully marketing to a small, static customer base. The segment continued to climb in 1989 as the economy improved. Collectibles are expected to establish stable below average growth in the early nineties.

Cosmetics

Cosmetics marketers have grown at the same rate as the total mail order industry at a steady six to seven percent rate. Mail order has increasingly become an accepted source for such personal products, lessening the dependance on department stores and boutiques. Key areas for the future include skin care products for both men and women, as well as a variety of new cosmetics for men.

Crafts

A shakeout in the crafts market in the early eighties contributed to strong sales growth among the survivors; several major marketers withdrew and the remaining companies pursued aggressive mail order marketing strategies and invested substantially. The early eighties also experienced renewed consumer interest in creative and functional craftwork. The strong growth of the early eighties continued through 1987. In 1988 and 1989, sales settled down to an average growth rate; the growing percentage of working women contributed to this drop. Leaders in the segment expect to see a flattening of the growth rate in the nineties.

Educational Services

Fluctuation in sales of educational services can be attributed to a number of factors: first, an increased emphasis on direct mail marketing for technical training programs; second the segment is economy sensitive, reflecting a growing trend in the consumer market to pursue additional training for improved and secondary incomes. With the improvement of the economy, the majority of firms have stepped-up mail order marketing efforts and have focused on the rapidly expanding self-help industry by appealing to a large, diverse customer base. Increased competition for job placements and advancements have added to correspondence education.

Electronic Goods

The electronics segment boomed in the mid eighties with an increased number of electronics specialty catalogs marketing carefully edited lines of upscale merchandise and an increased need for specialized electronic and computer products. An above average growth rate is expected for the nineties as the consumer's fascination with electronic gadgets continues.

Food

Growth in the mail order sales of gift and general food items was slow throughout the early eighties. The seasonality of the industry, increasing costs, and the recession forced many of the leading companies in the segment to adopt conservative marketing strategies for mail order campaigns. Customer expectations have risen; consumers want more value per dollar and expect products faster. The popularity of gift foods is rising with increasing quality and variety available due to new shipping and handling procedures. Growth in the early nineties is expected to level off. Innovators in the segment can and will do substantially better by offering unique products.

Gardening/Horticultural Products

Gardening mail order marketers are constantly at the mercy of seasonal sales and unpredictable weather. The early eighties showed erratic growth periods. The mid to late eighties showed a renewed interest in gardening. Overall, the late eighties saw a heightened interest in home gardening. The improved economy enabled consumers to spend more discretionary dollars and the trend towards organic gardening methods (avoiding chemicals and pesticides) increased sales as well. A growth rate slightly below average is expected to continue into the nineties.

General Merchandise/Housewares/Gifts

Sales growth in the early eighties for general merchandisers was strong, but dropped in the mid eighties with the economic recession. As the economy improved through the mid to late eighties, the segment re-established healthy sales increases, and trends in the mail order industry as a whole have lifted sales growth substantially. There is an increasing need for the segmentation of buyer bases in the broad merchandise segment. Marketers expect a climb in growth rate in the nineties.

Health/Nutritional Products

Mail order marketers in the health and nutrition segment are gaining a wider customer base through the aging population, an increased number of consumers over 65, increased discretionary income, and a previously untapped disabled market. Companies in the segment expect conservative, steady growth through the nineties; marketers foresee roadblocks in tapping the disabled market -- names are protected and not available. The interest in vitamins is dropping and consumers are becoming more aware of healthful eating and exercise; the non-direct marketing health care industry is downplaying supplementary nutrition products. Growth is expected to match the overall mail order industry.

Insurance/Financial Services

Throughout the 1980s insurance and financial services direct marketing grew at an above average rate. Consumers have accepted direct marketing as a legitimate buying mode for insurance and investment, a general increase in discretionary income and the improved economy has led to increased investing and a rising interest in life insurance. Health insurance in the eighties has undergone frequent upheavals, forcing consumers to shop for themselves rather than rely on agents exclusively. A number of new insurance options have effectively utilized the visibility of direct marketing. The dramatic increase of credit card and bank card companies have contributed to this segment's growth substantially, and the nineties are expected to see a continuation of the above average growth rate for several years.

Jewelry

The strong growth experienced by marketers in the jewelry industry over the past decade has been attributed primarily to stable, or slowly rising prices for precious metals, precious gems and semi-precious gems, though the late 1980s felt a rise in precious gemstone prices, slowing growth. Jewelry in the 1980s became more attractive to consumers as investment items, though market saturation led to a slight decline in growth in the late 1980s. Marketers in the segment now emphasize a strong merchandise mix, increased market penetration and competitive pricing. Leaders expect a continuing average growth rate into the nineties.

Magazine Subscriptions

Publishing companies offering magazine subscriptions through direct marketing continue to provide the industry with marketing innovations. Through the use of sweepstakes, games, premiums and incentives, mail order efforts have succeeded in posting strong sales ranging from seven to thirteen percent growth rates. The postal increase in 1988 affected sales adversely and the 1991 increase is expected to cut revenues as well. Sales are expected to continue at a slightly below industry average rate.

Photofinishing

The growth rate for direct marketing photofinishing rose dramatically during the early and mid 1980s and leveled off in late 1980s. Competition from grocery stores and quick-stop photofinishers has cut into mail order margins. Video tape mixing and finishing are adding to the mail order segment while remaining relatively untapped by quick-stop retailers. Growth is expected to continue at lower than average industry rate for the early nineties.

Prescriptions

Mail order marketers of prescription drugs have continually reported substantial growth throughout the 1980s. A small segment, prescriptions cater to a growing customer base of elderly people and those who take regular medications, a group which is expanding as the population ages. Lower prices and faster delivery continually establish new consumers, and the small but growing group of companies in the segment expect to continue their steady above average growth rate.

Records and Tapes

Direct marketers of records, compact disks and tapes through single item, multiple and continuity programs are dependent upon the fluctuations of discretionary income. The segment's growth curve is erratic, though it remains mainly above six percent. In the late eighties, increased production and marketing costs decreased financial growth; however, growing awareness and acceptance of mail order stabilized revenues. Leaders expect sales to grow at an average industry growth rate.

Sporting Goods

The 1980s experienced a strong fitness craze which sustained sales growth for direct marketers throughout the decade. American awareness and concern for good health created a substantial and sustained market, enabling direct marketers to maintain a dynamic above average growth rate. Adult "toy stores" also discovered a previously untapped niche, adding to the segment's success. Leaders in the industry continue to produce new product innovations, better operations and fulfillment, and cater to an ever widening health market. Growth expectations target a continuing above average rate of growth for the nineties.

Tools/Home Repair

Mail order companies marketing tools and home repair products experienced strong sales growth in the early eighties, despite a troubled economy. Many consumers were interested in "do it yourself" home improvement. However, discretionary income for the average worker declined during the period, resulting in uneven sales growth in the mid eighties. Sales in the nineties are anticipated to be better than the average rate of growth.

Chapter 3

Direct Marketing

To

Businesses

BUSINESS-TO-BUSINESS MAIL ORDER SALES

Business-to-business mail order sales in the 1980's showed strong growth throughout the decade, averaging fifteen percent. Since 1985, the industry has grown at an average of seventeen percent. A growing number of business people discovered that quality products, competitive prices, and good service are readily available for "in-office" as well as "in-home" shopping. One key factor influencing the substantial growth of business-to-business mail order sales is the comparative cost advantages of mail order over other forms of selling. The average cost of a personal sales call is markedly more than that of creating and mailing a catalog, prompting direct marketers to include not only low-end merchandise in catalogs but high-ticket business and industrial products as well. Time is also a factor; in retail, employers tend to prefer that employees place orders rather than waste time and resources shopping. A number of direct marketers respond to business demands for time by offering overnight shipping and other fast-as-retail services.

Direct marketers found that mail order proves to be a profitable way to sell a wide array of business products, from custom designed consumable products, business and financial services to sophisticated, high-tech equipment. The complete penetration of computers and computer network systems in the office gives rise to the fastest growing segment of business mail order: computer supplies, accessories, and software. Merchandisers and marketers view mail order as a synergistic adjunct to distribution through wholesalers, dealers, and distributors. As mail order enters the nineties, expectations target a continuing high growth rate, exceeding consumer mail order sales growth.

Business-to-Business Projected Growth

The chart below indicates the projected growth of the Business-to-Business mail order market in terms of sales volume in billions of dollars. By 1992, revenues are expected to grow beyond one hundred billion dollars.

1988	1989	1990	1991	1992	1993
$53.22	$64.90	$73.63	$88.06	$103.03	$121.58

The following chart is a breakdown of the major product categories in the business-to-business mail order market by sales and growth rates.

BUSINESS-TO-BUSINESS MAIL ORDER SALES

	1980 Billion $		%MO
Gen Office Supply Equipment	0.397		2.3%
Specialty Office: Medical, Dental	0.166		0.9%
Educational Services	0.193		1.1%
Subscription Product	0.353		2.0%
Industrial	0.410		2.3%
Computer Supplies & Accessories	0.185		1.1%
General Business-to-Business	15.880		90.3%
BUSINESS-TO-BUSINESS TOTAL	17.584		

	1981 Billion $	%CHANGE	%MO
Gen Office Supply Equipment	0.516	30.0%	2.8%
Specialty Office: Medical, Dental	0.179	7.8%	1.0%
Educational Services	0.193	0.0%	1.0%
Subscription Product	0.385	9.1%	2.1%
Industrial	0.451	10.0%	2.4%
Computer Supplies & Accessories	0.278	50.3%	1.5%
General Business-to-Business	16.674	5.0%	89.3%
BUSINESS-TO-BUSINESS TOTAL	18.676	6.2%	

	1982 Billion $	%CHANGE	%MO
Gen Office Supply Equipment	0.619	20.0%	3.1%
Specialty Office: Medical, Dental	0.195	8.9%	1.0%
Educational Services	0.212	9.8%	1.1%
Subscription Product	0.443	15.1%	2.2%
Industrial	0.487	8.0%	2.5%
Computer Supplies & Accessories	0.473	70.1%	2.4%
General Business-to-Business	17.340	4.0%	87.7%
BUSINESS-TO-BUSINESS TOTAL	19.769	5.9%	

BUSINESS-TO-BUSINESS MAIL ORDER SALES (continued)

	1983 Billion $	%CHANGE	%MO
Gen Office Supply Equipment	0.774	95.0%	3.3%
Specialty Office: Medical, Dental	0.236	42.2%	1.0%
Educational Services	0.229	18.7%	1.0%
Subscription Product	0.478	35.4%	2.1%
Industrial	0.580	41.5%	2.5%
Computer Supplies & Accessories	0.710	283.8%	3.1%
General Business-to-Business	20.114	26.7%	87.0%
BUSINESS-TO-BUSINESS TOTAL	23.121	31.5%	

	1984 Billion $	%CHANGE	%MO
Gen Office Supply Equipment	1.006	30.0%	3.7%
Specialty Office: Medical, Dental	0.293	24.2%	1.1%
Educational Services	0.252	10.0%	0.9%
Subscription Product	0.521	9.0%	1.9%
Industrial	0.701	20.9%	2.5%
Computer Supplies & Accessories	0.993	39.9%	3.6%
General Business-to-Business	23.735	18.0%	86.3%
BUSINESS-TO-BUSINESS TOTAL	27.501	18.9%	

	1985 Billion $	%CHANGE	%MO
Gen Office Supply Equipment	1.241	23.4%	4.0%
Specialty Office: Medical, Dental	0.310	5.8%	1.0%
Educational Services	0.297	17.9%	1.0%
Subscription Product	0.621	19.2%	2.0%
Industrial	0.776	10.7%	2.5%
Computer Supplies & Accessories	1.365	37.5%	4.4%
General Business-to-Business	26.437	11.4%	85.2%
BUSINESS-TO-BUSINESS TOTAL	31.047	12.9%	

    Maxwell Sroge Publishing

BUSINESS-TO-BUSINESS MAIL ORDER SALES (continued)

	1986 Billion $	%CHANGE	%MO
Gen Office Supply Equipment	1.536	23.8%	4.4%
Specialty Office: Medical, Dental	0.349	12.6%	1.0%
Educational Services	0.314	5.7%	0.9%
Subscription Product	0.733	18.0%	2.1%
Industrial	0.837	7.9%	2.4%
Computer Supplies & Accessories	1.815	33.0%	5.2%
General Business-to-Business	29.324	10.9%	84.0%
BUSINESS-TO-BUSINESS TOTAL	34.908	12.4%	

	1987 Billion $	%CHANGE	%MO
Gen Office Supply Equipment	2.069	34.7%	4.8%
Specialty Office: Medical, Dental	0.431	23.5%	1.0%
Educational Services	0.426	35.7%	1.0%
Subscription Product	0.905	23.5%	2.1%
Industrial	0.991	18.4%	2.3%
Computer Supplies & Accessories	2.801	54.3%	6.5%
General Business-to-Business	35.471	21.0%	82.3%
BUSINESS-TO-BUSINESS TOTAL	43.094	23.5%	

	1988 Billion $	%CHANGE	%MO
Gen Office Supply Equipment	2.766	33.7%	5.2%
Specialty Office: Medical, Dental	0.532	23.4%	1.0%
Educational Services	0.565	32.6%	1.1%
Subscription Product	1.170	29.3%	2.2%
Industrial	1.163	17.4%	2.2%
Computer Supplies & Accessories	3.830	36.7%	7.2%
General Business-to-Business	43.198	21.8%	81.2%
BUSINESS-TO-BUSINESS TOTAL	53.224	23.5%	

     Maxwell Sroge Publishing

BUSINESS-TO-BUSINESS MAIL ORDER SALES (continued)

	1989 Billion $	%CHANGE	%MO
Gen Office Supply Equipment	3.633	31.3%	5.6%
Specialty Office: Medical, Dental	0.649	22.0%	1.0%
Educational Services	0.635	12.4%	1.0%
Subscription Product	1.427	22.7%	2.2%
Industrial	1.413	21.5%	2.2%
Computer Supplies & Accessories	5.320	38.9%	8.2%
General Business-to-Business	51.823	20.0%	79.9%
BUSINESS-TO-BUSINESS TOTAL	64.90	21.9%	

	1990 Billion $	%CHANGE	%MO
Gen Office Supply Equipment	4.371	20.3%	5.9%
Specialty Office: Medical, Dental	0.743	14.5%	1.0%
Educational Services	0.676	6.5%	0.9%
Subscription Product	1.650	15.6%	2.2%
Industrial	1.584	12.1%	2.1%
Computer Supplies & Accessories	7.014	31.8%	9.4%
General Business-to-Business	58.592	13.1%	78.5%
BUSINESS-TO-BUSINESS TOTAL	74.63	15.0%	

PERFORMANCE ANALYSES OF BUSINESS-TO-BUSINESS PRODUCT SEGMENTS

The following are individual analyses of the primary business/industrial product segments of the mail order industry; each short analysis looks at the growth rate for the past decade for sales and the factors influencing this growth.

General Office Supplies

General office supplies marketers enjoyed substantial growth throughout the eighties, with a mild cooling-off of growth in 1989. Leading marketers in the segment reported that the economic conditions of the eighties led businesses to seek more efficient, cost effective ways of meeting office needs, thus fueling mail order growth. Marketers in the segment found that they could maintain better, more inexpensive, more readily available inventories than most retailers. In 1989, rising costs of mail order operations led to the slowed growth rate, along with greatly increased competition within the segment. The segment as a whole continues to capture a growing percentage of the mail order market. Solid sales increases into the nineties are expected while the industry experiences some shake-out of smaller, poorly positioned companies.

Specialty Office Supplies

Marketers of supplies, equipment and furniture for medical, dental, optical and other professional offices, as well as for hospitals, schools, laboratories, etc., continue to find solid advantages in targeting specialized clients by mail; mail order proves to be the most economical and efficient way to reach a specialty customer base. The trends in the national economy affected the segment much like they affected general office supplies; as the economy demanded more efficient operations, businesses turned to mail order and away from personal sales forces. The segment as a whole maintained a steady market share of business-to-business mail order through the eighties. The general increase in costs and competition in 1989 slowed growth to what is the expected growth rate of the early nineties.

Educational Services

Through the eighties, educational services experienced slower growth than the business-to-business direct marketing industry as a whole. Sales in 1981 were flat due to federal budget cuts while sales grew during the mid eighties from newly added programs and renewed marketing efforts to induce participation on the part of business people. As the economy cooled in 1989, Educational Services dropped in growth. A substantial part of the Educational Services segment is subject to federal and state legislation and budgeting; as the United States takes a fresh look at education and public awareness rises, growth in the industry is expected to rise in the early nineties as well as the segment's share of the mail order market, which remained steady through the early and mid eighties, growing slightly in the late eighties.

Subscription Products

Publishers and mail order marketers of different types of business subscription products indicated vastly differing performances over the past decade. While subscriptions may be perceived as additional costs, and therefore expendable, they may also be turned to in times of need for valuable information on "weathering storms." In general, Subscription Products grew equal to or higher than the business to business mail order industry. Leaders in the industry reported that mail order is the most natural form of marketing open to them. As the segment fluctuated during the eighties, it slowly captured slightly higher percentages of the mail order market.

Industrial Products

Leading mail order marketers in the Industrial segment include marketers of tools, scientific supplies, electronics, major machinery, and various other manufacturing related products. Sales grew through the eighties at a markedly lower rate than the business to business direct marketing industry as a whole, but the segment still reported strong growth. Since 1985, the segment's growth dropped while the industry as a whole grew. In the late eighties the segment's market share dropped due to the depressed manufacturing base in the United States. Many marketers in the segment originally developed mail order marketing operations as an adjunct to, or in some cases a replacement for, costly direct sales agent forces.

Computer Supplies, Accessories, and Software

The computer products segment has enjoyed phenomenal growth through the eighties and continues to control a growing percentage of the business to business mail order market. In 1980, the segment held a small market share; in 1989 the segment had grown to capture a major market share. Sales rose throughout the decade at generally double or higher than double the industry's growth rate (in 1982, the segment out-grew the industry by nearly 12 times). In the late eighties every computer mail order marketer still in business without exception reported substantially increased competition and price erosion within the segment. Growth slowed in 1989. As the segment experiences a great deal of shake-out and price competition, its growth in the nineties will be somewhat slower but still outpace the business to business direct marketing industry.

Chapter 4

Marketing

Analysis

COMPARATIVE ADVERTISING STATISTICS FOR ALL MEDIA

The 1980's saw generous overall increases in advertising budgets, and direct mail advertisers were no exception. Total dollars spent on advertising by mail were an average three percent higher than dollars spent on national advertising as a whole. From the beginning of the decade in 1980 until its close in 1989, direct mail advertising spending nearly tripled while total advertising saw even stronger growth. The advertising breakdown supplied by McCann-Erickson, Inc. illustrates the phenomenal growth direct mail enjoyed throughout the eighties, consistently out in front as the largest advertising medium.

The picture changed in 1989. Higher postal rates drove the number of mail advertising pieces down sharply. For the first time in a decade, average 13.7 percent annual growth in expenditures fell to a mere 3.9 percent in 1989 over 1988. Advertising as a whole suffered similarly due to a sluggish economic environment necessitating tighter advertising budget controls. Total ad dollars increased five percent in 1989 compared to 1988. Analysts predict that growth will be modest in the short term, expanded advertising activity is long overdue and will once again show strong growth as the 1990s progress. Advertisers will find increased pressure to provide more power to their punch, and in light of ever increasing postage rates, direct mailers and direct mail advertisers may be in for bumpy times ahead.

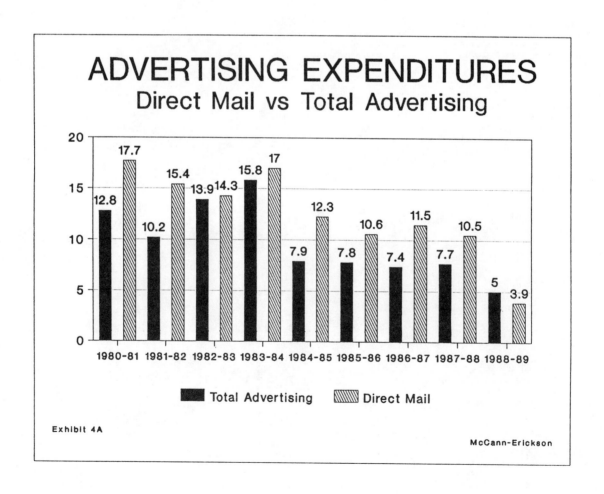

TOTAL ADVERTISING IN THE U.S.

MEDIUM	1980	1981	1982
Newspapers (national ads)	$1.96	$2.26	$2.45
Magazines	$3.15	$3.53	$3.71
Network TV	$5.13	$5.58	$6.21
Spot TV	$3.32	$3.81	$4.51
Direct Mail	**$7.60**	**$8.94**	**$10.32**
Other National Media	$8.66	$9.77	$10.59
Total National Advertising	$29.82	$33.89	$37.79
Newspapers (local ads)	$12.83	$14.27	$15.24
Local TV	$2.97	$3.35	$3.76
Other Local Media	$7.94	$8.92	$9.80
Total Local Advertising	$23.74	$26.54	$28.80
TOTAL ADVERTISING	$53.56	$60.43	$66.59

MEDIUM	1983	1984	1985
Newspapers (national ads)	$2.73	$3.08	$3.35
Magazines	$4.23	$4.93	$5.16
Network TV	$7.02	$8.53	$8.29
Spot TV	$5.10	$5.77	$6.00
Direct Mail	**$11.80**	**$13.80**	**$15.50**
Other National Media	$11.65	$13.58	$15.06
Total National Advertising	$42.53	$49.69	$53.36
Newspapers (local ads)	$17.85	$20.44	$21.82
Local TV	$4.32	$5.06	$5.71
Other Local Media	$11.16	$12.63	$13.87
Total Local Advertising	$33.33	$38.13	$41.40
TOTAL ADVERTISING	$75.86	$87.82	$94.76

MEDIUM	1986	1987	1988	1989
Newspapers (national ads)	$3.38	$3.49	$3.59	$3.72
Magazines	$5.32	$5.61	$6.07	$6.72
Network TV	$8.34	$8.50	$9.17	$9.11
Spot TV	$6.57	$6.85	$7.15	$7.35
Direct Mail	**$17.15**	**$19.11**	**$21.12**	**$21.95**
Other National Media	$16.09	$17.07	$18.51	$20.14
Total National Advertising	$56.85	$60.63	$65.61	$68.99
Newspapers (local ads)	$23.61	$25.92	$27.61	$28.65
Local TV	$6.51	$6.83	$7.27	$7.61
Other Local Media	$15.17	$16.28	$17.56	$18.68
Total Local Advertising	$45.29	$49.03	$52.44	$54.94
TOTAL ADVERTISING	$102.14	$109.66	$118.05	$123.93

Exhibit 4B

McCann-Erickson

CATALOG MAIL VOLUME

While the U.S. population grew about 15 percent in the 1980s, the number of American adults who shop by mail or phone has increased a phenomenal 59.7 percent. For direct marketers, that equates to 91.7 million potential customers. In just one decade, the number of catalogs mailed has more than doubled. In 1980, mail order marketers mailed 5.8 billion catalogs to the consuming public. By 1985, the number of catalogs had doubled to 11.1 billion, and in 1989, 13.4 billion catalogs were mailed. Catalogs are big business, and experts predict that social and economic projections such as the rise of non-traditional and dual-income families will propel this trend into the 90s as well.

The increasing dollars going into direct mail haven't been wasted. According to results from Simmons Market Research Bureau, there was a 30.34 percent increase in the number of total buyers from 1987 to 1988. Total buyers represent those consumers who ordered any merchandise or services by mail or phone due to offers in magazines, newspapers, television, radio, catalogs, or direct mail pieces.

MAIL ORDER BUYERS
1987 VS 1988

(MILLIONS)	ADULT 1987 POPULATION	ADULT 1988 POPULATION	POPULATION % CHANGE	
MALES	82.598	84.066	1.78%	
FEMALES	91.083	92.184	1.21%	
TOTAL ADULTS	173.681	176.250	1.48%	

(MILLIONS)	ADULT 1987 BUYERS	ADULT 1988 BUYERS	BUYERS % CHANGE	INCREASE IN BUYERS
MALES	27.558	37.142	34.78%	9.584
FEMALES	40.365	51.392	27.32%	11.027
TOTAL ADULTS	67.923	88.534	30.34%	20.611

Exhibit 4C   McCann-Erickson

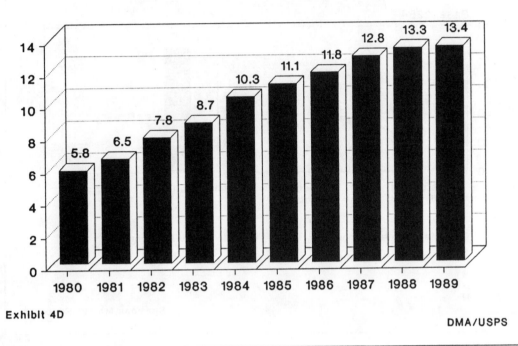

NUMBER OF CATALOGS MAILED
Estimated (In Billions)

Exhibit 4D

DMA/USPS

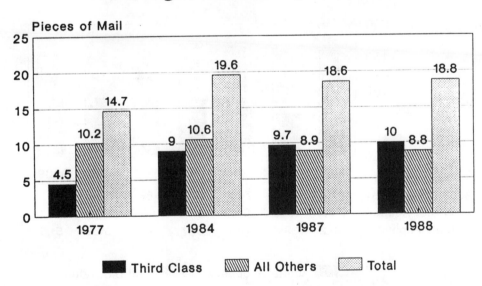

MAIL PIECES RECEIVED
Average Number per Week

Third Class   All Others   Total

Exhibit 4E

USPS Household Diary Study
1978, 1985, 1988, 1989

38

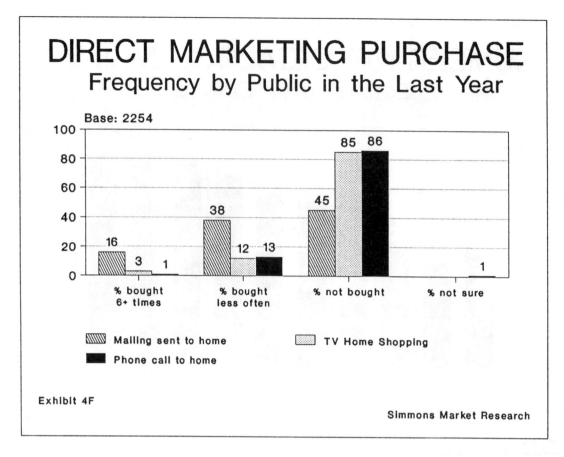

DIRECT MARKETING PURCHASE
Frequency by Public in the Last Year

Base: 2254

Exhibit 4F

Simmons Market Research

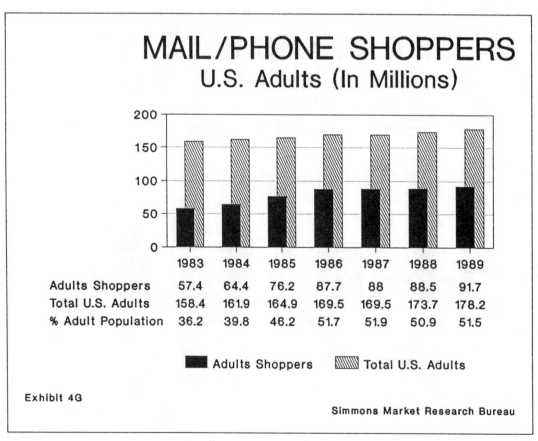

MAIL/PHONE SHOPPERS
U.S. Adults (In Millions)

	1983	1984	1985	1986	1987	1988	1989
Adults Shoppers	57.4	64.4	76.2	87.7	88	88.5	91.7
Total U.S. Adults	158.4	161.9	164.9	169.5	169.5	173.7	178.2
% Adult Population	36.2	39.8	46.2	51.7	51.9	50.9	51.5

Adults Shoppers   Total U.S. Adults

Exhibit 4G

Simmons Market Research Bureau

PERSONALIZED DIRECT MAIL

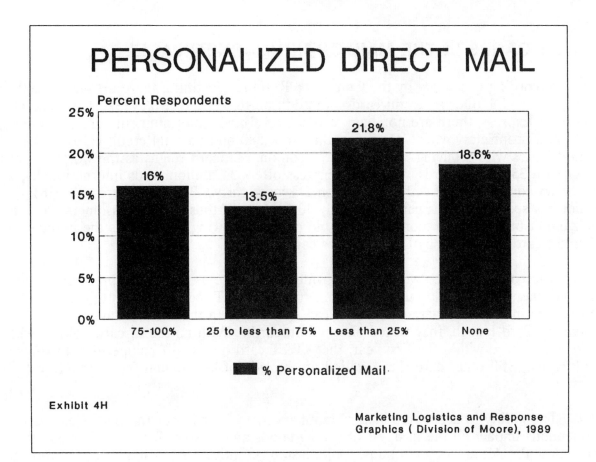

Exhibit 4H

Marketing Logistics and Response
Graphics (Division of Moore), 1989

SATISFACTION WITH MERCHANDISE
Received Through the Mail 1987-88

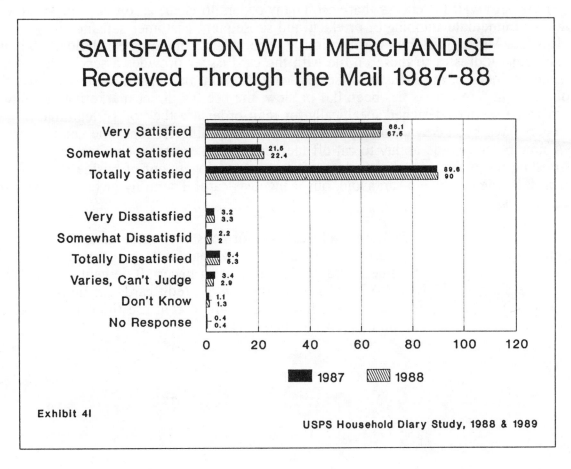

Exhibit 4I

USPS Household Diary Study, 1988 & 1989

CREDIT CARDS IN THE MAIL ORDER MARKETPLACE

According to a study by the Consumer Resource Institute, there are over 3,000 banks in the U.S. offering credit cards. In addition to MasterCard, VISA, Discover, and American Express, there are non-bank cards, Travel and Entertainment cards, gasoline cards, and proprietary cards. Currently there are 880 million total credit cards in the United States with a buying power of $2.75 trillion. Citicorp reigns as the world's largest issuer with 35 million cards, American Express offers 34 million cards internationally, and Sears comes in third with 32.8 million Discover cards. The average credit card holder has six cards in his name, and only 40 percent of those same consumers pay off their credit balance each month. The table on the following page shows the percentage of credit card ownership by United States consumers.

The competition between card providers is intense as bank card proprietors vie for consumers' loyalty and business. Front-runner AT&T has 70 million telephone subscribers in their database which they can solicit, and in the first 78 days of their Universal Card launch, they issued one million cards. With no fee to card holders who make a purchase within the first year, the AT&T card offers stiff competition to some bank cards. Still other cards have rallied on the side of low annual fees and interest rates.

The ability to accept credit card numbers by mail and over the phone has had a tremendous impact on the business of selling goods and services by mail. For one thing they allow the American consuming public instant gratification. Instead of the requisite time it takes to wait for checks that accompany orders to clear, credit card processing allows for immediate shipping of product, and subsequent customer satisfaction. Services like VISA's "Address Verification Service" which compares cardholder's billing and shipping addresses to those on file with the card issuer provides a service tailored to the specific needs of the industry while reducing fraud in mail order. Whereas use of credit cards in retail areas has been flat or slow, the use for direct marketing purchases has soared. Services designed specifically for mail order are the nod of legitimacy catalogers have been craving since the early 80s. Unfortunately for some catalogers, VISA now possesses the ability to cut-off merchants with excessive chargebacks, superseding the banks and effectively putting many catalogers out of business. This drawback is one catalogers can avoid, but it involves careful scrutiny of both banks and credit issuers.

Mail order buyers often use credit cards. For consumer catalogers, the percentage of customers paying by credit card is an average of 41 percent. Consumers of business catalogs, on the other hand, utilize credit at a lower 10 percent. An AT&T Telephone Shopper Study in 1987 broke down the use of credit cards for non-store shopping: Of all consumers, 61 percent have a card, 40 percent use the card, 21 percent do not use the card, and 38 percent do not have a card.

CREDIT CARD OWNERSHIP

CREDIT CARD	1983	1984	1985	1986	1987
HAVE CREDIT CARDS	82%	81%	79%	79%	77%
RETAIL CARDS	71%	69%	68%	68%	62%
Sears	53%	50%	49%	51%	44%
JC Penney	37%	35%	34%	35%	34%
Montgomery Wards	21%	23%	20%	17%	15%
Other retail cards	45%	41%	41%	39%	35%
BANK CARDS	58%	57%	56%	57%	60%
VISA	45%	43%	43%	45%	46%
Mastercard	36%	35%	34%	34%	36%
GASOLINE CREDIT CARDS	40%	35%	34%	35%	30%
TELEPHONE CREDIT CARDS	24%	26%	26%	25%	26%
THIRD PARTY CARDS	13%	13%	12%	14%	13%
American Express	11%	11%	12%	13%	12%
Diner's Club	2%	2%	2%	2%	1%
Carte Blanche	1%	1%	0%	1%	1%
Discover	NA	NA	NA	3%	9%
AIRLINE CREDIT CARDS	4%	3%	3%	3%	3%
CAR RENTAL CREDIT CARDS	3%	3%	3%	3%	2%

Exhibit 4J   Money Magazine, 1987

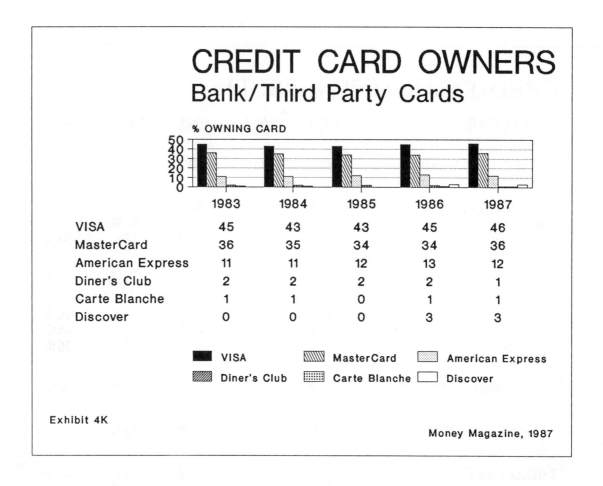

CREDIT CARD OWNERS
Bank/Third Party Cards

% OWNING CARD

	1983	1984	1985	1986	1987
VISA	45	43	43	45	46
MasterCard	36	35	34	34	36
American Express	11	11	12	13	12
Diner's Club	2	2	2	2	1
Carte Blanche	1	1	0	1	1
Discover	0	0	0	3	3

■ VISA ▨ MasterCard ▨ American Express
▨ Diner's Club ▦ Carte Blanche □ Discover

Exhibit 4K

Money Magazine, 1987

Fraud

The growing utilization of credit cards has given rise to the prevalence of telefraud. In fact, the Alliance Against Fraud in Telemarketing estimate that Americans lose billions of dollars each year to bogus sales pitches made over the phone. Mail-in orders aren't free from corruption either. Many banks are aware that mail order is subject to losses from fraud, and some small-sized and startup catalogs have suffered from the revocation of their existing credit card processing ability, or have been unable to offer credit cards. Technology that cross checks customer information to prevent abuses may counteract this problem, but consumer fraud poses a very real problem for direct marketers.

Credit Record Privacy

In recent years the consuming public has been concerned that too much of their private lives is open to be scrutinized and used without its knowledge. Without corporate attempts to challenge or change this perception, the issue moves closer and closer to the legislative arena. It's not unlikely that restrictions could be placed on the commercial use of consumer information garnered from credit applications and histories. Indeed, many state and national legislatures are already working to amend the Fair Credit Reporting Act (FCRA) to curtail the amount of information credit bureaus can make available, and to give the public more control over their credit files. Then, too, consumers have the ability to have their names taken off of lists that are sold to direct marketers by credit bureaus -- lists that have been the backbone of the mail order business. The clear picture of the customer provided by consumer databases, while a distinct advantage to direct marketers in terms of relevance marketing strategies, will continue to be a worry for consumers. The catalog marketers' challenge in the decade ahead will be to stem abuses of the system and sell consumers on the advantages of database information.

Chapter 5

International

Mail Order

INTERNATIONAL MAIL ORDER BUSINESS

The Popularity of Direct Marketing

The United States developed direct marketing to a greater extent than other nations and has remained far in the lead in the global direct market. Over the past ten years, however, Europe, the Far East, and Canada have gradually closed that gap. Just a decade ago, many nations felt direct response worthy of distrust and were connected to poor quality service and shoddy merchandise. Now more consumers than ever before rely on direct marketing as a reliable purchasing method. As more women enter the work force, limiting the time for retail shopping and increasing discretionary income, direct marketing is often the preferred alternative to retail.

Just a few years ago, only select nations felt the need to establish their own direct marketing associations. West Germany, Great Britain, Switzerland, Finland, the Netherlands, and Canada have all conducted and published extensive studies on their nation's direct response progress. Most of the European Economic Community's member states report a booming direct mail business, as does Australia, Japan, Hong Kong, South Africa, and Mexico.

Expansion of U.S. Direct Mail

Changes in the economic world are making international expansion of established American direct mail operations a very appealing prospect. In 1992, when the EEC drops the remaining trade sanctions and cross-border taxation, commerce within the wealthiest nations in Europe will be easier than ever before. The Free Trade Agreement between the United States and Canada will add opportunity for catalogers that have been eyeing our own continent as an expansion alternative to Europe or Asia. With Canadian consumers traditionally responsive to many successful American catalog efforts, Canada represents a fairly effortless expansion opportunity. The primary consideration is to determine the amount and type of modifications necessary to a catalog and existing products, so that they will be appealing in a foreign market. Of course, thought must be given to the preferred language of the target audience. For example, Hong Kong prefers Chinese, Belgium prefers French, and various regions of Switzerland will respond better to German, Italian, or French. Other countries have stringent social customs that would interpret personalized mailings which include a customer's first name as an intrusion into his or her privacy. One region might look more for technological advances in a product, another might respond better to a certain unique styling, while yet another may find ad mail containing discount pricing or contests and other sales gimmicks as more appealing. As a rule of thumb, European, Asian, and Canadian consumers expect more quality than the average American. Those catalogers that do not carefully study their target audience's expectations and make the necessary modifications to their products can expect a much higher return rate than they would in the United States. Many companies are already launching foreign editions of their catalogs and acquiring partners abroad in order to ease transition into new markets. The key will be, as is the case in the United States, to determine a customer's needs, and meet them effectively.

List Brokers and Data Processing

Although list brokers are widely used in the industry, list management still has a long way to progress in the foreign market. Capabilities from nation to nation vary in terms of data storage, merge/purge ability, and avoiding address duplication. Although some are on par with the United States, others have no reliable way to obtain new addresses or validate existing ones. List prices are often much higher than in the United States. A Japanese name can cost between twenty-five cents and one dollar, compared to the U.S. figure of eight cents to fifteen cents. Some nations also guard their psychographic and demographic information violently, as personal privacy has become a worldwide issue. Until a time when laws concerning lists and direct marketing become more homogeneous it will be costly for catalogers to pioneer into new foreign markets. Once a solid, profitable list has been established for an individual company, however, it should be easy to maintain and grow from there.

ANALYSIS OF INDIVIDUAL FOREIGN COUNTRIES AND THEIR DIRECT MARKETING OPERATIONS

The European Economic Community

The European Economic Community is an economic pact between twelve nations which dates back to 1958 and the Treaties of Paris and Rome. Its single goal was to replace nationalism and fierce economic competition among various European countries with a single, unified marketplace. This was thought to strengthen Europe's market efficiency and make it more competitive against outside markets. Its long term destiny was to unite Europe into a single entity, with the same political goals and demographic tendencies, becoming the European equivalent of the United States of America. Each nation would maintain its own local government, yet would abide by central EEC laws similar to federal laws in America. Its founding members were West Germany, France, Italy, and the three Benelux states (Belgium, the Netherlands, and Luxembourg). In 1973, Great Britain, Ireland, and Denmark joined, followed in 1981 by Greece, and finally by Spain and Portugal. By the year 1992, these twelve nations will be united into an economic marketplace that must be acknowledged. Although there are still problems which must be solved, such as homogenizing value-added taxes, setting quality standards for products, and most importantly, creating an unified European Monetary Unit, most changes have already been successfully implemented. Such a united marketplace eliminates the previous need to deal with twelve separate nations on commerce issues, and instead allows a single agreement to be effective in all member nations. The EEC will open monumental opportunities for direct mail. When retail and wholesale trade regulations are completely standardized within the EEC, mail order can only follow. Once a consistent postal system has been established, the final barrier for successful catalogs will be eliminated, opening the doors for American catalogers waiting to expand. Additional statistics show that this union will increase the standards of living for all nations concerned, positively affecting their disposable income. This in return will make direct mail an even more appealing purchasing tool for the consumers of the EEC.

Great Britain

According to latest studies, The United Kingdom is ranked sixth in expenditures among European direct marketing nations, having a 7.2 percent share of the total United Kingdom advertising expenditure pie. Total costs attributed to direct marketing were 530 million pounds (roughly $980 million U.S.) in 1988. Britain mailed 1.766 billion items of addressed direct mail that year, representing a 7.6 percent growth from 1987. The United Kingdom's inland pieces of direct mail grew approximately twelve percent, compared to the 8.6 percent growth of total inland mail from 1987 to 1988. The average piece of direct mail was reported to cost twenty-four cents (U.S.) in postage and thirty-six cents (U.S.) to produce. Additionally, British direct mail has reported an average annual growth rate of at least 7.5 percent since 1986.

Denmark

The Danish Direct Marketing Association reported over six thousand member companies in 1989. Denmark has a population of 5.1 million, with 2.6 million households. The total direct mail volume in 1988 amounted to 200 million pieces, thirty-five percent of Denmark's advertising expenditures for that year. Approximately 3.25 billion Danish Kroner were spent on direct mail in 1988 (nearly $542 million U.S.). An estimated 40 pieces of direct mail were received per head of population.

Although lists are available on a limited basis, they are primarily business to business, on which large companies can be sorted by number of employees and/or annual revenues. Consumer lists are scarce, although one list company is reported to have compiled a list of individuals in middle to upper-level managerial positions. It is not possible to merge/purge list in order to separate business from private addresses at this time. Saturation mail can be delivered to a certain recipient by the post office. Target groups available are apartments, houses, offices, retail stores, farms, and/or summer residences.

Switzerland

Swiss direct marketing expenditures have been growing steadily over the years with 1.63 billion Swiss Franken (approximately $1.18 billion U.S.) spent in 1987, 7.9 percent more than the previous year. Pre-addressed mail rose 6.5 percent and saturation mail climbed 8.3 percent in the number of pieces mailed from 1986 to 1987. About 1.9 billion pieces of direct response mail were sent in 1987 (620 million pre-addressed and 1.6 billion saturation mail; 638 pre-addressed mail were sent in 1988, a 2.9 percent increase for that segment).

The Schweizerische Verband fuer Direktmarketing (Swiss DMA) comments that in 1986 and 1987, the amount spent on direct response equaled that spent for advertisements in newspapers and magazine, or approximately thirty-seven percent of the total Swiss advertising expenditures for those years. In 1988, Switzerland is reportedly the highest saturated European nation, receiving ninety-eight pieces of direct mail per head of population.

The Netherlands

The Netherlands reported an overall growth in direct mail of 10.8 percent from 1988 to 1989, or 476 million pieces. Close to fifty-six pieces were received per head of population in 1988. Addressed direct response grew six percent to 897 million pieces in 1989, and saturation mail increased by twelve percent, to 3.972 billion pieces mailed that year.

Germany

The Federal Republic of Germany spent 12.8 billion Deutsche Mark (roughly $7.5 billion U.S.) in 1988 on direct mail. This represents approximately 6.7 percent of the comparable United States figure of $118.05 billion. An estimated fifty-nine pieces of mail were received per head of population in 1988, dwarfed by the more than 630 pieces received per head of population in the United States. The unification of East and West Germany will not significantly increase Germany's mail order business. But as tests by Reader's Digest and Avon have shown, the East German consumer is hungry for western products, by mail or otherwise.

Direct marketing has been used by seventy-seven percent of all West German banks and fifty-seven percent of all insurance companies. Fifty-two percent of all publishers used some form of direct marketing, as did fifty-one percent of all travel agencies. The Deutscher Direkt Marketing Verband (German DMA) estimates that direct marketing will grow nineteen percent from 1988 to 1990; telemarketing and direct response catalogs are expected to grow the fastest. In 1988, one out of every three West German companies utilized at least one form of direct response advertising, totalling 415,000 firms. Business to business direct marketing was reported slightly more popular than consumer direct response, making up fifty-four percent of the total West German direct mail industry. Although fifty-eight percent of the larger West German corporations utilized direct response in 1988, eighty-three percent of the total activity originated from small firms. Telemarketing was the least frequent form of direct response, as only thirty-eight percent of all direct marketers utilized it.

Computerized shopping became more dominant in West Germany, as American companies like CompuServe begin to expand internationally. Btx (short for "Bildschirmtext", or monitor text) is the German version of Prestel, a networking system similar to CompuServe and Prodigy, which allows consumers to acquire stock reports, complete financial transactions, and even shop at home. Television and radio were still being used infrequently as direct marketing vehicles, although advertiser-funded cable networks were reportedly popularizing home shopping.

Eastern Europe and U.S.S.R.

Eastern Europe and the Soviet Union are still virtually untouched by direct mail. Although borders are dropping rapidly around the world, the economies of the eastern countries are still weak. Their consumers often do not have the discretionary income to take part in the mail order phenomena of the West. Perhaps in another eight to ten years, the economies of these countries will have prospered enough to afford initial catalog expansion. At the present time, the necessary infrastructure has simply not been established. Until knowledge about the extent of fulfillment, facilities, copy writing skills, and creative abilities exists, the Eastern Bloc will remain a difficult market to tap into. As the reunification with West Germany comes closer, so comes the German Democratic Republic's improvement in standard of living.

The following charts represent the amount of addressed direct mail pieces mailed in some of the leading European countries and the number of pieces of direct mail received per head of population.

ADDRESSED DIRECT MAIL VOLUME
1981-88 (Millions of items)

COUNTRY	1981	1982	1983	1984	1985	1986	1987	1988
Belgium	312	344	409	449	474	506	533	566
% Change		10.3	19.9	9.8	5.6	6.3	5.4	6.1
Denmark	130	135	140	150	165	190	225	235
% Change		3.8	3.7	7.1	10.0	15.2	18.4	4.5
Finland	154	156	171	199	213	220	240	216
% Change		1.3	9.6	16.4	7.0	3.3	9.1	9.6
France	1401	1553	1603	1737	1973	2000	2376	2500
% Change		10.8	3.2	8.4	13.6	1.4	18.8	5.0
Ireland	N/A	7.0	7.1	8.6	13.3	19.4	20.2	20.0
% Change			1.4	21.1	54.7	45.9	4.2	1.0
Netherlands	444	454	451	512	541	558	680	780
% Change		2.2	-0.6	13.5	5.6	3.1	21.9	14.7
Norway	105	108	121	135	177	204	215	225*
% Change		2.9	12.0	11.6	31.1	15.3	5.4	
Portugal	N/A	83	58	58	61	66	85*	85*
% Change			-30.1	--		5.2	8.2	28.8
Sweden	373	383	404	434	457	481	511	541
% Change		2.7	5.5	7.4	5.3	5.3	6.2	6.0
Switzerland	467	496	534	542	565	582	615	638
% Change		6.2	7.7	1.5	4.2	3.0	5.7	2.9
United Kingdom	1034	1102	1084	1261	1303	1401	1626	1766
% Change		6.6	-1.6	16.3	3.2	7.5	16.1	8.6
West Germany	3013	2996	3004	3113	3078	3261	3357	3607
% Change		-0.6	0.3	3.6	-1.1	5.9	2.9	7.6

* Estimate

Exhibit 5A   Danish Direct Marketing Association

ADDRESSED DIRECT MAIL VOLUME
PER HEAD OF POPULATION
(Number of Items Per Year)

	1981	1982	1983	1984	1985	1986	1987	1988
Belgium	32	35	41	45	48	51	54	57
Denmark	25	26	27	29	32	37	43	45*
Finland	32	33	36	41	44	46	50	45
France	26	28	29	32	36	37	41	45*
Ireland	N/A	2	2	2.4	4	5	6	6
Netherlands	30	31	31	35	37	38	40	56
Norway	25	26	29	32	42	49	52	55
Portugal	N/A	8	6	6	6	6	8	8*
Sweden	45	46	49	52	55	58	62	66
Switzerland	72	76	82	83	87	90	95	96
United Kingdom	18	20	19	22	23	25	29	32
West Germany	49	49	49	51	50	53	55	59

* Estimate

Exhibit 5B   Danish Direct Marketing Association

Canada

The Canadian population of twenty-six million represents about 10.4 percent of the people residing in the United States. Canadian mail order generates only 4.6 percent of the comparative U.S. revenues. Sales through Canada's mail order industry for 1989 were 7.1 billion Canadian dollars -- $4 billion came from ad mail, $1 billion resulted through telemarketing, and a combined $2.1 billion was generated through coupons and free-standing ads. According to the Canadian Direct Marketing Association, the 1990 direct mail income is expected to reach 7.7 billion Canadian dollars, an 8.4 percent increase over the previous year. This figure is consistent with the average eight to ten percent increase in direct response revenues which the CDMA expects to attain annually. Canada's mail order is projected to increase proportionally to its population, but the CDMA admits that this may take a few years. Canada is made up of only a few large cities, the rest of its population lives in areas without prime shopping facilities. This factor explains why some American catalogs have performed up to fifty percent better in Canada than in the domestic market.

The CDMA advises Americans considering catalog expansion to Canada to release bilingual editions of its catalogs in English and in French since the province of Quebec is eighty-five percent Canadian French and prefers correspondence in that language. Canadian English also retains many of the British English spelling -- experts agree that a Canadian consulting firm or copy writers will provide best results when Americans expand north.

The Free Trade Agreement between Canada and the United States, passed January 1, 1989, will be gradually phased in over the next nine years. It will eliminate many of the strict duties that have restricted commerce between the two nations in the past. Tariffs on over four hundred products have already been cut in an effort to implement the majority of changes prior to 1994. When the Free Trade Agreement is fully phased in, it should lessen the impact on those American companies that did not jump on the bandwagon for European expansion.

As an indication of the positive progression of direct mail in Canada, the CDMA reports less demand for introductory direct marketing courses and instead reports an ever increasing attendance at intermediate level seminars. Overall response to catalogs and trust in mail order is growing, although telemarketing is reported as very unpopular by the Canadian consumer. The market has not yet been saturated with direct response advertising and leaves excellent opportunity for expansion to the American cataloger. Current top sellers which have expanded their U.S. products to Canada are primarily apparel-based -- L.L. Bean reports a 70,000 Canadian past buyers list, Lands' End mailed its initial Canadian test catalog in Spring 1990 and will repeat that test in fall. Talbots, Spiegel, and J. Crew are also eyeing the Canadian market, some planning expansion as soon as Spring of 1991. Canadian Sears is Canada's largest cataloger with annual revenues of 900 million Canadian dollars. Regal Greetings and Gifts is another large player on the relatively sparse roster of Canadian direct response teams, mailing 1.5 million catalogs a year. Seed companies and office product suppliers are also doing well; Canadian Moore leads the latter segment in yearly revenues.

Similar to the United States, Canada's direct marketing community has its problems. The most active issues currently are privacy/data protection, postal affairs, the collection of accurate statistics, and post secondary education about direct marketing. Currently two statistical studies are underway -- one is entitled "Rationalization of Standards," which concerns the metric system and adaption of U.S. products. The other, "Government Subsidies," focuses on wide-spread provincial and federal level subsidies, and whether they conform to fair business practices.

Japan

While Japanese retailers and department store chains have been buying American firms such as Talbots and Gump's, American direct marketers such as REI and Austad's are mailing catalogs in Japan and the Far East. Japanese consumers traditionally prefer face to face shopping to catalogs, accounting for the limited acceptance rate of the latter. Americans who wish to launch Japanese versions of their catalogs do have one significant advantage over Japanese retail - U.S. prices are a tremendous bargain over the comparatively high cost of Japanese products. The primary difficulties presented in establishing a successful catalog operation in Japan are similar to those in European nations. The largest problem is establishing a reliable list, as few list sources are available, and even fewer have the proper technology and skills to merge/purge or otherwise manipulate a list. Lists meeting specific demographic needs are virtually non-existent, meaning that names have to be personally solicited by each cataloger through ads in Japanese vertical publications. List cost is another factor; most Japanese names cost three to four times more than names in America. Finding acceptable letter shops is also difficult. This makes state-side production, shipping the catalogs to Japan, and having them alternately delivered there the least expensive, most reliable way of distributing U.S. catalogs in Japan.

"It will take money, time, and manpower to succeed as a direct marketer in Japan," states Bob Overton of Direct Marketing Services International. An American company that goes to Japan must be willing to take losses for a while and consider initial progress as a first step anticipating the time when catalogs become widely accepted. U.S. companies must also invest in translating catalogs and developing an effective, quick fulfillment plan. "A reliable source of mine in Japan calculated that the average [American] catalog will take four years and seven months before it breaks even. Many small to medium-sized companies will not be able to afford such losses. A company must be committed to its Japanese market and must possess financial staying power [in order to succeed there]." The best selling items are expected to be similar to those in the U.S., namely housewares, soft goods, and jewelry. Overton does not, however, foresee a significant change in the next five years in how catalogs are brought to the Japanese consumer, and maintains that stateside production will be the least expensive method, at least until Japan becomes more receptive to American catalogers.

Many changes are occurring in Japanese society, positively influencing the Japanese mail order industry. As more women enter the work force, less leisure time exists and discretionary income is increased. In 1980, fifty percent of the Japanese work force was comprised of women; in 1989, the Japanese work force was made up of nearly seventy-five percent women. With less time available to indulge in retail shopping, many consumers are abandoning the retail tradition and are instead reaching for the mail order catalog. Japanese retailers have also noticed this trend and are quick to jump onto the mail order bandwagon. Takashimaya, Daimaru, and Mitsukoshi are some of the leading department store chains that have increased their revenues through mail order sales. Takashimaya mail order sales for 1988 were estimated to be more than $400 million, Mitsukoshi's at $240 million, and finally Daimaru's revenues at $135 million. The Japanese mail order service is another factor in the improving conditions of Japanese mail order. Although the distance from the north end to the south end of Japan are approximately that of the East to West Coast of the United States, mail and parcels usually arrive within three days, with minimal delay or non delivery. Current predictions are that Japan's mail order industry will pass the $62 billion mark by 1998, a twenty percent growth over 1988.

Australia

Australia Post was reported to have handled 470 million pieces of direct mail in its 1989 fiscal year, or 12.7 percent of the total mail volume. A recent Australian Direct Marketing Association survey showed that 58 percent of Australians responded to direct mail. Nineteen percent of those expenditures were attributed to clothing, fifteen percent to charitable donations, ten percent to books, eight percent to wine and spirits, seven percent to tools or kitchen appliances, followed by six percent, which was spent on magazine subscriptions. Reportedly, Australian consumers respond similarly to American mail order buyers. "We've found that what works in America generally works in Australia, except for catalogs. Catalogs are difficult," said Bob Overton, president of Direct Marketing Services International. Due to the large amount of geography which isolates many Australians, fifty-three of those that responded to the ADMA survey felt that direct marketing actually kept them in touch with the outside world. With no need for translation, both Australia and neighboring New Zealand present excellent, inexpensive expansion opportunities for American catalogers.

AUSTRALIAN GOODS PURCHASED THROUGH DIRECT MARKETING (1988)

Books	10%	Magazines	6%
Jewelry	3%	Toys	3%
Clothing	19%	Footwear	9%
Tools	7%	Cosmetics	5%
Pharmaceuticals	4%	Wines & Spirits	8%
Records	6%	Videos	4%
Furniture	5%	Crockery/Tableware	4%
Kitchen Appliances	7%	HiFi, TV, VCR	3%
Entertainment	7%	Investments	3%
Insurance	3%	Superannuation	2%
Real Estate	2%	Motor Vehicles	3%
Professional Services	2%	Travel	4%
Charity Donations	15%	Film Processing	4%
Lottery Tickets	9%	Office Equipment	2%
Computers	2%	Political Support	1%
Collectibles	2%	Environment Donations	4%
Other	4%		

Exhibit 5C   Australian Direct Marketing Association

Summary

Around the world, direct mail marketing is becoming more accepted and gaining momentum every year. The stronger a country's economy, the more likely is it to realize the strong marketing potential cached in direct marketing. With the world economy becoming more accessible though such implementations as the Free Trade Agreement between the United States, Canada and the European Economic Community, catalogs will be the ultimate sales vehicle. Catalogs are relatively inexpensive to produce and distribute. They can also have an edge over retailers who need regional sales representatives to solicit sales. Additionally, catalogs can work as a comparatively inexpensive testing vehicle. If a catalog fails, the cataloger has lost only what it invested for that single test, while retailers have to consider divesting or liquidating facilities and assets held in the foreign marketplace. Of course, catalogs can be even more powerful if used conjunctively with retail as a tandem marketing vehicle. Those companies which can expand both their retail and catalogs internationally will be the sales giants of the future.

Chapter 6

Demographic

Trends

DEMOGRAPHIC TRENDS

More and more, success in direct marketing can be equated with knowledge of customer's buying patterns and lifestyle. Changes in the social and economic composition of the country have benefitted an alternative, viable marketing form -- mail order. In 1983, 24.5 percent of the total adult population of 158.4 million people used mail order. By 1989, that percentage grew to 51.4 percent, or 91.7 million potential customers. And as more non-traditional, two income households experience less leisure time and more discretionary income, they'll continue to reward catalogers providing ever-improving prices, quality, and service. However, customers demand more targeted marketing and services that meet their changing needs. These needs have led to the birth of new industry segments.

According to the census, households grew 13.9 percent from 1980 to 1988 while population grew 8.5 percent. Nine states experienced 20 percent or higher growth rates. While the population grew 12.5 percent since 1983, the number of Americans shopping by mail and telephone increased 59.7 percent.

Changing Age Distribution of the U.S. Population

The eighties were touted as the decade of the baby boomer, people born between 1945 and 1955. In the nineties, this group is aging. By the year 2000, the 45 to 55 year-old segment will jump 46 percent. This is good news for direct marketers because no other group earns or spends more. In addition to their spending abilities, the middle-aging trend is producing a segment that is historically stable--they stay at their jobs longer and move less often. This group values service over price, quality over quantity, and they insist on having fun. As such, they're excellent target customers for mail order. So, while the population will continue to grow throughout the 1990's, that growth will slow, society will age, and consumer markets will begin to fragment.

Changing Housing/Marital Status of Individuals

In many ways, the eighties were a time of relative stability after the dramatic changes in people's modes of living in the seventies. While the number of households grew by 27.4 percent between 1970 and 1980, that growth had dropped to 13.9 percent between 1980 and 1988. Similarly, whereas non-family households grew 77.7 percent and one person households grew 68.6 percent during the seventies, nonfamilies and single households experienced 22.2 percent and 19.6 percent respectively in the eighties. As has been the case for two decades, the traditional family has become less prevelant with 15.7 percent growth rate during the seventies and a slight 9.4 percent between 1980 and 1989.

   * In 1980, 11.3 million women were living alone. By 1987, that number had grown to 12.9 million, a 15.4 percent jump.

   * In 1980, 7.0 million men were living alone, a figure which rose 18.4 percent to 8.2 million by 1987.

* Single persons comprised 32.3 percent of all U.S. households in 1980. By 1987 that figure grew to 38.2 percent.

* Unmarried couples nearly tripled from 523,000 to 1.6 million between 1970 and 1980. This segment "stabilized" like all other groups, reaching 2.0 million in 1985 and then 2.3 million in 1987.

* Although both groups have grown less during the last decade, nonfamily households continue to outpace family households in terms of growth rate:

	Nonfamily	Family
% change 1970-1980	15.7	77.7
% change 1980-1988	9.4	22.2

Marital status has also undergone changes in the past. Since 1980, the number of divorces has fallen slightly while marriages have risen slightly. The traditional family household with a husband and wife present increased only 4.9 percent from 49.1 million in 1980 to 51.5 million in 1987. However, there was a simultaneous 20 percent leap in the number of households maintained by a woman with no husband present; whereas there were 49.1 million in 1980, there were 51.5 million by 1987. The majority of households are almost exclusively totally employed where all adult members work either full or part-time. As such, they require alternate shopping means to fill their needs, and buying by mail becomes a preferred, and necessary, alternative.

Dual Income Families

In today's family, often both parents work. Wages have increased and leisure time shrinks accordingly. These wealthy baby boomers with a median age of 45 years old are looking for convenience, and mail order provides them with all they want and more. Now, 35 percent of U.S. households have a net worth of $100,000.

Of interest to catalog marketers, consumers have said that 36 percent of those who use catalogs do so due to the convenience factor, of those 39 percent are women and 34 percent are men. Of those 25 years and older, 39 percent cited convenience; those under 25 cited it at a rate of 21 percent. The working family's most valuable asset is time. The proof is in the rise of telemarketing, convenience banking and automated teller machines -- and the mail order industry. The sensitive economy of the late 1980's caused a slight constriction in the growth of the industry, but consumers have not turned their backs on mail order. As women emerge in increasing numbers as the heads of households, the rise of catalog use will continue into the 1990's. Successful marketers will incorporate this fact into their marketing strategies.

The 50+ Market

The rise of the mature, age 50 and over market created its own market specific strategy. This trend will continue as the baby boomers continue to age. The 45-to-54-year-old segment will grow 46 percent during the 1990s, and likewise, the 55-to-64-year-old segment will increase 46.7 percent between the year 2000 and 2010. Although traditionally seen as an extension of the 25 to 49 year old market, increasing emphasis on the "golden years" has fostered a market concerned with its unique needs and lifestyles. Unlike their younger counterparts, this market values guarantees and quality over price. They are generally health oriented, but finance, travel, and leisure products and services also do very well. In terms of marketing, intangibles are less effective; more concrete terminology is necessary and less obvious benefits must be played up. Most important, however, is that older people identify with products targeted for their age group.

Less active, mature market also has shown implications for marketing to home-bound consumers. The disabled have historically been an untapped resource for mail order marketing. In many cases, these customers are difficult to target, because of their highly specialized needs. At the same time, however, a large portion of mail order activity focuses on the educational mission and home-bound related goods. The same is true for the 50+ market.

The Net Effect

These are by no means the only changes within the demographic make-up of the country, but they do stress the importance of careful target marketing. The typical consumer is a myth of the past, and today's catalog marketers must incorporate an increasingly complex number of issues and values if they are to become and then remain lucrative players in the industry.

BREAKDOWN OF THE UNITED STATES POPULATION

Population Statistics

The total population of the U.S. is expected to grow from its current 250.4 million to 260.1 million in 1995 and to 268.3 million in the year 2000 -- a 7.1 percent growth rate during the nineties. In 1988, U.S. consumer mail order sales accounted for $64 billion. By 1989, consumer mail order sales totaled $70.4 billion -- 1.4 percent of the $5.2 trillion GNP. The chart below and U.S. Census projections confirm that the population as a whole is gradually aging. Whereas the gross national product grew 41 percent between 1976 and 1988, forecasters predict that GNP growth will slow to 31 percent between 1988 and 2000. This slowing comes as a result of society's aging and the subsequent slowing growth of the labor supply.

POPULATION STATISTICS

DOLLAR FIGURES IN BILLIONS POPULATION IN MILLIONS	1980	1985	1990
Gross National Product	$2,732.0	$4,014.9	$5,524.0
Disposable Personal Income	$1,918.0	$2,838.7	$3,822.8
U.S. Population	227.8	239.3	250.4

	1995	2000	2010
Gross National Product	$5,855.4	$6,313.0	$7,070.6
Disposable Personal Income	$4,052.2	$4,335.8	$4,856.1
U.S. Population	260.1	268.3	282.5

% Persons By Age	1980	1985	1990
Under 18	28.2%	26.9%	25.6%
Ages 18-24	13.3%	11.5%	10.4%
Ages 25-34	16.5%	17.6%	17.5%
Ages 35-44	11.4%	13.3%	15.1%
Ages 45-54	10.1%	9.5%	10.2%
Ages 55-64	9.6%	9.3%	8.5%
Ages 65 and over	11.3%	11.9%	12.6%

% Persons By Age	1995	2000	2010
Under 18	25.1%	24.5%	22.2%
Ages 18-24	9.7%	9.4%	9.6%
Ages 25-34	15.6%	13.8%	13.3%
Ages 35-44	15.9%	16.4%	13.2%
Ages 45-54	12.1%	13.9%	15.3%
Ages 55-64	8.8%	9.0%	12.5%
Ages 65 and over	12.8%	13.0%	13.9%

Population
% change 1980-1990 = 9.9%
% change 1990-2000 = 7.1%
% change 2000-2010 = 5.3%

Demographic Statistics

Along with continued growth in the amount of disposable personal income held by the U.S. labor force, the growth rate of those moving in and out of metropolitan and non-metropolitan areas has slowed, and education level has increased. At the beginning of the 1980s, 51.5 percent of women were in the workforce. That number increased to 56 percent by the end of the decade. On the other hand, the number of men who worked (as a percentage of all U.S. men) fell slightly in the period from 77 percent to 76 percent. The following chart/graph illustrates the changing national picture in relation to major economic indicators. The sensitive nature of the economy during the late 1980's caused a slight constriction in the growth of the mail order industry. However, as more households experience greater earnings potential, more discretionary income, and less leisure time, in-home shopping becomes increasingly more attractive to consumers.

DEMOGRAPHIC STATISTICS

(Millions)	1980	1985	1986	1987
Births	3.6	3.8	3.8	3.8
Households	80.8	86.8	88.5	89.5
Single-Person Households	18.3	20.6	21.2	21.1
Families	59.6	62.7	63.6	64.5
Labor Force Participation Rate				
Men	77.4%	76.3%	76.3%	76.2%
Women	51.5%	54.5%	55.3%	56.0%
Total	63.8%	64.8%	65.3%	65.6%
Civilian Labor Force	106.9	115.5	117.8	119.9
Place of Residence:				
Metropolitan Areas	172.3	182.6	185.3	187.1
Non-Metropolitan Areas	54.2	56.1	56.1	56.3
Educational Attainment Rate:				
High School 1-3 years	17.1%	12.2%	11.9%	11.7%
High School Graduates	34.0%	38.2%	38.4%	38.7%
College 1-3 years	10.2%	16.3%	16.9%	17.1%
College Graduates	11.0%	19.4%	19.4%	19.9%

Exhibit 6B   Statistical Abstract of the U.S. 1990

CHANGING BUYING PATTERNS

Despite the spectacular gains made by direct marketing in the past decade, retail stores are the primary means of distribution for the majority of goods and services. But, opportunistic mail order marketers are capitalizing on the problems that plague retail shopping and play up the benefits of catalog shopping. Ten major problems have been identified as contributory factors to the shifting trend on behalf of American consumers away from in-store shopping, and towards "in-home" shopping. The following is a delineation of these problems and how mail order marketers have turned them into selling advantages.

Consumer In-Store Shopping Problems

1. Inadequate customer service for both sales and returns.
2. Inadequate communication of product information.
3. Deteriorating product satisfaction.
4. Increasing cost of transportation to shopping areas.
5. Inconvenient shopping hours.
6. Inconvenient delivery schedules.
7. Increased customer confusion due to product proliferation.
8. Increased personalization of consumer demand running counter to conventional mass marketing.
9. Increased sophistication of consumer tastes.
10. Decreased pleasure in shopping.

Mail Order Shopping Benefits

1. Perceived full service given to every mail order purchase and customer complaint.
2. Comprehensive product information in writing provided by direct mail.
3. Mail order guarantees assuring product satisfaction.
4. Economy of shopping at home.
5. Convenience of shopping at any hour.
6. Unlimited mail order delivery days.
7. Preselected merchandise in catalogs simplifying purchaser's decision making.
8. Mail order tailored to specific wants of large but scattered consumer segments.
9. Mail order providing access to worldwide shopping.
10. Fun shopping by mail in the relaxed atmosphere of the customer's home.

Analysis of Shopping Problems

(1&2) INADEQUATE CUSTOMER SERVICE AND INADEQUATE PRODUCT INFORMATION. Customers have long complained about the difficulty in getting a salesperson's attention, and then the subsequent rudeness and/or product ignorance of that person. In many stores, sales personnel staffing is inadequate. In mail order, full merchandise descriptions provide necessary details that lead to buying decisions. Additional information is usually a phone call away with the one-on-one assistance to telephone service representatives. If personal in-store service becomes a luxury of the past, catalogs will make more sense than ever.

(3) DETERIORATING PRODUCT SATISFACTION. Catalog returns are becoming easier. Most mail order marketers accept returned merchandise as a way to insure product satisfaction and improve customer service. Unlike mail order customers of the past, today's mail shopper is more likely to return an item if it doesn't meet their expectations. As mail order becomes more sophisticated, consumers demand satisfaction and their expectations increase.

(4) INCREASED COST OF TRANSPORTATION. With the increased cost of gasoline and the new emphasis on environmental concerns, in-home shopping cuts down on the necessity of trips to shopping centers. Even with increasing postage and delivery costs, the convenience far outweighs the hindrances.

(5) INCONVENIENT SHOPPING HOURS. With the rise of single person households and dual income families, and the subsequent whittling away of leisure time, fewer consumers (especially women) are able to shop during conventional store hours. Despite the growing prevalence of this trend, few stores have responded with "off-hour" shopping hours. As a result, the "at-home" shopper finds additional convenience and flexibility in their ability to order merchandise at home at just about any hour of the day.

(6) INCONVENIENT DELIVERY SCHEDULES. Most stores deliver only on certain days to certain areas, but mail delivery occurs six days a week and reaches even the most remote areas. With the growing trend toward overnight shipping, mail delays are becoming a thing of the past, and the mail order shopper has also become an impulse buyer.

(7) INCREASED CUSTOMER CONFUSION BECAUSE OF PRODUCT PROLIFERATION. Many mail order marketers believe mail order is successful because it eliminates choices and subsequently makes decisions easier for many shoppers. Since the merchandise is preselected, decision-making dilemmas are minimized. The onslaught of specialized catalogs has also simplified the selection process by catering to the specialized needs of the consumer.

(8) INCREASED PERSONALIZATION OF CONSUMER DEMAND RUNNING COUNTER TO CONVENTIONAL MASS MARKETING. Mail order marketers need not concern themselves with whether a large enough market for their product exists within a single community. Mail order marketers select their "community" from lists of people throughout the country who are logical prospects. Likewise, consumers with specialized buying interests need not turn only to local marketers for satisfaction as catalogs provide them with countrywide and worldwide selections of goods and services from which to choose.

(9) INCREASED SOPHISTICATION OF CONSUMER TASTES. Along with increased levels of consumer awareness and education have come increased expectations of consumers. Simultaneous increases in discretionary income enable consumers to satisfy their more sophisticated tastes with products of equal sophistication. As a result, consumers demand products which are unique.

(10) DECREASED PLEASURE IN SHOPPING. Lack of trained personnel, the sparsity of product information and less available shopping time for employed persons have taken much of the pleasure out of shopping. City-dwellers have joined their rural counterparts in promoting mail order as an increasingly necessary alternative to store shopping. The fun of ordering rather than the hassle of shopping, the anticipation of receiving ordered products, and the eventual satisfaction with those products have all contributed to more frequent shopping by mail among consumers.

New Consumer Issues

The other trend in buying patterns that is emerging for both retail and catalog marketers is the push toward social and environmental consciousness among consumers. Case in point: Eddie Bauer has institutionalized a company house volunteer program where they pay their employees for time donated to favored charity Easter Seals, and they also encourage their employees to match those hours with unpaid volunteers as well.

In addition, Eddie Bauer catalogs have begun to carry a message asking customers to recycle its catalogs when they're finished shopping. And Rodale Press has instituted its own in house recycling program. On the catalog side, the DMA has formed an Environmental Task Force to look at issues like recyclable paper, packing materials, and public image issues in light of the resurgence in environmental concern.

Unlike the environmental movement of the 1970's which heralded doom that never really materialized nor catalyzed the public to respond in active ways, the current global awareness and action was prompted by real issues. Americans may want to do their part, but current realities like waste management and dwindling resources make compliance a necessity. As consumers continue to look for personal ways to contribute to the global community and pick and choose the things they buy accordingly, moves akin to Eddie Bauer and Rodale's make not only good environmental sense, but good business sense as well.

SPECIAL INTEREST SEGMENTATION

Specialization was the key word in the past decade when it came to catalogs. It wasn't enough to have a catalog operation; specialty catalogs were the order of the day. Today, specialized catalogs are still prevalent, and additional books are unveiled just about every quarter.

But in the nineties, along with specialized catalogs will come the addition of four new areas of segmentation: overnight shipping, increased novelty marketing, ethnic markets, and ever-increasing micro specialization.

Overnight Shipping

Nothing has revolutionized mail order so much as the 800 number and overnight shipping. This change has allowed home shoppers to become impulse buyers. There's an increasing group that doesn't mind paying to get what they want, when they want it, and as a result, more and more catalogs are offering the express mail option. In addition, whole new operations are stemming from this phenomenon. Since September 1989, Federal Express has been producing a small catalog called "Dinners a la Federal Express." Consumers can order foods from around the country from companies including Ben & Jerry's ice Cream, Lou Malnati's Pizzeria, and the Great Maine Lobster Company. Marketing of this type offers both prestige and convenience -- something this group of consumers craves.

Interestingly, a new list has come into being called the Expressline Buyer File. Over 175 leading catalogs have included the names of their Fed Ex buyers, an up-scale, time sensitive group of consumers. Numerous catalogers have used the list as a test, and continuities are beginning to occur. The same time crunch that spurred the fax machine to its widespread acceptance in a short time period has also provided an environment where overnight is the outer limit to some consumers' patience.

Business-to-business consumers have begun to rely on immediate deliveries. Most office suppliers have necessarily added overnight shipping options. The business world demanded it.

Novelty Items by Mail

Along with the varied items included in the FedEx catalog of foods, other niche marketers have appeared on the home shopping scene. In many ways, mail order has made the world seem smaller, and exotic items are no longer isolated to their native regions. With mail order, the limits have expanded and variety is the spice of life. Consequently, things that early mail order pioneers would never have dreamed of have made their way to catalogs. Take, for example, the ability to provide a consumer with live seafood. At least three catalog marketers promote complete dinners with all the trimmings -- you can have a real clambake or lobster feast right in your own home, regardless of where that happens to be. Along with speedy delivery, the increasing sophistication of customers paired with marketers search for new and interesting products to sell have created some marvelously unique marketing opportunities for everyone. At this point, all that's necessary is a little imagination.

Ethnic Markets

Mail order marketers are just beginning to learn about the ethnic interest of consumers. Viewing their country as the great "melting pot," Americans pride themselves on their varied ethnic components. However, for many years, American marketing strategies reflected a flatter, more pointedly Caucasian mind set. But now that's changing. Advertising and marketing has begun to reflect national diversity.

The number of Hispanic Americans will triple by 2080, becoming 20 percent of the total population. The spending power of Hispanics increased from $104 billion in 1987 to $160 billion in 1989, and unlike popular misconceptions, they aren't a homogenized, downscale segment. Retailers have launched specific marketing campaigns directed specifically toward this group, and a few catalogers are beginning to follow suit. Most notably, J.C. Penney has produced brochures in Spanish which aid in catalog utilization, and they've also added an 800 number for their Spanish-speaking customers. Hispanic media is cheaper than Anglo, and the returns are traditionally higher. One stumbling block will be the subgroups within the Hispanic segment including Cubans, Central and South Americans, Mexicans and Puerto Ricans. In the coming decade, unsung groups will demand a greater voice if they're to contribute to the spending pool. Groups want to see themselves and their interests reflected in marketing forms.

Fine Tuning Specialization

In the past, the advent of specialty catalogs was the way many larger catalogers chose to diversify their product mix. Today, many catalog operations start out at a very specialized level. Fewer marketers go the route of big general merchandise players like Sears and J.C. Penney, rather they target potential buyers at a more specialized level like Talbots' upscale apparel offerings or the electronic specialties of The Sharper Image. In the last few years, even the specialists have become more specialized. Case in point: Placewares, a marketer of "organization products" is testing the idea of breaking its already specialized business of storage units down to separate catalogs for the work space, kitchen, or bedroom closet.

Micro-specialization progressed through the 1980's partly as a result of the sophistication of database information. Databases provide increasingly detailed looks at customers, and specialization has become the natural off-shoot of database technology. Ironically, publishing directories keeping track of nothing more than the more than 8000 different catalogs in the consumer marketplace have sprung up. Just keeping track of all of the players has become a job in and of itself.

Chapter 7

Major Factors

Affecting

Mail Order

Growth

USE TAX

In 1967, cataloger National Bellas Hess Company was taken to court by the state of Illinois. The issue was over "use tax," a tax which the cataloger would have to collect from its customers in Illinois and then pay to that state. Since Bellas Hess did not have any actual retail outlets, distribution centers, or other "physical presence" in the state of Illinois, the company felt that it did not need to pay taxes there, and that this attempt to collect was unconstitutional. The Constitution of the United States mandates that a state may not impose tax collecting burdens on a company which has no direct presence in that state, hence deriving no benefit from those taxes nor having the opportunity to take part in the state's political process. The U.S. Supreme Court sided with the cataloger, creating the now widely-debated Bellas Hess vs. State of Illinois precedent. This decision made it clear that a company with insufficient "nexus" (physical presence) in a state did not have to collect and pay use tax. However, no definitive description of a sufficient nexus was determined. Use tax simply presents a way to create additional state revenues without imposing new taxes on its residents. By law, the responsibility to pay use tax already lies with the mail order consumer. Since it is inherently difficult for the states to assure payment of taxes on every product ordered by mail, they are attempting to transfer such collecting and accounting responsibilities to the individual catalogers. Although the U.S. Supreme Court has sided with catalogers in every court case to date, strong arguments on both sides of the issue make a final outcome difficult to predict.

Twenty-seven states have already adopted use tax laws and four more are currently preparing such amendments to their legislation. Citing John Gibbs of the California State Board of Equalization, states feel that Bellas Hess is an outdated ruling since direct marketing has matured to the point at which "it is exploiting the industry as well as any retailer, and should therefore pay taxes." North Dakota just completed the first round of litigations against business product by mail supplier, Quill. "When compared to North Dakota retail stores [in terms of annual revenues], Quill is the seventh largest supplier of office products in the state. We feel it is justified to tax them," said Carla Smith of the North Dakota Tax Commissioner's Office. North Dakota argued that Quill's ninety day guarantee did not transfer title of ownership immediately, and that Quill actually retained physical property in the state for three months. Although the courts ruled in favor of Quill, the state plans to continue the case at a higher level.

The Quill vs. North Dakota case illustrates the dilemma created by the vague Bellas Hess decision of 1967. States feel that each case is different and that the precedent does not apply to their specific circumstances. The original case was decided for a company that mailed a relatively small circulation of catalogs into a limited region. Many states consider toll-free numbers within a state and credit cards drawn on local banks as sufficient nexus. California goes so far as to say that any service, such as a cataloger utilizing a collection agency in the state, constitutes a sufficient physical presence. States additionally point out that many nation-wide catalogers with retail operations (Spiegel, J.C. Penney, Sears, etc.) are already collecting taxes from most of their catalog orders and that others should have minimal difficulties in adapting as well. States also offer such incentives as tax credits in an attempt to help compensate retailers for the additional burden of collecting and accounting.

A few years ago, Spiegel settled out of court with an agreement to collect use tax through all of its catalogs. "At that time we had just acquired Eddie Bauer and Honeybee. With their retail stores, we had to already collect taxes on approximately seventy-five percent of our orders. Since the technology was already in place, it was never an issue to implement it. Had we not been in the same position, we would not have settled [out of court]," explained Spiegel's Debbie Koopman. Others may not adapt so easily. A small or medium-sized direct marketer might incur tremendous expense in implementing the necessary technology and would need to hire and train additional employees to keep track of the taxes collected.

Catalogers strongest argument is that they do not derive the benefits which their taxes are supposed to provide -police protection, the upkeep and use of state roads, etc. They also lack the constitutionally guaranteed political representation which the payment of taxes is supposed to insure. Another issue is that many consumers prefer mail order over retail because of the convenience. With the varying tax rates from state to state, consumers would have to spend more time calculating the proper amount. Catalogers reason that many consumers will miscalculate taxes, simply not pay, or worse, turn away from buying through the mail altogether. Current state legislation, according to catalogers, make little or no provisions for adequately reimbursing mail order companies for uncollected taxes or loss of business.

As more cases are decided by the U.S. Supreme Court, a more precise definition of "sufficient nexus" is becoming tangible. The state of Pennsylvania lost a case against Bloomingdale's By Mail recently, because the courts ruled that the cataloger was a separate entity from the Bloomingdale's retail stores. This decision will affect many catalogers whose separately operating retail divisions represent their only physical presence in a state where use tax collection is being attempted, by definitively declaring them as exempt. The DMA is currently searching for a direct marketer to sponsor that has as its only physical presence in Nevada, credit cards drawn there and toll free numbers. A U.S. Supreme Court victory for the cataloger would force other states to comply and would exclude credit cards and toll free numbers as determining factors for a sufficient nexus. The DMA hopes that such a decision would force states to realize that two of the most widespread tools in direct mail do not justify use tax collection.

The DMA suggests several ways in which the complex use tax issue may be lightened, if not solved altogether. Foremost, uniform taxes must be agreed upon. Many catalogers currently have to deal with varying states' taxes, and even taxation within a single state is inconsistent, different rates being effective on the state, county, and municipal levels. Congress should also define in current technology terms what exactly constitutes a sufficient nexus. This definition must be precise and comprehensive enough to allow catalogers to make their future business decisions. The DMA additionally suggests that toll free numbers and credit cards be omitted from the definition of sufficient nexus due to their widespread usage. After all, at the time of their implementation, catalogers assumed that their usage would be protected under the 1967 U.S. Supreme Court decision.

The last factor to consider is the widespread belief by catalogers and industry experts that use tax collection may actually backfire on the states attempting to enforce them. Various research statistics indicate that the states are often basing the potential for revenues generated through use tax collection on inflated figures. Additionally, they do not consider the tremendous expense involved in all phases of the new use tax laws. Administrative costs for both catalogers and the government will be tremendous. Many small and mid-sized catalogers could go out of business if they cannot meet the financial demands imposed by these additional tax collecting burdens. Although states favor use tax collection as an alternative to increasing local taxes, in all actuality, use tax is just another tax paid by that state's consumers. Loss of business due to the lessening of convenience in mail order will drastically decline revenues, in return lessening the use tax that can be collected. Some predict that states could actually lose tax revenues when all of these factors come into play.

REFINED DATABASE MANAGEMENT

The database is a computer file on a customer which includes name, address, telephone number, SIC code (for businesses) and a history of the customer's purchases, by item, price and date of purchase. This file gives the direct marketer a picture of who each customer is. However, it only becomes really effective when the marketer learns to manipulate the data in a way that fits his business objective.

A number of service companies specialize in database management. In addition to basic information, they can add demographic data such as the customer's age, income and family status. These databases are gathered not only from customer orders, but also from written questionnaires and telemarketing campaigns.

While major mail order companies purchase outside mailing lists and customer data, even small companies can benefit from maintaining a database of information on their customers which can be compiled on a personal computer.

One added benefit of database marketing is that it can be used to enhance a company's marketing program in all media. Print, radio and TV, as well as direct mail and catalogs, along with traditional sales channels, can be tied into a well maintained database.

The value of the data is only as good as its accuracy. The United States Postal Service National Change of Address Service (NCOA) provides a useful service for keeping files current. As shown on the chart below, not all catalog marketers have used this service, but when it has been employed, it has met with good success.

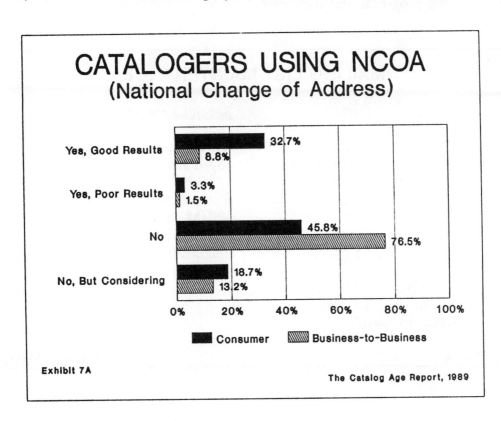

Moving Address Changes

During any given year in the 1980's an average 20 to 30 percent of the population relocated, making it difficult to maintain accurate addresses on mailing lists. Additionally, the USPS reports that 66.9 percent of its addresses are accurate and complete while 33.1 percent suffer from various omissions, errors, or are wholly inaccurate. The following list highlights the percentages of trouble addresses for the post office, and, consequently, for the mail order industry.

ACCURACY OF POSTAL ADDRESSES

66.9%	accurate
8.7%	moved
8.5%	missing altogether or inaccurate
6.1%	problem with street name or number
4.2%	problem with city, state, or zip code
3.0%	problem with apartment number or suite number
2.8%	problem with rural route

Exhibit 7B   The Catalog Marketer

As a response to relocation and information problems, the USPS and private service companies created list maintenance programs during the decade designed to combat change in address and to flag inaccurate addresses. The following table illustrates the main programs and their costs.

MAILING LIST MAINTENANCE

Program	Cost	Special Features
NCOA	$2.00-4.00/M	Set-up varies
ZIP+4	$1.00-3.00/M	$5/M savings
Dupe Elim	$2.00-3.00/M	1/2-30% found
CASS	no charge	Rates service
Mail Stops	no charge	$20/M savings
CRC	$3.00-7.00/M	bag tags and zip audits incl.
M.A.I.L.	no charge	diagnostic program in conjunction with USPS
Elim-I-Nix	$.03-.06/hit	
Finalist	$40,000	
Group 1	n/a	

Exhibit 7C   The Catalog Marketer

Most diagnostic programs can and should be run in tandem with other troubleshooting programs. Care must be used in choosing which to apply in which order, and when to apply the programs in the house cleaning process.

The National Change of Address (NCOA) program maintained by the USPS is updated every two weeks, is 97 percent accurate, and treats the 8.7 percent errors caused by relocation. The end result is a three to four percent corrected return, which costs $.05 to $.10 per name. The USPS also offers NCOA Nixie -- an alternative file which, when used in conjunction with the main file, provides a cross check and flags addresses known to be wrong. Together, the two programs serve mail order merchants effectively for the cost.

Using the ZIP+4 file of 25 million names as a cross check to a list serves as an effective way to troubleshoot as well. Additionally, the ZIP+4 system provides better and faster delivery, a $.005 discount per piece, and offers already compiled free demographic/psychographic information. The coding breakdown is as follows:

ZIP +4	ZIP CODES
10	Street Delivery
14	P.O. Box
18	Rural Route
20	High-rise
21	Firm/Organization
22	Postmaster
26	General Delivery

Exhibit 7D   The Catalog Marketer

ZIP+4 can enhance a list by providing free demographic information which can serve as a tool to better target mailings along with serving as a troubleshooter cross check.

Fraud

As a part of database management, many companies are instituting the use of "negative files." As a stay against mail order and credit card fraud, some companies use files of known fraudulent credit card numbers, prison inmate lists (which are available from the federal and state governments), known bogus mail stops and bogus addresses, and the names of individuals known to steal merchandise through the mail.

Some companies add problem customers to the list who have been chosen for excessive returns, bounced checks, and credit problems. For relatively little cost, mail order companies build their own "negative files" to weed out bad apples from their house lists; additionally, mail order companies are starting to freely share these lists among themselves.

Business-to-Business List Management

Special problems arise for business-to-business direct marketers. Business-to-business mail order sells to companies, but must still target individuals. This creates inefficient mailings when a company may receive many duplicate catalogs. List management gets more complicated when an employee, as opposed to the company itself, moves. So, marketers favor a list which emphasizes a company as a buyer.

Privacy

The population of the United States is becoming more concerned with personal privacy. As the growing distrust towards information sharing rises and resentment towards invasion of privacy mounts, the direct marketing industry faces a tough political issue in the nineties. As list sales blossomed in the eighties, so did consumer trepidation. The following tables outline consumer attitudes and concerns.

As the following table indicates, private citizens do not support the sharing of consumer information beyond mailing addresses. As direct marketers work towards better targeted lists and more complete demographic information, the general public attitude may hinder information acquisition. At present, little legislation stands in the way of direct marketing, but most trends indicate that change is on the way. Already some vote blocks support an affirmative consent requirement on all list sales by each specific consumer name. The consequences to mail order are obvious.

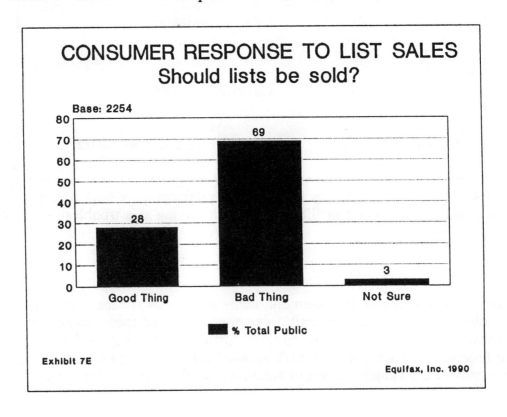

PAPER AVAILABILITY AND COSTS

As the following chart indicates, the paper industry during the 1980's experienced market fluctuations which closely followed the general trends in the economy. Earnings dropped during the 1982 recession, peaked in the mid-to-late eighties, and have recently slowed. Market analysts expect a mild cooling in the paper industry in the early nineties; earnings should drop 15 percent in 1990 from 1989 levels. The relative weakness of the dollar is expected to fuel exports (which accounted for 7.8 percent of paper production in 1988) and national supply and demand is not expected to shift significantly, thus countering the weak market.

Paper sales in the early nineties are expected to grow slowly. If the expected recession occurs, paper prices will not alter significantly; consolidation within the industry since the last recession has stabilized the industry with fewer, stronger companies controlling prices. As a result, prices have been relatively low and stable through the late eighties, stemming from the strong dollar of the mid eighties which cut into exports and drove domestic prices down. Paper prices are expected to stabilize in the early nineties as exporting strengthens, despite the expected recession.

Capacity increases have been moderate in the last few years as paper companies act conservatively and are cautious against spreading resources too thin. Escalating costs of new production facilities, the lack of soft wood mills in North America, and the increasing difficulty in obtaining operating permits inhibited expansion.

As a result of costly building, many companies opted instead to buy additional capacity. The Georgia-Pacific take-over of Great Northern Nekoosa indicates a change in the previously well protected and unified paper industry. Most companies have refrained in the past from take-over attempts and in some cases acted as white knights to protect the industry from outsiders. However, the industry is expected to quickly abandon tradition and enter into a more aggressive, less cooperative stance among its companies; the nineties should see many mergers, beginning with moderate sized targets owning attractive assets.

Market pulp prices have risen in the last four years and have topped out. Prices are expected to fall in the next few years due to pulp being the most volatile commodity in the paper industry. Market pulp is the main paper which catalog printers utilize; it rose to $830 per ton in 1989, up four percent from 1988. Prices are expected to hit a low in the $700 range in 1990. Coated paper, the other most utilized paper in the catalog business, dropped to $900 per ton, a three percent loss from 1988 to 1989. Coated paper, due to consistent demand, is expected to remain stable; growth in the nineties will be neither dramatic nor negative.

Wood costs are rising. The closing of some sawmills in the Pacific Northwest and lawsuits from conservationists have tightened the wood chip industry. In the nineties, wood prices are expected to continue to rise and will be the highest rising expense for paper producers.

Current social trends supporting recycling will affect the demand for virgin pulp, though presently industry leaders see no significant drop in paper demand for the future.

78

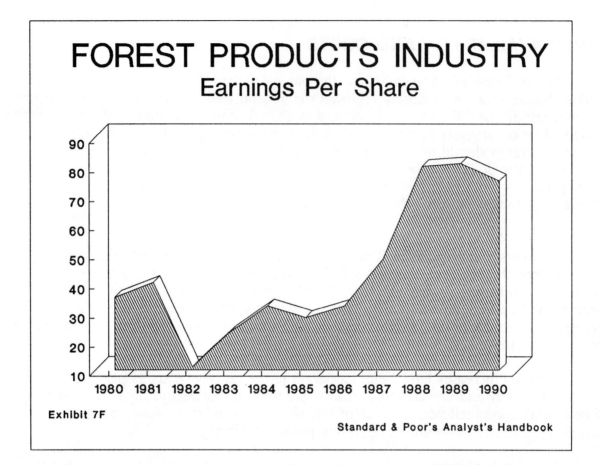

FOREST PRODUCTS INDUSTRY
Earnings Per Share

Exhibit 7F

Standard & Poor's Analyst's Handbook

POSTAL COSTS

The controversy over postal rates has been around almost as long as there's been mail. With the postal rate increase February of 1991 at the end of ten months of public hearings, direct mailers are again up in arms, and with good reason. The United States Postal Service (USPS) made three major rate changes during the 1980's, each one levying more damage to the direct mail industry. Since the USPS is making a push toward automation, and will rely more than ever on its optical Character Recognition (OCR) system, the current proposed increase signals a shift in the USPS attitude away from the interests of third-class advertising mailers. For the first time, non-letters or flats and catalogs will now have a higher rate than third class, letter-sized mail since they're not automatable.

The postal hike increased first class postage from its current 25 cents to 29 cents. Simultaneous increases for third class mailers ranged from 14 to 33 percent, and some estimates place total impact on direct mail marketers at $7.6 billion. Catalogs which aren't yet automatable could therefore be charged up to 3 cents more per piece versus automation compatible pieces.

Although the USPS rationalizes the rate increase based on their deficit situation since 1988, direct marketers have everything to lose and very little to gain. Perhaps the greatest strain will fall on the "little guys" whose small profit margins won't allow them to absorb the increased costs and who cannot afford to pass the costs on to their consumers. The law requires that each class of mail pays it's own expenses and other institutional, overhead costs. Still, the $7.4 billion USPS request isn't enough. They are also requesting a $1.4 billion contingency fund to cover unanticipated costs. Catalogers aren't the only victims. Philanthropic organizations and political campaigns will end up spending more as well.

Because of sky rocketing mailing costs, direct marketers must mail smarter. They must eliminate names of people from lists who aren't qualified for certain promotions or who have been ineffectively targeted. Eliminate duplicate mail, people who have moved or died, and addresses not meeting USPS deliverability standards. Improve the quality of the house list, and use compiled lists for prospecting. The National Change of Address (NCOA) system will go a long way to prevent undeliverable mail. Plus, database technology is making it easier to compose complete demographic pictures of clients, to refine lists accordingly.

Catalog marketers can also do a lot to fit into the new push toward automation. Advanced lettershop capabilities like electronic inserting, drop-shipping and pre-barcoding will ensure cost effective results. Palletization will also reduce postal costs by reducing the sorting at the post office's end. Indeed, work sharing may be the most effective way to cut costs by cutting down on the work of the USPS. Work sharing methods include various levels of pre-sorting and moving mail to USPS destination centers thereby eliminating previous USPS work steps.

The most radical response to the issue of postal rate hikes is to turn to alternative, private delivery methods. In this arena, two services have cornered the market. The Time-Warner venture Publisher's Express handles between 200,000 and

300,000 pieces each month. Alternate Delivery Systems (formerly United Delivery Systems) handles 800,000 monthly pieces. The DMA co-sponsored a software system with ADS. In the next five years, alternate delivery players expect to create national networks and expand aggressively. With their ability to undercut the USPS price per weight option with less expensive price per piece costs, alternate delivery systems will create serious competition for the USPS.

Regardless of outcome, the uncertainty surrounding the future of the postal service demand that direct marketers monitor the USPS and the Postal Rate Commission's activities throughout the duration of the current rate hike case, and in subsequent years. Ignoring the problem won't make it go away.

POSTAL RATE HISTORY FOR
BULK BUSINESS MAIL

(SHOWN IN CENTS)	1960	1963	1964	1965	1968	1969
Third Class/piece	2.50	2.63	2.75	2.89	3.60	3.80
First Class/piece	4.00	5.00	5.00	5.00	6.00	6.00

	1971	1972	1973	1974	1975	1976
Third Class/piece	4.04	4.85	4.80	6.10	7.70	7.50
First Class/piece	8.00	8.00	8.00	10.00	13.00	13.00

	1978	1981	1982	1983	1985	1987
Third Class/piece	8.40	10.40	10.90	11.00	12.50	16.70
First Class/piece	15.00	18.00	20.00	20.00	22.00	25.00

NOTES:

Rates for 1969-76 Third class reflect first 250,000 pieces/mailer/year rate.

Rates for 1978-1987 third class piece rates are regular bulk rates.
Lower rates are available if mail is sorted more precisely than minimum requirements (5 digit Zip Code, carrier route).

Exhibit 7G   Direct Marketing Association

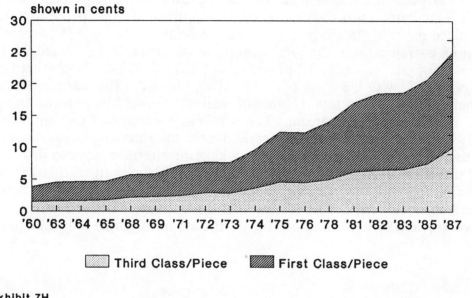

POSTAL RATE HISTORY
1st Class vs 3rd Class Cost Per Piece

Exhibit 7H

Direct Marketing Association

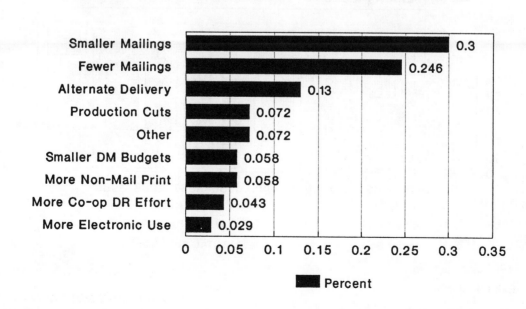

POSTAL RATE HIKE EFFECTS
Postal Rate Increase will Result in ...

Exhibit 7I

Advertising Age, 1990

Third Class Postal Statistics

During the 1980s, third class revenues continued to grow while third class volume slowed and, in the first half of 1990, actually dropped. In 1980, Third Class mail volume was 28.6 percent of the total mail distributed in the United States. In 1988, that ratio had grow to 39.17 percent, increasing steadily at approximately one percent annually. In 1988, the USPS increased third class rates, adding approximately 28 percent more expense per piece mailed. As a result, third class volume showed a 2.35 percent loss for that year and its overall ratio to the total number of pieces mailed declined 1.6 percent. Revenues, however, grew a steady 7.7 percent from 1988 to 1989. Comparing the first three quarters of 1990 with the same period in 1989, illustrates the alarming condition of third class mail. Although the total volume of mail has grown 1.98 percent, third class mail volume increased only .49 percent. The pending (average 16.7 percent) postal rate increase in 1991 will force catalogers to nearly double their mailing budgets within two years. Because of this, direct marketers are looking for alternate ways to distribute their catalogs and direct mail pieces, shrinking the USPS traditionally strong market share. Following the same trend, revenues for both third class and total mail have shown healthy growth since 1980; although, for the first three quarters of 1990, while total mail revenues have grown 2.98 percent, those for third class have grown only 1.34 percent.

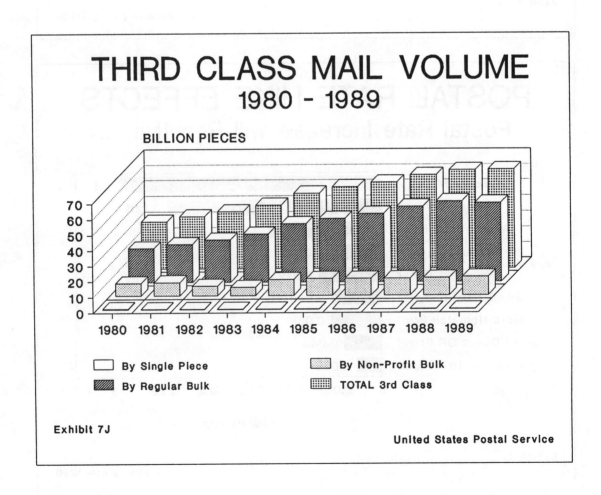

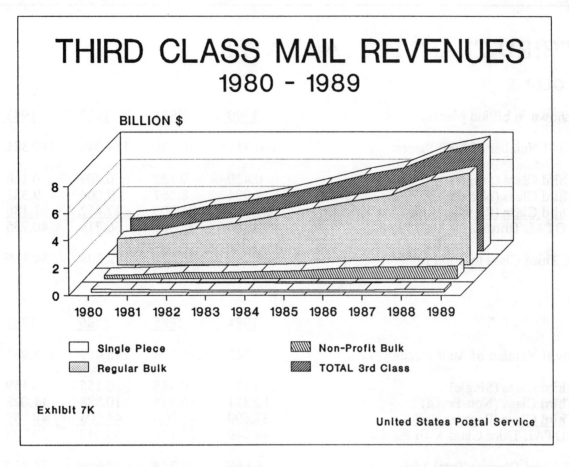

THIRD CLASS MAIL REVENUES
1980 - 1989

BILLION $

Single Piece

Regular Bulk

Non-Profit Bulk

TOTAL 3rd Class

Exhibit 7K

United States Postal Service

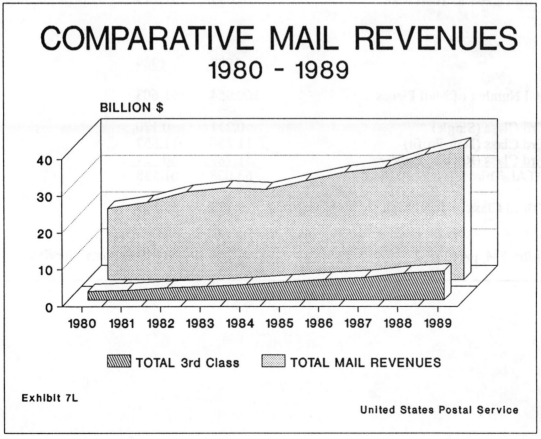

COMPARATIVE MAIL REVENUES
1980 - 1989

BILLION $

TOTAL 3rd Class

TOTAL MAIL REVENUES

Exhibit 7L

United States Postal Service

THIRD CLASS POSTAL RATES

VOLUME

(shown in billion pieces)	1980	1981	1982	1983
Total Number of Mail Pieces	106.311	110.130	114.049	119.381
Third Class (Single)	0.420	0.335	0.203	0.168
Third Class (Non-Profit)	7.964	8.567	9.064	9.381
Third Class (Regular Bulk)	21.997	24.706	27.452	31.186
TOTAL Third Class Mail Pieces	30.380	33.607	36.719	40.735
% Third Class to Total Mail	28.58%	30.52%	32.20%	34.12%

	1984	1985	1986	1987
Total Number of Mail Pieces	131.545	140.098	146.409	153.931
Third Class (Single)	0.178	0.168	0.155	0.159
Third Class (Non-Profit)	10.371	10.976	10.888	11.022
Third Class (Regular Bulk)	37.699	41.026	44.006	48.553
TOTAL Third Class Mail Pieces	48.249	52.170	55.049	59.733
% Third Class to Total Mail	36.68%	37.24%	37.60%	38.81%

	1988	1989
Total Number of Mail Pieces	160.954	161.603
Third Class (Single)	0.211	0.170
Third Class (Non-Profit)	11.250	11.857
Third Class (Regular Bulk)	51.789	50.731
TOTAL Third Class Mail Pieces	63.038	61.588
% Third Class to Total Mail	39.17%	38.11%

Exhibit 7M, part 1 of 2   United States Postal Service

THIRD CLASS POSTAL RATES

REVENUES
(shown in billion $)

	1980	1981	1982	1983
Total Mail Revenues	$19.261	$20.918	$23.741	$24.819
Revenue 3rd Class Single Piece	$0.216	$0.208	$0.178	$0.157
Revenue 3rd Class Non-Profit Bulk	$0.259	$0.302	$0.425	$0.443
Revenue 3rd Class Regular Bulk	$1.909	$2.104	$2.667	$3.039
TOTAL Revenue 3rd Class Mail	$2.412	$2.643	$3.303	$3.677
% 3rd Class Revenue to Total	12.52%	12.64%	13.91%	14.81%

	1984	1985	1986	1987
Total Mail Revenues	$25.216	$27.642	$30.002	$31.417
Revenue 3rd Class Single Piece	$0.156	$0.149	$0.149	$0.153
Revenue 3rd Class Non-Profit Bulk	$0.498	$0.561	$0.743	$0.836
Revenue 3rd Class Regular Bulk	$3.541	$4.136	$4.671	$5.112
TOTAL Revenue 3rd Class Mail	$4.241	$4.887	$5.606	$6.148
% 3rd Class Revenue to Total	16.82%	17.68%	18.69%	19.57%

	1988	1989
Total Mail Revenues	$34.894	$37.744
Revenue 3rd Class Single Piece	$0.200	$0.203
Revenue 3rd Class Non-Profit Bulk	$0.860	$0.899
Revenue 3rd Class Regular Bulk	$6.199	$6.769
TOTAL Revenue 3rd Class Mail	$7.311	$7.924
% 3rd Class Revenue to Total	20.95%	20.99%

Exhibit 7M, part 2 of 2   United States Postal Service

86

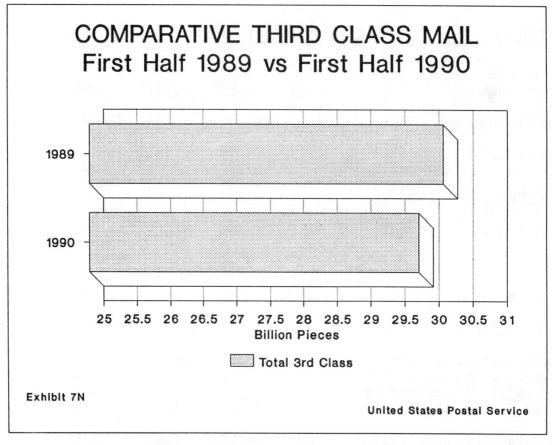

COMPARATIVE THIRD CLASS MAIL
First Half 1989 vs First Half 1990

Billion Pieces

Total 3rd Class

Exhibit 7N

United States Postal Service

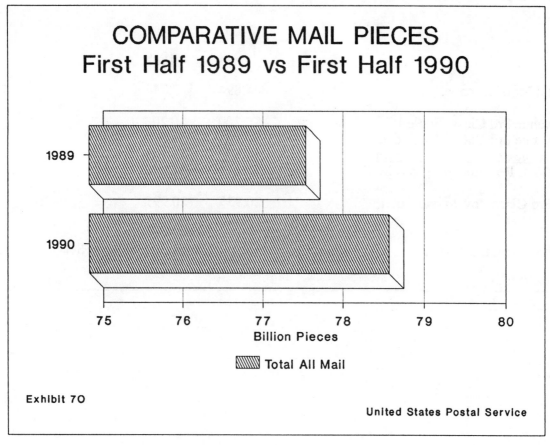

COMPARATIVE MAIL PIECES
First Half 1989 vs First Half 1990

Billion Pieces

Total All Mail

Exhibit 7O

United States Postal Service

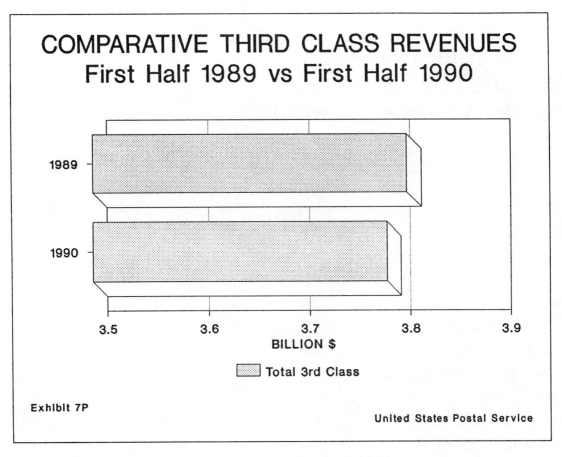

COMPARATIVE THIRD CLASS REVENUES
First Half 1989 vs First Half 1990

Exhibit 7P

United States Postal Service

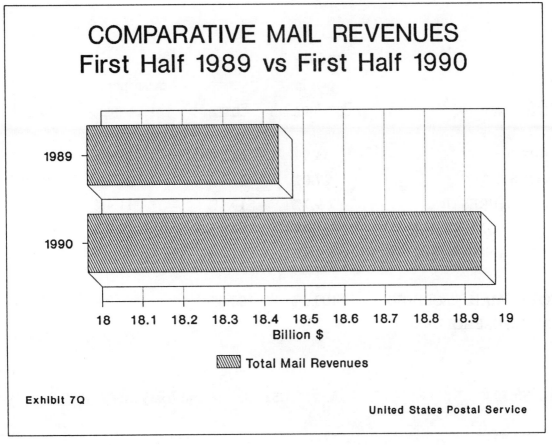

COMPARATIVE MAIL REVENUES
First Half 1989 vs First Half 1990

Exhibit 7Q

United States Postal Service

CONSUMER INTEREST
IN THIRD CLASS MAIL

(Percentage of Mail Received by Households, 1988)

Usefulness	Letter-Size Envelope	Larger Than Letter Envelope	Detached Label Card	Post-Card
USEFUL	32.4%	36.2%	25.7%	34.9%
INTERESTING	21.5%	28.0%	17.4%	18.3%
NOT INTERESTING	27.8%	22.9%	36.5%	33.0%
OBJECTIONABLE	7.0%	4.9%	7.5%	6.1%
DON'T KNOW/NO ANSWER	11.3%	8.1%	12.9%	7.7%
TOTAL MAIL RECEIVED BY HOUSEHOLDS	100.0%	100.0%	100.0%	100.0%

Usefulness	Catalog Not In Envelope	Flyers	Newspapers/ Magazines	Total
USEFUL	55.5%	44.3%	37.4%	40.3%
INTERESTING	27.0%	21.4%	19.3%	23.0%
NOT INTERESTING	9.7%	19.1%	11.4%	21.5%
OBJECTIONABLE	1.9%	3.4%	2.9%	4.6%
DON'T KNOW/NO ANSWER	5.9%	11.9%	29.1%	10.6%
TOTAL MAIL RECEIVED BY HOUSEHOLDS	100.0%	100.0%	100.0%	100.0%

Exhibit 7R   USPS Household Diary Study, 1989

Third Class Delivery Performance

In 1988 and 1989, Litle & Company conducted a test of third class postal delivery performance. Four hundred pieces were tracked during a normal week and then compiled into an aggregated statistic which reported how long the average piece took to get from region to region (see map below); also reported was the average percentage of pieces not delivered. As a comprehensive grade, judging the entire delivery system for third class mail, performance was poor. (A "C minus" in the words of T.J. Litle's Charles Perry.) This borderline performance is not entirely the USPS' doing, though; slowed and non-delivery could result during any number of steps along the total process, including at letter shops and with data base companies which may have processed list information incorrectly.

POSTAL DELIVERY REGIONS

Exhibit 7S

T. J. Litle & Company

It took an average of eleven days for third class mail into and out of all ZIP regions. Coincidentally, eleven percent of all third class pieces tracked during the test period was not delivered. Mailings within a single ZIP region took an average of two days, although one day delivery was not unusual.

The following is a listing of statistics during the period from August 1988 to July 1989:

Best delivery time:	1 day (nine occurrences)
Worst delivery time:	77 days (mailed from region three to eight)
Second worst delivery time:	63 days (mailed from region three to five)
Best average delivery time:	4 days (mail originating from region one)
Worst average delivery time:	40 days (mailed into region four)
Best percent not delivered:	0 percent (several occurrences)
Worst percent not delivered:	37 percent (mailed into region four)
Second worst percent not delivered:	36 percent (mailed into region four)

The following summarizes the best regions to mail into and out of:

Best to mail to:
Delivery days:	Region two (9 days)
Percent not delivered:	Region three (5 percent)
Best overall:	Region three (11 days, 5 percent)

Worst to mail to:
Delivery days:	Region one (12 days)
Percent not delivered:	Region four (18 percent)
Worst overall:	Region four (11 days, 18 percent)

Best to mail from:
Delivery days:	Region two (9 days)
Percent not delivered:	Region zero (8 percent)
Best overall:	Region zero (10 days, 8 percent)

Worst to mail from:
Delivery days:	Region eight (14 days)
Percent not delivered:	Region three (16 percent)
Worst overall:	Region three (10 days, 16 percent)

As a whole, ZIP region four (Michigan, Indiana, Ohio, and Kentucky) ranked worst. Although delivery days were sometimes on par with the best regions, its high non-delivery percentage brought down its rating. The following summarizes region four's performance:

Average days mailed to:	11 days
Average days mailed from:	10 days
Percent not delivered to:	18 percent
Percent not delivered from:	15 percent

Regions zero, three, five, and seven all came very close in comparative "best overall in/out" rating, with region seven the most consistent area throughout the test. However even an average eleven percent non-delivery is disappointing to direct marketers. That figure means that "eleven percent of your mailing budget is being totally wasted," according to Perry. The study also indicates an apparent relationship between the visual appearance of a mailing piece and its delivery; the more "promotional" it appears, the less likely it is to arrive. Additionally, the deliverability test suggests that the delivery process treats every third piece of mail as trash. Catalogers must examine the process of getting direct mail to the consumer and eliminate or improve poor connections.

ALTERNATIVE DELIVERY SYSTEMS

The Postal Reorganization Act, passed into law on August 12, 1970 made the United States Postal Service a business dependent on its own income rather than existing off federal supplements. Prior to this act, postage was kept low and funds necessary to keep the USPS in the black came from federal taxes. Taxes were used to pay for the Postal Service regardless of the amount of mail which any given citizen actually mailed. Postal rates prior to 1971 were simply lower than the actual cost of delivering pieces of mail. Since the Postal Reorganization Act, rates have increased steadily, faster than the rate of inflation, prompting catalogers to find alternate ways of catalog and direct mail distribution. Since second (magazines) and third class (catalogs and saturation mail) are exempt from the Private Postal Service Express Statute, those classes of mail provide the largest area for competition. In fact, since the early 1970s, many magazines and most newspapers have been privately delivered.

In the early 1980s, many companies sprang up in an effort to undercut USPS prices. Due to the large amount of investment capital necessary to launch a nation-wide delivery service, many smaller, poorly financed companies went out of business. After a shake out in 1981 and 1982, United Delivery Service walked away with the largest share of the newly established niche market. The company grew slowly, yet steadily, currently handling 800,000 pieces of private mail a month. By offering prices calculated by piece, rather than weight, UDS managed to recruit more and more catalog business away from the Postal Service's third class segment. The company, which changed its name in 1990 to Alternate Postal Service, Inc., estimates its prices to be fifteen percent lower than those of the USPS; even larger price differences are realized on heavier pieces. The Direct Marketing Association "estimates a [potential] loss of $100 million in revenues from the USPS and a shift of 26 billion pieces of mail [annually]" to alternate delivery methods in the years to come.

In 1988, a major postal rate increase raised catalogers' mailing costs by approximately twenty-eight percent. Because of this tremendous increase in costs and in preparation for any future postal cost increases, catalogers "made a commitment to test and develop alternate delivery systems," said Chet Dalzell of the DMA. As a direct response, Time-Warner's "Publisher's Express" was created in July 1989, joining Alternate Postal Service as the second largest alternate delivery service. "Publisher's Express" focuses primarily on magazine deliveries, although thirty-five percent of its estimated monthly deliveries are catalogs. In addition to the two large, nation-wide delivery services, regional services have developed in most cities throughout the United States. "Publisher's Express" and Alternate Postal Service plan to enlarge the scope of their operations by acquiring such companies with only a small, regional delivery area as independent affiliates, and then help them implement the technology necessary to run a successful alternate delivery business. They will additionally supervise the integration of services so that a universal format and price is used for them and their affiliates. With the enlargement of the two companies' reach, alternate delivery will have a nation-wide scope similar to the USPS, making it even more appealing as an inexpensive alternative to the steadily increasing third class rates of the United States Postal Service. Along with superior pricing, alternate delivery companies also have the benefit of being flexible toward customers' marketing needs. Alternate delivery offers inexpensive polybag "ride-along" packages, which the USPS only provides on a limited basis and for considerably higher fees. Magazines and pay-basis catalogs can be renewed through local delivery/sales representatives. The delivery person receives a list of those customers whose subscription is about to expire and can personally solicit their renewals.

Judging by the stunted growth which the USPS' third class volume experienced in 1989, and by the decline in volume for the first half of 1990, speculations based on the planned 16.7 percent postal rate increase in 1991 look optimistic for alternate delivery companies. More alternate delivery will appear around the country each year. Combined with such vehicles as CompuServe's shopping mall and increasing at home shopping vehicles which catalogers are utilizing as an alternative to mailing catalogs, the future for the USPS' third class segment looks poor. Predictions are that an increasing share of the Postal Service's market share will be deferred to alternate means each year. Phillip Miller of Alternate Postal Service said, "we plan to be the UPS or Federal Express of second and third class mail. Years ago, people didn't believe it was possible." The main task of the USPS is letter mail. Unfortunately, it has tried to specialize in a large area of mail delivery and has lost its cost effectiveness. Because the USPS is spreading itself so thin, alternate delivery will prosper as the competition for the second and third class niche market rises.

Chapter 8

Mail Order

Businesses

MAJOR CORPORATIONS WITH MAIL ORDER OPERATIONS

As mail order companies have begun to grow and prosper they have become attractive as corporate acquisitions. Corporations vary in approach; some add to existing retail operations, while others market unique lines of products which fit manufacturing and buying facilities. Some corporations simply see an opportunity to buy and finance profitable mail order operations with no direct tie to other in-house efforts.

Some foreign corporations turned recently to American mail order as a market with wide potential. Japanese giants Tobu Department Stores and the AEON Group ventured into mail order through the acquisition of direct marketers/retailers Gump's and Talbots respectively.

Expectations for the nineties favor mail order operations with strong capital bases. As shakeout in the industry consolidates the market in the future, those players with the most cash will maintain healthy profits. As mail order matures, like many other young industries in the past, from overnight success to sustainable profitability, corporate positions in the market strengthen.

CORPORATIONS WITH MAIL ORDER

Parent Corporation	Mail Order Segment	Year Added	Type of Product
Adler & Shaykin	Best Products	1988	Discount general merchandise
AEon Group (Jusco Co.) (Japan)	The Talbots	1988	Women's and children's apparel
American Protection Industries	The Franklin Mint	1985	Collectibles and gifts
Businessland	Businessland Catalog	1986	Computer hard/software
Dun & Bradstreet Corporation	Carol Wright Sales, Inc.	1979	General merchandise
Field Corporation	Field Publications	1985	Educational publications
FPL Group	Colonial Penn Group	1985	Insurance
Hachette S.A. (France)	Grolier	1988	Educational publications
Horn & Hardart	Hanover House (Direct)	1973	Gifts, Apparel, Furnish., & Acc.
J.C. Penney's	J.C. Penney's	1962	Apparel & general merchandise
Macy's	I. Magnin	1989	Apparel
Macy's	Bullocks-Willshire	1989	Apparel
Macy's	Bullocks	1989	Apparel
Playboy Enterprises, Inc.	Critic's Choice	1988	VHS films
Playboy Enterprises, Inc.	Sarah Coventry		Jewelry
Playboy Enterprises, Inc.	Playboy Catalog		Lingerie
Sara Lee Corporation	Wolferman's	1986	English muffins
Sara Lee Corporation	Coach Leatherwear	1985	Leather accessories & gifts
Sara Lee Corporation	L'eggs	1972	Women's hosiery
Sears, Roebuck and Company	Sears catalog	1895	Apparel & general merchandise
Spiegel Holding Co. (Otto Versand)	Spiegel	1982	Apparel and general merchandise
The Limited	Victoria's Secret Catalogue	1982	Lingerie & women's apparel
The Limited	Brylane Catalog Division	1982	Women's apparel
Tobu Department Stores Co. (Japan)	Gump's	1989	Gifts, fine art, & jewelry
Primerica	Fingerhut	1979	General merchandise & gifts

Exhibit 8A

Maxwell Sroge Publishing

COMBINED MAIL ORDER AND RETAIL BUSINESSES

Mail order operations and retail stores often combine well and provide companies with a stronger way to reach consumers. By operating mail order and retail marketing efforts in tandem, companies can offer the best of both worlds and meet the needs and wishes of all its consumers. The leading three direct marketers, Sears, J.C. Penney, and Spiegel, all maintain both retail and catalog operations, realizing the value of combined marketing. By operating retail stores, direct marketers can control inventory better (through the use of sales and discounting), and allow consumers who prefer retail to take advantage of the product range of a catalog. At the same time, companies have found that their retail and catalog customers may be quite different people.

Rather than competing with mail order customers, retail stores can often tap into or reinforce a new regional market and bring in more consumers who are unfamiliar with a company's catalog. This process also builds a company's house list. The three largest companies are not alone. Many smaller companies have increased sales and profits by expanding early into combined marketing efforts. Trends indicate that tandem marketing requires more resources and provides better penetration and outcome. The following four brief company highlights illustrate the specifics of turning toward tandem marketing.

Spiegel

Spiegel, which sells almost exclusively through catalogs, acquired Honeybee and Eddie Bauer in 1988. Both companies focused on retail sales, with their catalogs sustaining only a small fraction of their apparel markets. Spiegel felt that both Eddie Bauer and Honeybee could learn from its expertise in direct mail and continue to expand their relatively small catalogs. In return, Spiegel gained a foundation in retail and learned how to improve its own outlets (used to liquidate excess catalog merchandise) from the two retailers. Debbie Koopman, Manager of Spiegel's Investor Relations, stated that "many companies fail because they do not keep separate facilities for mail order and retail. It is often very difficult to run the two types of business under one roof." Spiegel has prospered by keeping the two facets of business separate, yet complimentary, and is leading Honeybee and Eddie Bauer down the road to success.

Banana Republic

Banana Republic garnered a strong reputation based on its unique, water color painted catalogs. The company was established in 1978 as a privately held apparel merchant of safari and outdoors clothing and accessories. After experiencing success in the apparel market, Banana Republic expanded; "Trips" magalog was added to its operations, selling books and information about travel. The new addition had an almost immediate negative impact on Banana Republic's core business, as the bottom line started dropping. In 1983, retailer The Gap bought Banana Republic's mail order apparel business and its two retail stores. Catalogs were circulated less frequently as Banana Republic's new parent refocused the company's energy on retail expansion. A final catalog was mailed to the Banana Republic list in early 1990, offering a toll free number for orders rather than an order sheet, and supplying the location of the retail store closest to any given customer. Banana Republic currently operates 118 retail outlets, supplemented by space ads for catalog inquiries in The Wall Street Journal. Under new ownership, the company has shifted its marketing venues away from catalogs and conducts primarily retail transactions. The catalog has lost its function as revenue generator and instead adopted the role of retail support vehicle.

The Sharper Image

In 1978, attorney Richard Thalheimer created the Sharper Image, following a successful ad in "Runner's World" advertising digital sports watches. The initial catalog, mailed in 1979 generated $500,000 in revenues for that year, and offered an expanded product line, including exercise items, electronic gadgets, and gifts. Seeing a way to capture previously unsolicited customers in the San Francisco area, The Sharper Image opened its initial retail outlet in 1985. Houston and Denver stores soon followed. The company began to focus on retail but continued to fuel catalog operations. Currently retail substantiates seventy-five percent of overall revenues, with seventy domestic and eight international outlets. Media/Public Relations Manager, Gary Schweikhart commented that when a new store is opened, the Sharper Image always reaches new customer. Initially, there may be some cannibalization away from the catalog business, which soon evens out as some of the newly acquired retail shoppers start to use mail order instead. He feels that the impact of opening the 70th store was obviously not as dramatic as when the initial outlets were opened, but the company still acquires a large amount of previously unreached consumers for its house list. "We added retail because it gives us the advantage of reaching non mail order people." The Sharper Image's successful utilization of both direct mail and retail shows how tandem marketing can improve a company's overall performance by accessing previously untapped retail markets and building on the existing mailing list in the same process.

CompuAdd

CompuAdd, launched in 1982, began by placing space ads in trade publications, supplemented by relatively small retail operations. The initial catalog was mailed in 1987 and sold IBM hard and software. This expansion from the limited reach of space ads proved to be a "major revenue generator," according to John Q. Pope, Director of CompuAdd's Corporate Relations department. "[A catalog] is much more cost effective than space ads and acts very much complementary [to our existing retail operations]." He admits that some cannibalization occurs when new retail outlets are opened, but counters that the new retail customers generated make up for that minimal loss in CompuAdd's mail order segment. In 1989, the company refocused on retail, yet insisted that all sales channels will continue their traditional growth. To bolster direct marketing, CompuAdd launched its second catalog, "MacAvenue," in early 1990, focused on Macintosh products. "Our philosophy is not to be wed to a single channel [of marketing]. We wish to have diversity and balance in our operations." Revenues that have increased from $28 million in 1985 to over $610 million in 1990, suggest that CompuAdd has managed to find a truly complementary balance between catalog and retail operations.

As these examples illustrate, a company must progress with caution when changing its marketing focus. Concentrating exclusively on one segment of business can cause the other to lose substantially, in some cases beyond rescue. As numerous companies have found out, poorly planned retail locations can take away from booming catalog areas. On the other hand, retail can also reach new, non mail order customers that have not yet been exposed to the company's products.

MERGERS AND ACQUISITIONS

Mail order and direct marketing expanded dramatically in the 1980's. The number of catalogs increased and flooded consumers with a myriad of shopping options. And consumers responded in kind. The mail order market showed wide growth in the eighties and promises further expansion in the nineties. Industry innovators made substantial profits, small mail order companies were formed, larger companies added specialty catalogs, and new approaches toward capturing consumer interest were implemented. Direct marketers generally experienced steady growth in the last decade. As a growth industry, mail order not only gained credibility with consumers, but also with investors. Mail order businesses themselves have become a commodity.

Although mail order was originally perceived solely as an add-on for retail operators, proven longevity and credibility brought the industry to the notice of investors. No longer a faddish afterthought, mail order has come into its own, demanding market attention. The Reagan administration's deregulation laws and lenient anti-trust policy brought on a barrage of stock market and investment activity in the early eighties. Mergers and acquisitions became the name of the game -- and mail order was not unaffected. The advent of leveraged buy-outs and consolidation led to company debt and monopolization, threatening the stability of many once secure corporations. Junk bonds, a hot item in the eighties, added to an already volatile market.

While the stock market cooled in the late eighties, mail order companies remained hot. The mail order industry suffered a low 1987 stock performance but quickly rebounded, outperforming the stock market by 12 percent in 1988. Since the market fray began, catalogers have employed anti-takeover measures through a variety of defense mechanisms including poison pill debt incurment, staggered boards, rights options, golden parachutes, and employee stock purchasing campaigns. Mail order companies have learned, many of them the hard way, that the time to employ such measures is before you need them, and not while in the throws of a hostile action.

Mail order not only caught the eye of the domestic investors, but also attracted foreign investors. Within the next decade, foreign investors will play an increasingly greater role in domestic marketing. Global influences and fluctuations will further affect mail order. The Common Market of 1992 Europe promises additional opportunities for international mail order, and state-side catalogers have already begun positioning themselves for the potential opportunities. Mail order has gone on to become an international commodity as well.

Mail order in the nineties will certainly continue to expand, and that expansion will in turn continue to breed interest in the industry as a stock commodity. In light of the increasing cost of expanding existing operations and spin-off catalogs, more companies are looking to their fellow, established participants as acquisition candidates. Acquisition has become an attractive expansion strategy, with the benefit of an established list and lower costs to buy rather than grow an operation.

MERGERS AND ACQUISITIONS 1986

DATE	COMPANY	SOLD BY	COMPANY SALES	SOLD TO	PRICE
FEB	Sturbridge Yankee Workshop	CML		Carlisle Capital Corp.	
	FPL Group	merge		Colonial Penn	$35/s
MAR	Goldberg's Marine Distributors		$20 mil	E & B Marine	
	UCI (Used Computers Inc.)			Sorbus	
MAY	Benefit Consultants			Comp-U-Card	
	Kobs & Brady			Ted Bates Worldwide	
	Micro Mart		$15 mil (Chapter 11)	Data Research Associates	
JUNE	Tandycrafts		$75 mil	Initio	$47 mill for 11% stake
	Browncor		$7.5 mil	W. H. Brady	
JULY	Fingerhut	AmCam		Maj. Cable Network	in return for stock
AUG	Stuart McGuire			Home Shopping Network	$5/s for 68%, rest in Oct.
	Boston Paper			E & B Giftware	
OCT	Marketing Outlooks & Certified Collateral Corp.			Comp-U-Card	
	Sportpages			Sporting Life	$900,000 in assets + $5 mil in scrip
	Russell Miller & A.A. Sales		$6 mil combined	Rapidforms	
	Pottery Barn			Williams-Sonoma	
NOV	Looart Press & Current	Dusty & Gary Loo		American Can Co. (Fingerhut)	$114 mil cash
DEC	Bear Creek (Harry & David, Jackson & Perkins)		$150 mil	Shaklee	$123 mil cash
	Just-For-Kids & Giggletree		$7 mil, a little less, respectively	Grolier	
	Brookstone & Jos. A. Bank	Quaker Oats		group of mgmt & investment bankers (Brookstone)	$215-220 mil

Exhibit 8B, part 1 of 5

Maxwell Sroge Publishing

MERGERS AND ACQUISITIONS 1987

DATE	COMPANY	SOLD BY	COMPANY SALES	SOLD TO	PRICE
JAN	Doubleday & RCA Record & Music Publishing	RCA Direct	$170 mil	Bertlesmann A.G.	$300 mil for balance RCA music ops.- 25% prev. owned
FEB	Baltimore Federal Financial			Home Shopping Network	$40 mil
APR	Giorgio		$18.5 mil	Avon	$185 mil
	Burpee	Clayton & Dublier		separate company (BT Capital, Wicks Capital, Burpee Execs.)	
MAY	Sycom Limited Partnership		$13 mil	NEBS (New England Business Service)	
JUNE	Western Ranchman Outfitters		$2.2 mil	Gander Mountain	
	Master Vaccine		$2+ mil	Gander Mountain	
AUG	Sunshine Shippers (Mission Orchards & Calif. Cuisine)		$5 mil	Hormel (George A. Hormel & Co.)	
	Avon Direct Response Division (renamed New Hampton, Inc.)			Avon Products management team	$151.2 mil
	Krames Communications		$17 mil	Grolier	
SEPT	ACI Financial Corporation			National Liberty	
NOV	Misco	Gillette		Electrocomponents P.L.C.	undisclosed
DEC	Current (Looart Press & subsidiary Current)		$125 mil	Deluxe Check Printers	$150 mil cash
	National Card Control, Inc.			CUC	$15.5 mil

Exhibit 8B, part 2 of 5

Maxwell Sroge Publishing

MERGERS AND ACQUISITIONS 1988

DATE	COMPANY	SOLD BY	COMPANY SALES	SOLD TO	PRICE
JAN	Jerry Leonard Retail Stores	Allied Corp.		King Size Company	undisclosed
FEB	Abercrombie & Fitch	Oshman's Sporting Goods	$50 mil	The Limited	$47 mil
	Hills Court			DM Management	
MAR	Grolier			Hachette S.A.	$450 mil
	Childcraft	Hatchette		Walt Disney	$52 mil
	Honeybee		$33 mil	Spiegel	$23 mil
	Yield House	Standex	$4.2 mil (fiscal 3rd qtr.)	ASM Group (NY investment firm)	$6.6 mil charge
APR	Eczel			Pryor Corp.	
	Jenifer House		chapter 11	DM Management	
MAY	Golf Day			DM Management	
	Eddie Bauer	General Mills	$250 mil	Spiegel	$260 mil
	Talbots	General Mills		Jusco	$325 mil
	Bullocks, Bullocks Wilshire, & I. Magnin	Federated Dept. Stores of Calif.		Macy's	$1.1 bil
JUNE	Brooks Brothers	Campeau	$250 mil	Marks & Spencer	$770 mil
	Johnny Appleseed		$32 mil	Jelmoli	
JULY	Nicole Summers & Winterbrook Fulfillment Center			DM Management	
	Funk & Wagnalls			Field Publications	
AUG	Direct Marketing Technology		$22 mil	Maxwell Communications	
SEPT	Primerica	merge		Commercial Credit Group	$1.7 bil in stock + cash
	Kron Chocolatier	merge		Casa Nova Chocolate	
OCT	American Accents	McCormick Spices		DM Management	
	Horchow		$125 mil	Neiman Marcus	$125 mil
	Career Guild	Aparacor	$15 mil	Hanover Companies	
	America's Shopping Channel		chapter 11	CVN Companies & Cox Cable	
NOV	The Very Thing!	Swiss Colony	$15 mil	DM Management	
	Crown Publishing & subsidiary Publisher's Central Bureau			Random House	

Exhibit 8B, part 3 of 5

MERGERS AND ACQUISITIONS 1989

DATE	COMPANY	SOLD BY	COMPANY SALES	SOLD TO	PRICE
JAN	Direct Action Marketing	Ocilla Industries		The Meadow Group	340,000 shares at $5.125/s (26% stake)
MAR	Shaklee & Bear Creek mail order subsidiary			Yamanouchi Pharmaceutical	$395 mil
	General Nutrition Catalog		$23 mil	Nature's Bounty	$7 mil
	Direct Action Marketing	Ocilla Industries		The Meadow Group	$6.3 mil (74% stake)
APR	Devoke	NEBS		Devoke management	$1 mil after-tax charge on sale in its 3rd fiscal qtr. (NEBS)
MAY	Hamilton Group		$485 mil	Stanhome Inc.	
	Lerner Women Division	The Limited		management-led investment group	
JUNE	Curriculum Innovations Group	General Learning Corp.		Field Publications	
	The Sportsman's Guide			Vincent Shiel	controlling interest of stock for $500,000; $500,000 term loan; $750,000 short-term secured bridge financing.
AUG	The Company Store (majority interest)			Ardshiel	
	Down's Collectors Showcase	Johnson Worldwide Associates		First Provident Group, Inc.	
SEPT	Golf Day	DM Management		Stan Black	
OCT	Western Ranchman Outfitters	Gander Mountain	$113 mil	management buyout to exec vp & cfo, Frederick Wojik	$3.1 mil
	CVN (all of common stock)			QVC	
NOV	Popular Science Book Club	Grolier Inc.		Meredith Corp.	
	CPS Direct	Carson Pirie Scott		P.A. Bergner	$282 mil bid

Exhibit 8B, part 4 of 5

Maxwell Sroge Publishing

MERGERS AND ACQUISITIONS 1990

DATE	COMPANY	SOLD BY	COMPANY SALES	SOLD TO	PRICE
JAN	King-Size Catalog Business	King-Size		WearGuard	
FEB	Universal Direct			Reliable	
MAR	Joan Cook	Jim & Joan Cook		Investor group headed by Harold Schwartz	
	Sybervision	CML		Shansby Group	
APR	Hedly Taylor PLC	Hedly Taylor	$40+ mil	Nashua	

Exhibit 8B, part 5 of 5   Maxwell Sroge Publishing

MAIL ORDER FIRMS

Many direct mail companies have chosen to "go public." A public stock offering allows a company to grow quickly and expand its horizons with newly generated funds. The following list is representative of the many catalogers and direct response marketers who have chosen to go public in the last decade:

Company's Name	Public Offering Date	Service/Product Description
Businessland (San Jose, CA)	December 1983	Computer accessories
CML Group, Inc. (Acton, MA)	September 1983	Apparel and gifts
Collectors Guild Int'l Inc. (Bronx, NY)	February 1981	Home decorations
Dell Computer Corporation (Austin, TX)	June 1988	IBM PC compatibles
E&B Marine (Edison, NJ)	April 1983	Marine and boating supplies
Epic Health Group (Elmsford, NJ)	January 1986	Medical prescriptions
Fashion Channel Network Inc. (Irvine, CA)	October 1987	Apparel, accessories and gifts
Gander Mountain, Inc. (Wilmont, WI)	April 1986	Outdoor equipment and apparel
Home Shopping Network Inc. (St. Petersburg, FL)	May 1986	Consumer and insurance products
Inmac Corporation (Santa Clara, CA)	1986	Computer and data communication products
Land's End Corporation (Dodgeville, WI)	1986	Apparel
Lillian Vernon Corporation (Mount Vernon, NY)	August 1987	Gift, household and children's accessories
Medi Mail, Inc. (San Diego, CA)	April 1987	Generic prescriptions and health products
Primerica Corporation (New York, NY)	November 1986	Financial services, consumer goods (Fingerhut)
QVC Companies Inc. (Westchester, PA)	September 1986	Shop-at-home consumer products
Reader's Digest Association (Pleasantville, NY)	February 1990	Publisher, books and magazines
Regal Communications Corp. (Moorestown, NJ)	September 1986	Publisher for lottery segment
The Sharper Image Corp. (San Francisco, CA)	April 1987	Electronics, health/fitness items and gifts
Spiegel, Inc. (Oakbrook, IL)	October 1987	Apparel, accessories and general merchandise
TJX Companies (Framingham, MA)		Specialty apparel (Chadwicks of Boston)
Viking Office Products Inc. (Los Angeles, CA)	March 1990	Office products
Williams-Sonoma, Inc. (San Francisco, CA)	July 1983	Cooking accessories, home furnishings and garden accessories

Exhibit 8C

Maxwell Sroge Publishing

PERFORMANCE OF SELECTED FIRMS

The following nine publicly held mail order companies represent a diverse group of industry leaders. While they cannot serve as guides for the mail order industry as a whole, they do serve as examples for sales and earnings fluctuations for large corporations.

While the cumulative fluctuations on this table of nine companies is more dramatic than the industry's trends as a whole, the slow-down in the 1987 marketplace, along with the accompanying growth in 1986, is clearly apparent. As cash and credit flow tightened, the dollar's value dropped, and competition and costs rose, consumer spending slowed earnings to a cumulative -3.03 percent in 1987. This follows the industry's 1987 performance and parallels the 9 percent loss in earnings overall. These nine companies tended to perform better than the industry in profits; most had the resources to weather economic storms and take advantage of the 1987 slow-down. As the nation entered a recession, some large mail order businesses profited by offering inexpensive, convenient merchandise to consumers who had turned away from retail shopping. Profits dipped in 1988, in contrast to the industry as a whole which experienced mild growth, indicating that these large companies also fall victim to economic fluctuations and that the 1987 rise in profits cut into 1988 expenses. The market further cooled in 1989, meeting industry norms; sales continued to level off as profits remained stalled. As large, publicly held mail order corporations enter the nineties, steady sales growth is expected and profits will climb at a slower rate than that of the mid eighties, continuing the trends in the late eighties.

SELECTED COMPANIES
ANNUAL SALES

Thousand $	1984	% CHANGE	1985	% CHANGE
Commerce Clearing House	422.65	86.60%	435.95	3.15%
Dreyfus	143.63	13.04%	134.95	-6.04%
Frederick's of Hollywood	44.04	-2.26%	46.62	5.86%
GEICO	994.97	14.01%	1219.41	22.56%
G-R-I	111.91	14.19%	83.70	-25.21%
New England Business Svc	147.03	19.19%	166.26	13.08%
Safecard	52.11	20.63%	64.81	24.37%
Shopsmith	75.78	5.21%	50.01	-34.01%
Williams-Sonoma	52.14	20.03%	68.30	30.99%
TOTAL	2044.26	12.71%	2270.01	11.04%

Thousand $	1986	% CHANGE	1987	% CHANGE
Commerce Clearing House	519.39	19.14%	551.50	6.18%
Dreyfus	231.89	71.83%	272.96	17.71%
Frederick's of Hollywood	50.84	9.05%	58.97	15.99%
GEICO	1429.80	17.25%	1582.20	10.66%
G-R-I	77.70	-7.17%	82.37	6.01%
New England Business Svc	229.29	37.91%	203.64	-11.19%
Safecard	87.98	35.75%	118.68	34.89%
Shopsmith	44.00	-12.02%	36.54	-16.95%
Williams-Sonoma	84.63	23.91%	127.16	50.25%
TOTAL	2755.52	21.39%	3034.02	10.11%

Thousand $	1988	% CHANGE	1989	% CHANGE
Commerce Clearing House	612.39	11.04%	677.45	10.62%
Dreyfus	267.78	-1.90%	272.10	1.61%
Frederick's of Hollywood	65.03	10.28%	80.07	23.13%
GEICO	1548.99	-2.10%	1621.40	4.67%
G-R-I	79.11	-3.96%	64.86	-18.01%
New England Business Svc	202.42	-0.60%	225.93	11.61%
Safecard	107.00	-9.84%	115.14	7.61%
Shopsmith	38.74	6.02%	43.23	11.59%
Williams-Sonoma	174.18	36.98%	218.17	25.26%
TOTAL	3095.64	2.03%	3318.35	7.19%

Exhibit 8D, part 1 of 2   Maxwell Sroge Publishing

SELECTED COMPANIES
ANNUAL PROFITS

Thousand $	1984	% CHANGE	1985	% CHANGE
Commerce Clearing House	40.27	61.60%	44.84	11.35%
Dreyfus	38.63	13.62%	55.64	44.03%
Frederick's of Hollywood	0.21	-77.17%	0.16	-23.81%
GEICO	131.31	15.44%	170.58	29.91%
G-R-I	-1.32	-160.00%	-5.67	-529.55%
New England Business Svc	12.71	5.48%	14.06	10.62%
Safecard	6.19	12.96%	14.64	136.51%
Shopsmith	0.74	-72.18%	-2.70	-464.86%
Williams-Sonoma	-0.04	-105.56%	2.43	5975.00%
TOTAL	228.70	16.27%	293.98	28.54%

Thousand $	1986	% CHANGE	1987	% CHANGE
Commerce Clearing House	47.55	6.04%	52.79	11.02%
Dreyfus	80.60	44.86%	95.81	18.87%
Frederick's of Hollywood	-0.63	-493.75%	1.21	92.06%
GEICO	217.74	27.65%	177.90	-18.30%
G-R-I	1.25	77.95%	2.13	70.40%
New England Business Svc	21.96	56.19%	22.02	0.27%
Safecard	22.55	54.03%	28.51	26.43%
Shopsmith	0.70	74.07%	-0.45	-164.29%
Williams-Sonoma	2.04	-16.05%	1.92	-5.88%
TOTAL	393.76	33.94%	381.84	-3.03%

Thousand $	1988	% CHANGE	1989	% CHANGE
Commerce Clearing House	49.49	-6.25%	34.34	-30.61%
Dreyfus	92.31	-3.65%	147.88	60.20%
Frederick's of Hollywood	1.72	42.15%	3.04	76.74%
GEICO	189.04	6.26%	213.05	12.70%
G-R-I	-5.58	-361.97%	-2.96	-153.05%
New England Business Svc	22.43	1.86%	22.19	-1.07%
Safecard	23.30	-18.27%	24.60	5.58%
Shopsmith	0.45	200.00%	1.47	226.67%
Williams-Sonoma	5.21	171.35%	8.97	72.17%
TOTAL	378.37	-0.91%	452.58	19.61%

Exhibit 8D, part 2 of 2

Maxwell Sroge Publishing

110

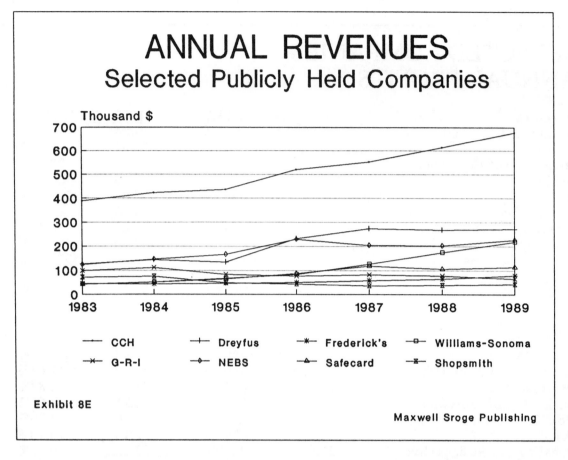

ANNUAL REVENUES
Selected Publicly Held Companies

Thousand $

Legend: CCH, Dreyfus, Frederick's, Williams-Sonoma, G-R-I, NEBS, Safecard, Shopsmith

Exhibit 8E

Maxwell Sroge Publishing

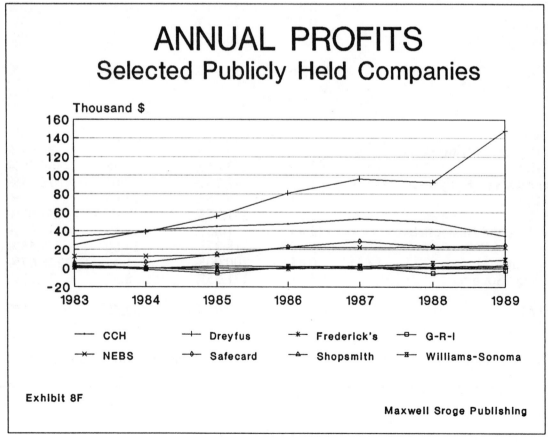

ANNUAL PROFITS
Selected Publicly Held Companies

Thousand $

Legend: CCH, Dreyfus, Frederick's, G-R-I, NEBS, Safecard, Shopsmith, Williams-Sonoma

Exhibit 8F

Maxwell Sroge Publishing

CORPORATE PROFIT RATIOS

Overall, mail order posted a strong performance in the eighties.

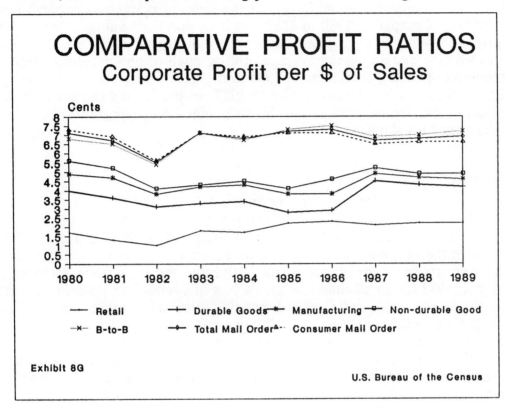

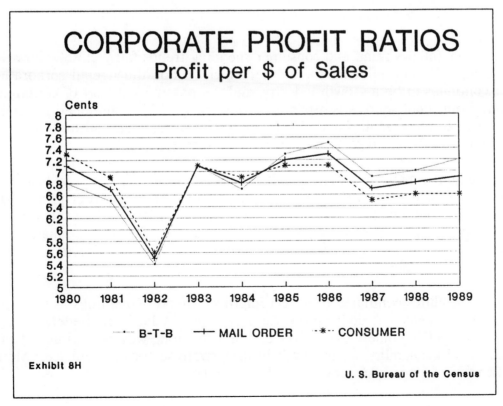

Retail

The retail industry reports lower proportionate profits than manufacturing or mail order, but is the most stable of the three industry groups. Its trends closely match economic and socioeconomic national factors as the industry is solely dependent upon consumer spending. Comparing 1980 to 1989, retail corporations gained twenty-three percent in profits to sales; an aggregate total for the industry shows a 1.9 cent profit to dollar of sales average and an overall average profit growth of one percent. The improved economic spending conditions of 1985 and 1986 allowed for the greatest gain of the decade, though, as the slight recession in 1987 cut profits, the market leveled out in the later part of the decade. Growth in the early nineties is expected to be slow as the marketplace remains sluggish.

Manufacturing

Goods producers had the hardest time in the 1980's. In 1981, Federal debt demanded tighter money policy and looser fiscal policy in order to stimulate the economy without making major spending cuts and control rising interest rates. The resulting effect on the economy reduced credit availability and lowered domestic savings rates, thus leaving less funds for private sector businesses and higher interest rates. Manufacturing in 1982 hit an all time low with a loss of twenty-four percent. During the mid-eighties, the foreign trade deficit stifled manufacturing sales, again creating an all-time low for goods producers in 1985. Conditions improved in 1987 as the economy improved and interest rates dropped. The manufacturing market has yet to reach 1980 profit levels and the current market has leveled off. The Federal Reserve is again tightening money availability and the nineties may create a restricted environment for manufacturers.

Mail Order

Mail order follows retail and consumer spending trends fairly closely; however, a number of unique factors influence the market which do not affect retail corporations. Mail order continues to be a growth industry, and the potential market of consumers turning away from retail sources is expanding. The early 1980's continued to reflect the booming growth of the seventies and also reflected the predominant attitude that mail order served as an adjunct to retail and direct sales forces.

As an adjunct, mail order sharply felt the recession of 1982 as many businesses trimmed what they saw to be alternative marketing programs; mail order profits per dollar of sales dropped eighteen percent from 1981 levels, a loss of 1.2 cents per dollar. As discretionary income and cash availability increased in 1982 and 1983, mail order proved to be a resilient, strong industry of its own by jumping to its previous 1980 profit ratio of 7.1 cents per dollar.

The mid-eighties continued to reflect improved market conditions as mail order reached a peak 7.3 cents per dollar profit ratio in 1986. In 1987, the Federal Reserve's tightened money policy hindered cash flow and add to, along with rising interest rates and limited credit availability, a slow down in the private sector marketplace. Mail order profit ratios dropped 0.6 cents, or eight percent.

In addition to standard economic and demographic factors, mail order in the late eighties has had to absorb continually rising postal costs, higher printing costs, and cope with increased competition. Due to these rising costs, mail order marketers have relied heavily on the strengths of targeted marketing: controlling outside list rental and prospecting, controlling volume, frequency, and timing of mailings, and implementing pricing and merchandising strategies aimed at specific segments of their customer bases. These measures have enabled them to better weather the economic storms of the late eighties.

Proportional mail order growth is expected to slow in the early nineties as its market share increases; this reflects both rising competition and the increased size of the industry. Nevertheless, while proportionate growth may slow, sales and profits will continue their established momentum into the nineties.

Consumer Mail Order

Consumer mail order in the early 1980's controlled a higher proportion of mail order profits than business-to-business market segments. It enjoyed phenomenal growth rates before and after the 1982 recession; profits per dollar climbed 1.5 cents from 1982 to 1983, a 21 percent climb. In the mid-eighties consumer marketing profits continued strong growth; however, the untapped opportunities in business markets allowed business-to-business mail order to increase profits at a higher proportional rate. In 1986, consumer mail order hit its peak on 7.5 cents per dollars of sales. The stifled marketplace of 1987 affected consumer mail order, especially apparel, more severely than other mail order segments. Competition increased substantially in the consumer mail order market, costs rose, and consumer discretionary income dropped. These conditions created the flat 6.6 cents profit per dollar of sales ratio in 1988 and 1989. Consumer mail order is expected to experience some shake-out in the early nineties and will continue its ten percent sales growth. Profits are expected to climb as the industry segment continues to streamline its operations.

Business-to-Business Mail Order

Business-to-business mail order in the early eighties provided direct marketers with open-door potential. The rising needs in the office-place demanded efficient, cost effective services. After the 1982 recession, business-to-business mail order climbed 1.6 cents profit per dollar of sales, a twenty-four percent rise from the previous year. During the optimal conditions of the mid-eighties and utilizing the growing needs of the computer users and manufacturers industries, business-to-business mail order climbed to the lead of mail order profits. In 1985, consumer mail order profits rose 0.2 cents per dollar of sales, whereas business-to-business mail order profits increased 0.6 cents per dollar of sales. These profits are due mainly to the rapidly expanding computer supplies and accessories market and due to the needs for streamlining in the American office-place. As the 1987 slowdown occurred, businesses turned to mail order as an efficient way to shop for supplies and equipment. Profits are expected to rise in the early nineties; however, rising costs and competition, especially within the computer mail order segment, are expected to curb profit growth.

Chapter 9

New
Marketing
Technologies

NEW MARKETING TECHNOLOGIES

Despite the enormous number of catalogs in circulation, direct response marketers have diversified their marketing techniques through a number of new technologies of which mail order pioneers might only have dreamed.

The Computer Age

It didn't take long for the personal computer to infiltrate the American household, and it took marketers even less time to realize the PC has applications beyond word processing and games. The rise of the computer and increasing computer literacy has opened up an entirely new and expanding arena for direct response marketing, helping busy people get things done faster and easier.

Videotex

The PRODIGY two-way interactive personal computer service (videotex) has emerged as the leader of the industry. Forged through a partnership between IBM and Sears, the available services continue to expand. At a $10 flat rate a month, PRODIGY offers customers everything from financial services to travel to shopping to entertainment to grocery shopping to information. Interactive computer systems boast customer ease in use and colorful graphics, and simply requires a compatible PC, a personal password, a phone line and modem, and a disk drive. At the end of 1989, total users stood around 250,000 with PRODIGY taking in approximately $2 million a month in subscription revenues.

As videotex ventures like PRODIGY and CompuServe (approximately 550,000 subscribers) become more popular, more companies will join the videotex marketing revolution. The benefit to marketers is the ability to conduct surveys, generate leads, test marketing concepts and build a database based on customer behaviors.

Consumers enjoy the control they have in an interactive system. But the market hasn't grown as rapidly as anticipated and a number of major companies failed to find a niche in two-way computer services in the 1980s.

Ad Disks

Another important advance for the developing home computer market is the prevalence of ad disks. Stemming from the growing saturation rate of PC's and the difficulty to tap the elusive PC users group, the diskette has become a cost effective way to reach people. Once inside the diskette menu, users can access in-depth information on a myriad of products in unusual ways. This marketing format has proven especially useful, and the consumer applications are growing more attractive for direct marketers; PC users are collectively falling in to the $45,000 median income level and able to satisfy "high ticket" marketers.

From the marketing point of view, the cost associated with production and distribution of ad disks is highly competitive with print and video, and considering an ad disk audience is usually more attentive and views a disk more than once, returns are higher. At this point the only limits on the technology are computer illiteracy and equipment computability constraints. In their favor, these little wonders boast a high pass-along rate and a long shelf life, something most catalogers wish they could say about their catalogs.

The FAX Revolution

Almost overnight the Fax machine became a fixture in offices and even homes and cars. The fax has changed the nature of business. Overnight is no longer fast enough -- business is handled in terms of minutes and hours, not days and weeks. For direct marketers, the fax machine offers one more way for customers to place an order, and it also represents an intriguing direct mail alternative.

Along with the positive results, the fax has become the latest arena for debate. The fax has bred its own nuisance in the form of the "junk fax." Unsolicited and unwanted ads have the industry in an uproar since they tie up an important piece of office equipment and waste supplies. Some legislators have rallied to promote anti-fax laws restricting and banning unsolicited faxes promoting goods and services in response to the growing prevalence of junk fax transmissions. While the technology won't go away, it's just a matter of time before it becomes regulated, especially if the industry fails to utilize self-regulation.

Electronic Marketing

Television

The television continues to experience its own renaissance within the industry. Commercials, although by no means new, are changing as well. There's a trend away from the usual two minute spots that direct marketers were used to, and instead they've resorted to either 30 and 60 second spots with 800 numbers, or the extended format of 30 to 60 minute programs. By extending the time and producing paid programming rather than spot advertisements, direct marketers tap into the credibility and potential associated with programming versus commercial advertising.

The newest television, however, is low power television (LPTV) which works like regular broadcast television but at a lower power covering a smaller radius. It can be used in major cities to reach a large group of people in a small geographic area. The original programming on LPTV taps a new market, generates leads, and offers marketers the opportunity to produce long-form programs with one sponsor. To the consumer, it simply appears to expand the number of their available broadcast channels; to marketers, it offers a viable alternative to longer, expensive television ads while maintaining the inherent credibility associated with programming.

Cable Home Shopping

In the early 1980s, cable networks expected home shopping to become a significant part of their business. Despite a thinning out of the field in recent years, this format will continue to experience growth into the next decade as well. While the home shopping side has begun leaning toward consolidation and liquidation, cable television experiences incredible growth. Present cable penetration stands at 57 percent or 52.6 million households. By 1992 that figure is expected to exceed 65 percent. It is predicted that by 1993, 67.7 percent of the 83.7 million dwelling units passed by cable will be subscribers. Annual rate of cable penetration growth increased from 305,5000 to 327,250 homes per month, and that's just the beginning.

The shop-at-home marketplace hasn't been as lucky, and the electronic retailing industry has fallen victim to a shakeout during the last two years. Since 1988, two companies have literally cornered the market: Home Shopping Network and QVC Network (Quality, Value, and Convenience). Although the nineties will see fewer start-ups in the area of home shopping, the home shopping venue will continue to be profitable for savvy marketers. It just won't be as easy as it was in the 1980's. Marketers are learning that more attention needs to be placed on viewer credibility and media acceptance. Electronic marketing had to learn from its mistakes. If nothing else, the few remaining players are getting better at programming using increased knowledge of audience demographics.

Telephone Services

Increasingly, the telephone has become the alternative media of choice among marketers. Along with the now standard 800 numbers, 900 numbers and recorded advertising messages are gaining popularity because they offer cost benefits for marketers and diversity for customers.

The 900 number is changing the focus of telemarketing. Offered by long distance companies who bill customers for services and products sold by independent businesses, these numbers allow marketers to pass on some of their telecommunication costs to the consumer. For the first time, telemarketers can turn their phone options into another source of revenue, and if all proceeds according to plan, 900 services could eliminate the need to send bills and replace the credit card as a billing method.

Although originally spurred on by the 1980 Carter-Reagan debates where an estimated 500,000 people called in to choose the winner, 700 and 900 services accounted for about $455 million in 1988. The 1992 market should be $2.9 billion. The future of these services will depend on whether the major phone networks want to act as credit card companies, billing for purchases that cost more than the cost of the phone call. One option would be to have the local phone companies handle the billing and charge a user fee. With the look, feel, and options of 800 services, the diversity and speed of this technology is turning even the harshest critics into believers.

Unlike its original use for pornography, advice lines, and polling, the new telephone options are drawing attention from large corporate advertisers such as RJR Nabisco, General Foods, and Anheuser-Busch. Consumer products form the phone-ad industry's growth segment; consumers currently spend $1 billion a year to receive phone ads, and that figure could climb as high as $4 billion by 1992. After the AT&T breakup in 1984, local companies began offering a variety of over-the-wire services, and today a legion of phone-ad agencies have sprung up to arrange phone lines and messages and to create print and broadcast ads publicizing the numbers.

Still, there is a high potential for abuse of 900 numbers. Many states now require recorded messages warning users of the cost of the call, and some phone companies are required to install blocking devices which prevent children from making unwanted calls.

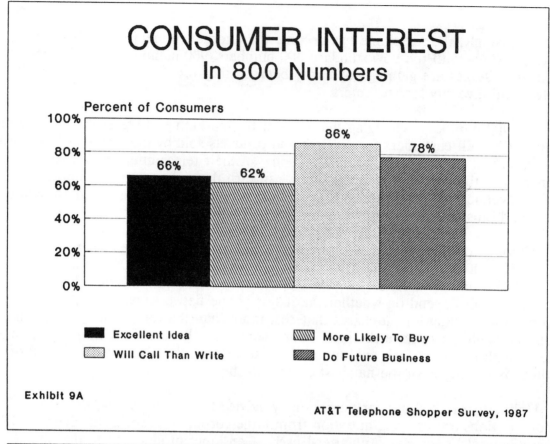

CONSUMER INTEREST
In 800 Numbers

Percent of Consumers

Legend:
- ■ Excellent Idea
- ▨ Will Call Than Write
- ▨ More Likely To Buy
- ▨ Do Future Business

Exhibit 9A

AT&T Telephone Shopper Survey, 1987

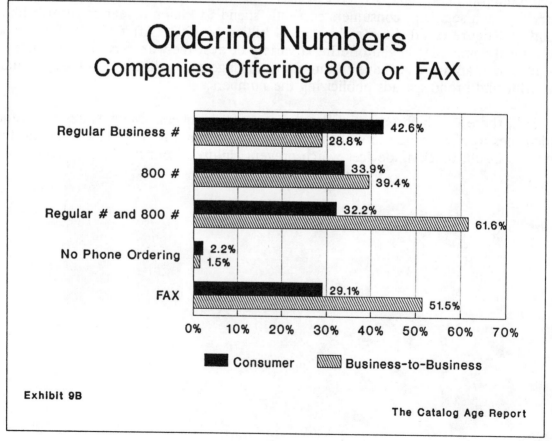

Ordering Numbers
Companies Offering 800 or FAX

- Regular Business # — 42.6% / 28.8%
- 800 # — 33.9% / 39.4%
- Regular # and 800 # — 32.2% / 61.6%
- No Phone Ordering — 2.2% / 1.5%
- FAX — 29.1% / 51.5%

Legend:
- ■ Consumer
- ▨ Business-to-Business

Exhibit 9B

The Catalog Age Report

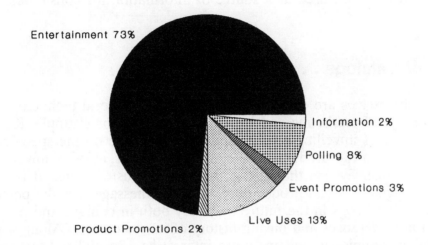

USES OF 900 NUMBERS
Telephone Services

Entertainment 73%

Information 2%

Polling 8%

Event Promotions 3%

Live Uses 13%

Product Promotions 2%

Exhibit 9C

Link Resources

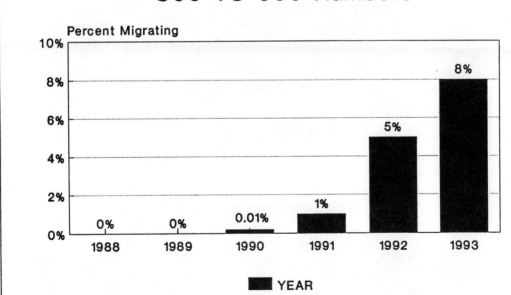

CHANGE PHONE SERVICE
800 TO 900 Numbers

Percent Migrating

0%	0%	0.01%	1%	5%	8%
1988	1989	1990	1991	1992	1993

YEAR

Exhibit 9D

Strategic Telemedia

Laser Disk Kiosks

Laser disk kiosks are free standing units with an internal laser disc and player linked to a microprocessor that responds to touch options displayed on a television screen. They can be formatted to handle credit cards, link with telephone lines, or print out a variety of coupons and receipts. Kiosks have been tested nationwide with the greatest success in mega-supermarkets. Although the potential of kiosks is still unknown, they currently are used as a source of information for consumers.

The Future of Catalogs . . .

Catalogs themselves are changing with the times. Several technologies are creating better targeted marketing and increased interest. For example, Kodak is just one of many companies unveiling mechanisms that capitalize on the specificity of database information in the production of specialized books. Kodak unveiled a 4400 Binding Line Controller System that allows true catalog customizing. It is capable of changing printed signatures and producing customized messages for the person receiving the book. Finished catalogs in the future may vary both in content and page count depending on the preferences and buying history of its customers. Along with specific marketing, catalogs promise to become more interesting. Specialized technology like scent strips and talking microchips add yet another dimension to direct marketing.

Chapter 10

Business Profiles

of 25

Consumer

Mail Order

Companies

CALSTAR, INC.

Calstar, Inc.
7401 Cahill Road
Minneapolis, MN 55435
Telephone: (612) 941-0110

ADDRESS, PHONE

Calstar is publicly held. Its stock is traded OTC under NASDAQ symbol "CSAR".

OWNERSHIP

James Goetz, Chairman; William Beddor, Board of Directors; Ronald Shiftan, President and CEO; Jay White, Vice President Merchandising; Robert W. Beel, CFO and Treasurer.

MANAGEMENT

Mail order.

TYPE OF MARKETER

Calstar is a marketer of a broad selection of collectible products ranging from non-manufactured collectibles, such as coins and stamps, to manufactured items such as dolls and fine porcelain. Non-manufactured items account for 90 percent of sales. All merchandise is sold by mail through continuity programs, solo promotions and catalogs. In addition to manufacturing, Calstar has in-house creative for all promotional activity.

BUSINESS

The business was founded as Calhoun's Collectors Society in Minnesota by former chairman and president, Stafford Calvin. Operating and financial difficulties forced the company to seek protection under Chapter 11 bankruptcy in 1984. The business was renamed Calstar and taken from Chapter 11. In 1988 an over aggressive growth strategy resulted in renewed financial problems.

COMPANY HISTORY

Calstar markets throughout the U.S. and Canada, with limited overseas sales. The customer base is 60 percent men.

MARKETS

CALSTAR, INC. (continued)

FACILITIES	Headquarters, production and distribution operations are located in the company owned facility in Minneapolis, MN.
PRODUCTS, BRAND NAMES, PRICE RANGE	Calstar's primary focus is on coins, stamps, porcelain, gems and jewelry. The company's brand names include: Calhoun's Royal Cornwall, American Heirloom Porcelain, Kyoto Imperial and Royal Regency. The average ticket for continuity purchase is $350.

FINANCIAL INFORMATION

	SALES	NET INCOME	PROFIT MARGIN
1987	$13,711,901	$1,220,691	8.9%
1988	$13,796,242	$ 300,784	2.2%
1989	$16,075,000	-$ 160,000	-1.0%

TYPE OF ADVERTISING, PROMOTION

The majority of promotions for the company's collectible products are direct mail packages for continuity offers and solo promotions for single products or lines. The company is developing specialty catalogs for new lines.

LIST INFORMATION

Quantity Mailed:	12,000,000*
Average Order:	$350
Active Buyers:	44,505
Total List:	178,000
List Source:	direct mail

COMMENTS

Following emergence from Chapter 11, the company successfully met its term debt obligations in the period ending April 30, 1987. In 1988, management took steps toward an aggressive expansion with a new catalog. The costly gamble resulted in a need for cash to maintain the company's business. Management met that need by selling $400,000 of Calstar stock to two outside directors. They now own 55 percent of the company. Despite financial setbacks, Calstar plans to continue developing specialty catalogs.

CAROL WRIGHT SALES, INC.

Carol Wright Sales, Inc.
70 Seaview Avenue,
Stamford, CT 06904
Telephone: (203) 353-7200.

ADDRESS, PHONE

Carol Wright is a subsidiary of Dun & Bradstreet Corp., reporting through the Donnelley Marketing division.

OWNERSHIP

Robert Ginsberg, Executive Vice President, General Manager and COO; David Brace, Vice President, Operations; Deborah Heilig, Vice President, Marketing; Nicholas Parrinelli, Vice President, Merchandise; Alan Ross, Vice President, Finance.

MANAGEMENT

Mail order.

TYPE OF MARKETER

Carol Wright Sales, including the Carol Wright Gifts catalog operation, is the mail order marketing arm of Donnelley Marketing. The company sells a wide variety of home furnishings, kitchen and auto accessories, apparel, electronic devices and novelty items. Merchandise is sold through catalogs, space advertising and an extensive co-op direct mail package program. The company employs between 630-700 people at its Lincoln, NE plant and a staff of 35 in Stamford, CT.

BUSINESS

The business started as a mail order operation for the Donnelley Marketing division of the Reuben H. Donnelley Corp. It became a separate mail order division in 1972. The name Carol Wright has been used by Donnelley for its co-op mailing program since 1970 and was later applied to the entire mail order products division. In 1979, Carol Wright Sales, Inc. was incorporated as a wholly owned subsidiary of the Dun & Bradstreet Corp.

COMPANY HISTORY

Carol Wright sells throughout the U.S., 75 percent of buyers are women with median household incomes of $38,000.

MARKETS

CAROL WRIGHT (continued)

FACILITIES	The company headquarters are located in Stamford, CT; fulfillment and customer services are in Lincoln, NE.
PRODUCTS, BRAND NAMES, PRICE RANGE	The company's product line includes tools, decorative lamps, tables, towel and coat racks, pots, pans, food processors, knife and scissors sets, rain gear, travel bags, adult and children's gifts, apparel and footwear. Prices range from $2.95 to $29.95.

FINANCIAL INFORMATION

	SALES	NET INCOME	PROFIT MARGIN
1987	$ 76,000,000	N/A	N/A
1988	$105,000,000	N/A	N/A
1989	$105,000,000	N/A	N/A

TYPE OF ADVERTISING, PROMOTION	Carol Wright uses catalogs to market its full merchandise line and direct mail co-op inserts to promote individual products.

LIST INFORMATION

Quantity Mailed:	45,000,000, catalog
Average Order:	$24 catalog, $12 co-op
Active Buyers:	6,000,000
Total List:	12,000,000
List Source:	direct mail, space

COMMENTS

Management predicts Carol Wright's 1990 revenues will be slightly above the 1989 level. The company mailed approximately 45 million catalogs in 1989 and another 1.8 billion co-op inserts. Mailings were targeted at an existing 6 million name active house file and extensive rented lists. The catalog was expanded from 48 to 112 pages in 1986. 8 editions of the company's 5 1/2" x 8 1/4" catalog are mailed annually. Promotional inserts are also placed in Donnelley Marketing's "Coupons from Carol Wright" packages - 10 editions are mailed annually. The company sees its marketing niche as the low end of the consumer market.

128

E & B MARINE

E & B Marine
980 Gladys Court
Edison, NJ 08817
Telephone: (201) 819-7400

ADDRESS, PHONE

E & B Marine is publicly held. Stock is traded OTC under the symbol EBMI.

OWNERSHIP

Richard E. Kroon, Chairman; Kenneth Lever, President and CEO; Sam B. Slade, Jr., CFO and Senior Vice President of Direct Marketing; Randy Uner, Senior Vice President, Retail; Robert Defonti, Senior Vice President, Merchandising; Jack Howie, Director Real Estate.

MANAGEMENT

Mail order, retail, wholesale.

TYPE OF MARKETER

The company markets marine supplies and equipment for sailboats and powerboats through catalogs, a chain of discount centers along the eastern seaboard and a group of eastern-based retail outlets purchased in 1985. The company recently acquired Goldberg's Marine Distributors and claims to be the largest retailer of marine supplies serving recreational and commercial boating markets in the U.S. The heaviest sales occur during the second quarter.

BUSINESS

Ernest Bench and his son, Robert, founded the business in 1956 as a government and industrial surplus store on Staten Island, NY. The company entered the discount pleasure-boating business in 1958. The company went public in 1983. E & B acquired James Bliss & Co. in 1985 and Goldberg's Marine in 1986. E & B and Goldberg's operations consolidated in Edison, NJ in 1987. Richard Kroon heads an investment group which purchased a 60 percent interest in the company in March, 1989.

COMPANY HISTORY

Customers are primarily upscale men, ages 24 to 55; owners of sailboats and powerboats throughout U.S.

MARKETS

E & B MARINE (continued)

| FACILITIES | Headquarters and fulfillment operations are located in the warehouse facility in Edison, NJ. |

PRODUCTS,
BRAND NAMES,
PRICE RANGE

E & B's product line includes ship-to-shore radios, depth-finders, automatic pilots, navigational equipment, boating supplies and apparel. New Sea Ranger electronics products include EHF radios and a navigational device, both highly rated in boating circles. Prices range from $2 to $1500.

FINANCIAL
INFORMATION

	SALES	NET INCOME	PROFIT MARGIN
1987	$18,425,310	N/A	N/A
1988	$21,598,629	N/A	N/A
1989	$23,000,000*	N/A	N/A

TYPE OF
ADVERTISING,
PROMOTION

E & B promotes primarily through national mail order catalogs and direct mail packages in retail regions. The company advertises in national sports and boating magazines and attends annual in-water boat shows.

LIST
INFORMATION

Quantity Mailed:	5,000,000*
Average Order:	$95
Active Buyers:	150,000
Total List:	300,000
List Source:	direct mail

COMMENTS

Total sales reported are for mail order only. In 1988, mail order represented about one quarter of total sales, a figure which has remained constant over the past years. E & B underwent major management changes when the founders stepped down in 1988. The company closed its distribution center in St. Petersburg, FL and consolidated in Edison, NJ. The firm also consolidated buying in its Edison headquarters, writing off a total of $2,303,000, charged to operations.

130

EDDIE BAUER

Eddie Bauer, Inc.
15010 N.E. 36th Street
Redmond, WA   98052
Telephone: (206) 882-6100

ADDRESS,
PHONE

Eddie Bauer is a subsidiary of Spiegel, Oak Brook, IL.

OWNERSHIP

Wayne Badovinus, President; Jim Cannataro, Vice President
Finance; Rick Fersch, Senior Vice President, Retail Stores;
Frank Jennings, Vice President Retail Operations; Ray McCready,
Vice President General Merchandise Manager; Ken Wherry, Vice
President Direct Marketing Operations; Bill Michel, Division Vice
President Direct Marketing.

MANAGEMENT

Mail order, retail.

TYPE OF
MARKETER

Eddie Bauer manufactures and markets a variety of sportswear,
footwear, and outerwear, as well as some specialty gift items. The
company is best known for its line of goosedown jackets, parkas
and vests. Merchandise is marketed through a chain of 100 retail
stores and through mail order catalogs. Retail generates
approximately 55 percent of sales; the remainder comes from mail
order. Company mails 10 editions of its catalog annually, plus
specialty books: "All Week Long," and "Eddie Bauer, a Legend for
Four Generations."

BUSINESS

Eddie Bauer founded the company in 1920 as a sporting goods
shop. He later developed the goosedown jacket and the concept
was used to develop down sleeping bags and other outdoor gear
and apparel. Bauer later launched the catalog and the firm
became primarily mail order. In 1968, Eddie Bauer was sold to
the Neimi family. General Mills bought it in 1971, and in the
1980s began opening stores again. In May, 1988, Eddie Bauer was
sold to Spiegel.

COMPANY
HISTORY

Customers are upscale outdoor enthusiasts throughout the U.S.
and Canada.

MARKETS

EDDIE BAUER (continued)

FACILITIES

Headquarters, offices, and fulfillment facilities are located in Redmond, WA.

PRODUCTS, BRAND NAMES, PRICE RANGE

Bauer sells men's and women's casual sportswear and outdoor apparel, including goosedown outerwear, sweaters, flannel and chamois shirts, slacks and dresses, footwear, and soft luggage. The company also sells a line of gift related hard-goods. Prices range from $3 to $1,000.

FINANCIAL INFORMATION

	SALES	NET INCOME	PROFIT MARGIN
1987	$191,400,000	$15,400,000	8.0%
1988	$250,000,000	$22,000,000	8.8%
1989	$400,000,000	$35,860,000	9.0%

TYPE OF ADVERTISING, PROMOTION

Bauer produces 10 full color, 64+ page catalogs each year, in addition to several specialty book slated to launch in 1990.

LIST INFORMATION

Quantity Mailed:	42,000,000
Average Order:	$88
Active Buyers:	1,500,000
Total List:	N/A
List Source:	direct mail, space.

COMMENTS

Financial information for 1987 and 1988 reported while owned by General Mills. In the spring of 1985, Eddie Bauer underwent significant restructuring and repositioning. Merchandising emphasis went from outdoor and recreational equipment/apparel to casual apparel, sportswear, footwear and gifts. Bauer is expected to expand dramatically under the ownership of Spiegel; Spiegel opened 40 retail stores in 1989 for Eddie Bauer.

FIELD PUBLICATIONS

Field Publications
245 Long Hill Road
Middleton, CT 06457
Telephone: (203) 638-2400

ADDRESS, PHONE

Field Publications is an affiliate of The Field Corporation, Chicago, IL, which is privately held.

OWNERSHIP

Bruce Seide, President; Peter Igoe, Senior Vice President and CFO; Bob Mills, Senior Vice President, Operations; Kim Hostetler, Vice President, Human Resources.

MANAGEMENT

Mail order.

TYPE OF MARKETER

Field Publications is the leading provider of entertaining and informative products and services satisfying the learning needs of families and schools. It is best known for publishing the nation's pre-eminent school newsweekly, the 60 year old <u>Weekly Reader</u>. Field also operates the world's largest juvenile book club business. In-house marketing/advertising department handles all promotional activity producing more than 3,500 direct mail and space jobs annually.

BUSINESS

The company was started as American Education Publications in 1902. <u>Current Events</u> was launched in 1902. The nation's largest classroom periodical, <u>Weekly Reader</u>, launched in 1928. Wesleyan University purchased the company in 1949. It was subsequently sold to the Xerox Corporation in 1965 and the name was changed to Xerox Education Publications. The Field Corporation acquired the business from Xerox in 1985.

COMPANY HISTORY

Products are sold throughout the U.S. and Canada; 55 percent to families with children; 30 percent to schools; 15 percent to adults.

MARKETS

FIELD PUBLICATIONS (continued)

FACILITIES

Field Publications has headquarters and operating facilities in Middleton, CT and Columbus, OH.

PRODUCTS, BRAND NAMES, PRICE RANGE

Field's product line includes elementary and secondary school periodicals, books, continuity programs and instructional materials. Trademarks include Weekly Reader, Muppet Babies, Teen Works, and McCall's Cooking School. Prices range from $3 to $7.

FINANCIAL INFORMATION

	SALES	NET INCOME	PROFIT MARGIN
1987	$207,000,000	N/A	N/A
1988	$246,000,000	N/A	N/A
1989	$282,900,000	N/A	N/A

TYPE OF ADVERTISING, PROMOTION

Field reports heavy use of jumbo direct mail packages, direct mail solos and flyers; all produced in-house. The company also sells products through insert programs, telemarketing, cable promotions, and space ads in magazines.

LIST INFORMATION

Quantity Mailed:	55,000,000
Average Order:	varies
Active Buyers:	10,000,000
Total List:	12,000,000
List Source:	direct mail, space, telemarketing

COMMENTS

Field management reports a sales gain of 18 percent in 1988. Field claims the subscriber base for Weekly Reader family of periodicals at 9.1 million, exceeding that of Time and Newsweek combined. The company reportedly shipped more than 56 million adult and children's books in 1989. Hardcover book clubs brought in more than four million new members, while softcover clubs sold a combined volume of 13 million books. Eight new product lines have been introduced in the last two years, broadening Field's market. Funk & Wagnall's became affiliated with Field in 1988 and Field acquired Curriculum Innovations Group in Spring of 1989.

FRANKLIN MINT

The Franklin Mint
Franklin Center, PA 19091
Telephone: (215) 459-6000.

ADDRESS, PHONE

Company is a wholly owned subsidiary of privately held American Protection Industries, Los Angeles, CA.

OWNERSHIP

Stewart Resnick, President; Lynda Resnick, Executive Vice President; Martin Breisblatt, Vice President Sales; Thomas Durovsik, Vice President Marketing, Vice President Public Affairs; Alan Beer, Vice President Media; Jack Wilkie, Public Relations.

MANAGEMENT

Direct response, retail.

TYPE OF MARKETER

The Franklin Mint conceives, creates, and markets collectibles and "desirables" through five distinct product marketing divisions: Female Collectibles, Male Collectibles, House of Faberge, Jewelry and The Franklin Library. The company also operates four retail stores. The Franklin Mint has offices in 19 countries on 6 continents and employs approximately 4,700 people.

BUSINESS

Joseph Segal founded General Numismatic Corporation as the parent of the Franklin Mint. The corporate name became Franklin Mint Corp. in 1972. Firm began as a minter and marketer of numismatic products. In the mid-70s, it diversified into other product lines. The company merged with Warner Communications in March 1981. In March 1985, it was sold to American Protection Industries and the name was changed to The Franklin Mint.

COMPANY HISTORY

The Franklin Mint markets to upscale collectors and consumers in the U.S. and 18 foreign countries. Customers are increasingly more affluent and young.

MARKETS

FRANKLIN MINT (continued)

FACILITIES

Corporate headquarters and fulfillment facilities are in Franklin Center, PA, a suburb of Philadelphia.

PRODUCTS, BRAND NAMES, PRICE RANGE

Products include fine porcelains, designer jewelry, porcelain heirloom dolls, handcrafted sculpture, reproductions of original artwork, precision die cast cars, collectible board games, fine weapon replicas, and classic collectors' books.

FINANCIAL INFORMATION

	SALES	NET INCOME	PROFIT MARGIN
1987	$500,000,000*	N/A	N/A
1988	$605,000,000*	N/A	N/A
1989	$740,000,000*	N/A	N/A

TYPE OF ADVERTISING, PROMOTION

Products are offered through direct mail packages sent to existing collectors and outside lists. The company also uses extensive space and television advertising to generate new customers.

LIST INFORMATION

The Franklin Mint does not release numerical list information regarding its list.

COMMENTS

The Franklin Mint has undergone significant transformation during the past decade, moving aggressively from its original focus on numismatics. In the 70s it began broadening its scope to include various categories of collectibles. While the merchandise mix has continued to expand and diversify, the 80s have also marked the broadening of its customer base. The company's target market now consists not only of serious collectors, but consumers of quality, upscale "desirables" as well. Management reports that each product is marketed as its own business and profit center. The company's goal reportedly is to offer a product which appeals to every demographic profile conceivable; thus the increasing emphasis on space advertising in a wide range of diverse publications.

GANDER MOUNTAIN, INC.

Gander Mountain Inc.
Highway West
P. O. Box 128
Wilmot, WI 53192
Telephone: (414) 862-2331

ADDRESS,
PHONE

Gander Mountain is publicly held, stock is traded on NASDAQ under symbol GNDR.

OWNERSHIP

Ralph Freitag, Chairman and President; Tom Curry, Vice President.

MANAGEMENT

Mail order, retail.

TYPE OF MARKETER

Gander Mountain is a mail order marketer of outdoor recreational equipment and items of interest to hunters, fishermen and campers. While Gander maintains two retail outlets, sales are primarily through 13 catalogs. Gander recently sold its Western Ranchman Outfitters, which markets western clothing and accessories by mail. Master Animal Care, a mail order and retail marketer of veterinary supplies, was acquired in 1986. Recent strategy has been the development of various specialty catalogs.

BUSINESS

Robert Sturgis founded Gander Mountain Shooting & Supply in 1960 as a retail and mail order marketer of firearms, ammunition and hunting supplies. The name was shortened in the late 1960s. The company filed for bankruptcy in 1981, but completed a successful reorganization. Gander Mountain was sold to a group of private investors led by Ralph Freitag in September, 1984. The company went public in April, 1987. That same year, GM acquired WRO and Master Vaccine. WRO was divested in 1989.

COMPANY HISTORY

Gander Mountain markets to hunting, fishing and camping enthusiasts throughout the U.S., primarily men.

MARKETS

GANDER MOUNTAIN, INC. (continued)

FACILITIES	Headquarters, warehouse and retail outlet are housed in a 213,000 square foot, company-owned complex in Wilmot, WI.
PRODUCTS, BRAND NAMES, PRICE RANGE	Gander Mountain sells outdoor sporting goods and hunting equipment, plus some fishing and camping equipment. Emphasis is on brand name clothing and footwear. Prices range from $1 fishing lures to $500 optics.

FINANCIAL INFORMATION

	SALES	NET INCOME	PROFIT MARGIN
1987	$ 57,800,000	$1,535,000	2.7%
1988	$ 89,787,000	$1,414,000	1.6%
1989	$113,798,000	$ 829,000	0.7%

TYPE OF ADVERTISING, PROMOTION	More than 90 percent of the company's business is mail order through 13 Gander Mountain catalogs and 12 Master Animal Care books. The remainder comes from space advertising in outdoor magazines.

LIST INFORMATION

Quantity Mailed:	33,000,000
Average Order:	$67
Active Buyers:	1,100,000
Total List:	3,500,000
List Source:	direct mail, space.

COMMENTS

In 1986, the company positioned itself for substantial growth with new acquisitions. While Western Ranchman Outfitters and Master Animal Care contributed strong sales, they placed a serious drain on the bottom line. In late 1988, the Gander Mountain directors put the company up for sale. After six months, they abandoned that strategy. The company is currently making a number of operational and management changes.

GROLIER

Grolier Inc.
Sherman Turnpike
Danbury, CT   06816
Telephone: (203) 797-3500

Grolier is a wholly-owned subsidiary of Hachette S.A., a Paris, France-based publisher.

Jean-Claude Lattes, Chairman and CEO; Frederic J. Laffont, President and COO, Stephen Toman, Senior Executive Vice President, U.S. & Canada; Dante Cirilli, Group Vice President, Grolier Direct Marketing; Robert Palmerton, Group Vice President, Publishing.

Mail order, direct response.

Grolier is a worldwide marketer of encyclopedias, children's books, reference sets and educational materials. Subsidiaries include Franklin Watts, Childrens Press, and Krames Communications. Grolier Enterprises, its principal mail order division, sells adult and children's books, reference books, and encyclopedias through single-title, club and continuity programs.

Founded in 1895, the company reorganized as "The Grolier Society" in 1936. Direct marketing began with annual encyclopedia supplements and yearbooks to customers who owned Grolier reference sets. The company moved to Connecticut in 1977. In 1985, Grolier acquired Mystic Color Labs, Childcraft, Krames and Childrens Press. Hachette acquired Grolier in April 1988 and sold Childcraft and Mystic Color Labs.

Grolier markets to adults, parents, schools, libraries, and medical establishments; sales are international.

GROLIER, INC. (continued)

FACILITIES	Headquarters are located in Danbury, CT. Offices are located in NY, Canada, Mexico, Latin America, Europe and the Far East.
PRODUCTS, BRAND NAMES, PRICE RANGE	Grolier's product line consists of encyclopedia annuals, reference sets, children's book clubs, continuity series, educational materials, collectibles and photofinishing services. Reference set prices range from $200 to $950; continuities and encyclopedia annuals range from $150 to $500.

FINANCIAL INFORMATION

	SALES	NET INCOME	PROFIT MARGIN
1987	$424,154,000	$15,458,000	3.6%
1988	$437,515,000*	N/A	N/A
1989	$451,300,000*	N/A	N/A

TYPE OF ADVERTISING, PROMOTION

Promotional emphasis is on direct mail, package inserts, billing inserts and co-op advertising. Television spots and space ads are used to promote children's book clubs.

LIST INFORMATION

Quantity Mailed:	80,000,000
Average Order:	varies by program
Active Buyers:	4,000,000
Total List:	8,000,000
List Source:	direct mail, space, rental

COMMENTS

Grolier restructured operations several times in the 70s and early 80s due to heavy long-term debt. Refinancing and a debenture offering in 1985 was used by Grolier Enterprises for its acquisition program. Beginning in the fall of 1985, Grolier diversified through non-publishing direct marketing acquisitions. Since the purchase by Hachette, the focus has returned to publishing and non-publishing companies have been divested. Grolier sells encyclopedias worldwide through an extensive sales force and in the U.S. through independent distributors. Direct marketing sales in the U.S. and Canada for 1988 totaled $248 million, 53 percent of overall revenues.

GUMP'S

Gump's
250 Post Street
San Francisco, CA   94108
Telephone: (415) 982-1616

ADDRESS, PHONE

Gump's is privately owned by Tobu Departments Store Co. and Charterhouse Equity Partners L.P.

OWNERSHIP

Kenneth Watson, Chairman; Bill Sharp, Vice President, Jewelry Group; Bill Gonlet, Vice President, Advertising and Corporate Gifts Group; Joe Pickard, Vice President, Mail Order and Merchandising.

MANAGEMENT

Retail and mail order.

TYPE OF MARKETER

Gump's sells a high-quality line of specialty gift items including crystal, china, jade figurines, and other objects d'art. The company is well known for its imported oriental jewelry, art, and decorative merchandise. Gump's markets by mail and through its four retail stores located in San Francisco, Dallas, Houston, and Beverly Hills. The company designs many of the products it sells, but does no manufacturing. Sales reportedly are heaviest during the Christmas season. Gump's has 430 employees.

BUSINESS

The Gump family founded the company in San Francisco in 1861, retailing saloon mirrors for bars and bordellos. The merchandise line was expanded to its current mix at the turn of the century and mail order was added in 1950. Gump's was acquired in 1969 by Macmillan, Inc. In June, 1989, Gump's was sold to Japanese Tobu Department Store Co., Ltd. for $36.5 million.

COMPANY HISTORY

Sales occur primarily in the U.S. to mid to upscale women with an average age of 35.

MARKETS

GUMP'S (continued)

FACILITIES

Merchandising and marketing headquarters are located in San Francisco, CA; warehousing and shipping in De Soto, TX.

PRODUCTS, BRAND NAMES, PRICE RANGE

Gemstone jewelry, figurines, china, brass and crystal items, oriental gifts, and fashions for women comprise Gump's product line. Prices range from $10 to over $35,000.

FINANCIAL INFORMATION

	SALES	NET INCOME	PROFIT MARGIN
1987	$ 8,200,000*	N/A	N/A
1988	$11,800,000*	N/A	N/A
1989	$15,600,000*	N/A	N/A

TYPE OF ADVERTISING, PROMOTION

Gump's mails four editions of its catalogs in January, March, May, July and September, with a special mailing during the Christmas season. Gump's fashion book, "Palette," mails three times a year, in February, August and November.

LIST INFORMATION

Quantity Mailed:	2,300,000*
Average Order:	$150
Active Buyers:	64,000*
Total List:	105,000*
List Source:	direct mail, space

COMMENTS

Gump's sale to Japanese Tobu Department Store Company, Ltd. was in line with its former owner's plan to focus on publishing, instruction and information-oriented concerns. About 25 percent of Gump's total revenues are attributed to mail order sales, reportedly Gump's fastest growing business segment.

HAMMACHER SCHLEMMER

Hammacher Schlemmer
212 West Superior
Chicago, IL   60610
Telephone: (312) 664-8170

ADDRESS, PHONE

Hammacher Schlemmer is privately owned by the MacArthur family.

OWNERSHIP

Richard Tinberg, CEO; John Semmelhack, President; Irene Wilson, Vice President of Advertising; Thomas Yocky, Director of Marketing; Brian Hyzy, Comptroller.

MANAGEMENT

Mail order, retail.

TYPE OF MARKETER

Hammacher Schlemmer markets a wide assortment of unique gift and general merchandise items for home, office and personal use. The mixture crosses into virtually all product categories. Merchandise is sold by mail through the company's catalogs and through company-owned retail stores. Hammacher Schlemmer employs approximately 100 people.

BUSINESS

William Tollner founded the company in 1848 as a hardware store in New York's Bowery district. Tollner's nephew, William Schlemmer, and an associate, Alfred Hammacher, invested in and eventually purchased the store. A catalog was published as early as 1881. The company has changed hands several times; Gulf & Western Industries acquired the business in 1975 and sold it to the MacArthur family in 1980.

COMPANY HISTORY

The domestic mail order customer base is upscale, primarily business and professional people.

MARKETS

HAMMACHER SCHLEMMER (continued)

FACILITIES	Marketing operations are located in Chicago, IL. Retail stores are located in New York, Chicago, and Beverly Hills.
PRODUCTS, BRAND NAMES, PRICE RANGE	The company specializes in unique products for home, garden, office, travel, personal care and recreation. Recent products are a Russian military watch ($99.50), personal indoor driving range ($199.50), remote control car starter ($309.50), and personal robot ($7,995.50).

FINANCIAL INFORMATION

	SALES	NET INCOME	PROFIT MARGIN
1987	$36,000,000	N/A	N/A
1988	$30,000,000	N/A	N/A
1989	$40,000,000	N/A	N/A

TYPE OF ADVERTISING PROMOTION	Marketing emphasis is mail order catalogs. HS uses space advertising in consumer and business magazines, as well as major newspapers including The Wall Street Journal and New York Times to generate catalog inquiries.

LIST INFORMATION

Quantity Mailed:	29,000,000
Average Order:	$115
Active Buyers:	400,000
Total List:	1,200,000
List Source:	direct mail, space

COMMENTS

Hammacher Schlemmer's mail order sales in 1989 were estimated at $40 million and shows strong growth for 1990. The company attributes its growth patterns to the increased variety of products offered. Hammacher Schlemmer continues to introduce new and original products and is selling more of its higher priced items. A switch was made from two-color to four-color catalogs in 1983. Hammacher Schlemmer now publishes a 64-page catalog 12 times each year. (The company mailed only 10 catalogs editions in 1988). Mail order sales are estimated to account for approximately 80 percent of the company's total revenues. The company stated that declined sales in 1988 were because the market was not appropriate for the upscale priced items of Hammacher Schlemmer that year.

144

J.C. PENNEY

J.C. Penney
P.O. Box 65900
Dallas, TX   75265-9000
Telephone: (214) 591-1000

ADDRESS,
PHONE

J.C. Penney is publicly held. The company is listed on the New York, Brussels and Antwerp stock exchanges.

OWNERSHIP

William Howell, Chairman; Robert Gill, Vice Chairman; Rod Birkins, President of Catalogs.

MANAGEMENT

Retail, mail order.

TYPE OF MARKETER

J.C. Penney is the second largest general merchandise catalog marketer in the U.S. The company operates department stores that offer a broad range of merchandise, predominantly family apparel, shoes, furnishings, and accessories for the home. In addition, products are sold through mass merchandise, specialty and sale catalogs. The company operates catalog sales centers, some of which are located within their stores. Penney employs about 190,000.

BUSINESS

James Cash Penney founded the company with his philosophy of "Always First Quality." The first store opened in Kemmerer, WY in 1902. The founder's dedication to quality led the company to establish the largest merchandise testing center in the world. J.C. Penney began catalog operations in 1962 by acquiring General Merchandise Co., a Milwaukee, WI firm. There are now 6 catalog distribution centers in the U.S.

COMPANY HISTORY

Penney's customers are from middle-income households throughout the U.S. and Puerto Rico.

MARKETS

J.C. PENNEY (continued)

FACILITIES

Headquarters are located in Dallas, TX. The company operates 1,800 catalog centers and 1,300 retail stores.

PRODUCTS, BRAND NAMES, PRICE RANGE

Merchandise mix is predominantly private label (75 percent), plus an offering of brands. Retail stores carry soft goods; catalog offers both hard and soft goods.

FINANCIAL INFORMATION

	SALES	NET INCOME	PROFIT MARGIN
1987	$15,745,000,000	$608,000,000	3.9%
1988	$15,296,000,000	$807,000,000	5.3%
1989	$16,405,000,000	$802,000,000	4.9%

TYPE OF ADVERTISING, PROMOTION

Penney's mails two main catalogs, Fall/Winter and Spring/Summer, and various specialty apparel books (large sizes, tall men's, big men's, extra tall men's, work clothes, bridal and others).

LIST INFORMATION

Quantity Mailed:	300,000,000
Average Order:	$30
Active Buyers:	20,000,000 (active cardholders)
Total List:	35,000,000 (total cardholders)
List Source:	direct mail, cardholders

COMMENTS

Sales have been slowly increasing over the past several years, due to Penney taking steps to improve profitability and plan for future growth. Headquarters recently moved from New York City to Dallas, TX, from where they will relocate in 1993 to Dallas suburb, Plano. 1988's income included $130 million from the sale of Penney's New York building. When that one-time sales income is removed from the figure, the company's 1989 operating income is actually up approximately 20 percent from the previous year. J.C. Penney's goal is "to be the largest catalog retailer by the mid-1990s." The company's subsidiary, J.C. Penney Telemarketing, Inc., operates 16 telephone sales centers, employing 8,000 order-takers; it reportedly handles over 100 million incoming calls a year. Inbound and outbound services are also sub-contracted to other catalogers. J.C. Penney's recently took two major steps in preparation for the 1991 postal rate increase: It signed up as a merchant on the 500,000-subscriber computer shopping network, CompuServe, and entered into agreement with QVC to substitute J.C. Penney's Televised Shopping Channel in place of the proposed QVC "multi-merchant network."

KNIGHT'S LTD.

Knight's Ltd.
1226 Ambassador Boulevard
St. Louis, MO   63132
Telephone: (314) 993-1516.

ADDRESS, PHONE

W. Grant Williams and other private investors own Knight's Ltd.

OWNERSHIP

W. Grant Williams, President; Steve Kessler, Vice President, Operations; Ann Lucas, Vice President, Inventory Control; Lisa Brougham, Director of Marketing; Kim Comer-Ross, Merchandise Manager.

MANAGEMENT

Mail order.

TYPE OF MARKETER

Knight's Ltd. is a catalog marketer of high ticket women's fashion apparel. Main book offers dresses, blouses, shoes, purses, watches, and related items. The gift line was discontinued in 1986. In January 1989, Knight's Ltd. added a second title, "City Spirit," focusing on sportswear. Company now publishes eight full-color fashion catalogs annually. A single outlet store, along with occasional warehouse sales, serves to liquidate overstock. Management reports 70 employees.

BUSINESS

Grant Williams founded Knight's in 1979 in San Francisco, mailing 40,000 catalogs to test the women's apparel market. Second book was changed to include 90 percent women's fashion and 10 percent gifts. The company moved to St. Louis in 1982. It grew rapidly, reportedly breaking even in less than four years. In 1986, testing prompted a return to strictly apparel as merchandise mix. Company launched sportswear specialty book in 1989.

COMPANY HISTORY

Customer base consists of upper income women, mostly age 40 and over, throughout the U.S.

MARKETS

KNIGHT'S LTD. (continued)

FACILITIES	Headquarters, warehouse, and fulfillment facilities are located in St. Louis, MO.
PRODUCTS, BRAND NAMES, PRICE RANGE	Product line consists of upscale women's fashions by Joanie Char, Bill Geoffreys, Susan Bristol, Elliot Lauren, and J. G. Hook, among others. Shoes by Joan & David, Calvin Klein, Unisa, and Jack Rogers are also featured. Prices range from $30 to $500.

FINANCIAL INFORMATION

	SALES	NET INCOME	PROFIT MARGIN
1987	$ 9,700,000	N/A	N/A
1988	$11,400,000	N/A	N/A
1989	$14,800,000	N/A	N/A

TYPE OF ADVERTISING, PROMOTION

The company relies exclusively on its 32-plus page full-color catalogs for advertising and promotion. Main book and "City Spirit" specialty catalog are each mailed four times annually.

LIST INFORMATION

Quantity Mailed:	8,300,000
Average Order:	$167
Active Buyers:	90,000
Total List:	300,000
List Source:	direct mail, rentals

COMMENTS

Profitable since 1983, Knight's Ltd. achieved a 30 percent sales growth in 1989, and management expects sales momentum to continue in 1990. With increased circulation and additional contribution of the "City Spirit" specialty catalog, gross sales are expected to increase by 44 percent, reaching $21.3 million in 1990. A new specialty catalog, as of yet untitled, will be launched in Spring of 1991; its target customer will be older than Knight's core customer, currently aged 40 to 50. The company reports exceptional performance of all catalog efforts for this year, hoping for good performance of traditionally strong Holiday books. Knight's Ltd. pays particular attention to sizing and all customer service reps are trained to answer "key fit" questions.

LANDS' END

Lands' End Inc.
Dodgeville, WI 53595
Telephone: (608) 935-9341

ADDRESS, PHONE

Lands' End is publicly held. Stock is traded on NYSE under the symbol LE.

OWNERSHIP

Gary C. Comer, Chairman and CEO; Richard C. Anderson, President and COO; Paul C. Kramer, Senior Vice President and CFO; Russel C. Gaitskill, Executive Vice President and General Merchandising Manager; David L. Schlotterback, Executive Vice President Administration and Operations.

MANAGEMENT

Mail order.

TYPE OF MARKETER

Lands' End markets traditionally styled casual apparel for men, women and children, plus accessories, shoes, and soft luggage. The company manufactures its own luggage. Products are sold through mail by catalogs and 10 outlet stores (principally for liquidation). Strong emphasis is on customer service and retention has been an important component of Lands' End strategy since its start. Roughly 40 percent annual sales volume is generated in holiday season. Management reports 3,000 employees.

COMPANY

Gary Comer founded Lands' End in 1963. Formerly an advertising copywriter, Comer began supplying sailboat hardware and equipment by mail. In 1965, Lands' End published the first edition of Yachtsman Equipment Guide, complete with clothing section. By 1976, the focus had shifted to clothing and soft luggage. The company launched a national ad campaign in 1981. Initial public offering was made in 1986.

COMPANY HISTORY

Lands' End markets to highly educated, professional people, 50 percent between 25 and 44, most with incomes above $35,000.

MARKETS

LANDS' END (continued)

FACILITIES	Headquarters are located in Dodgeville, WI; offices located in Chicago, IL; manufacturing plant in West Union, IA; phone center, in Cross Plains, WI.
PRODUCTS, BRAND NAMES, PRICE RANGE	Lands' End trademarks include the Authentic Rugby Shirt, Breezer Shorts, Drifter sweaters, Interlochen knit shirts, Perfect penny loafers, Roveralls playsuits, Serious sweats, Runaway jackets, and Lighthouse luggage. Prices are concentrated between $6 and $100.

FINANCIAL INFORMATION

	SALES	NET INCOME	PROFIT MARGIN
1988	$336,291,000	$22,805,000	6.9%
1989	$455,806,000	$32,282,000	7.1%
1990	$545,200,000	$29,070,000	5.3%

TYPE OF ADVERTISING, PROMOTION	Lands' End published a new catalog edition every four weeks during fiscal '89, for a total of 75 million catalogs mailed to 9 million people. A national space ad campaign also supported promotion.

LIST INFORMATION

Quantity Mailed:	75,000,000
Average Order:	$75-$80
Active Buyers:	1,300,000
Total List:	4,000,000
List Source:	requests, referral, space ads, rental

COMMENTS

Lands' End goal is to increase its size by an average of 15 to 20 percent annually. In fiscal '89, ending January 31, 1989, it far exceeded its goal with sales up 35 percent and net income up 42 percent. Investments in a new plant and equipment totaled $16 million (all reportedly paid out of earnings); investments in fiscal 90 will total $31 million. Continued strong commitment to customer service reportedly paid off: Lands' End reportedly added more new customers than in any previous year, repeat orders increased and ordering frequency improved. Inventory levels reportedly allowed the company to fill nearly 90 percent of orders immediately. Lands' End notifies mail order customers of back orders by phone.

150

LILLIAN VERNON

Lillian Vernon
510 South Fulton Avenue
Mount Vernon, NY   10550
Telephone: (914) 699-4131

ADDRESS,
PHONE

Lillian Vernon is publicly held, stock is traded AMEX under LVC.

OWNERSHIP

Lillian M. Katz, Chairman and CEO; Fred P. Hochberg, President and COO; David C. Hochberg, Vice President Public Affairs; J. Paul Bergmoser, Lilyan Affinito, Leo Salon, Directors.

MANAGEMENT

Mail order, wholesale, retail, manufacturer.

TYPE OF
MARKETER

This specialty catalog company offers low to medium priced gifts, household, gardening and children's items, many imported, often exclusive by design, price, or personalization. LV has buying/quality control offices in Florence, Italy, Taipei, Taiwan and Hong Kong. Overstock is sold through sale catalogs and outlet stores. The company also operates a $2 million wholesale division. Sales are heaviest from October to January. LV reports 1,200 employees during its peak season.

BUSINESS

Lillian Katz launched Vernon Specialties in 1951 with a single $495 ad for personalized purses and belts. The ad returned $16,000 in sales in six weeks. Lillian Vernon Corp. was formed as a mail order entity in 1965. The New Company, supplier of brass tree ornaments, was started in 1976. LV went public in 1987. A new 454,000 square foot national distribution center opened in Virginia Beach, VA in 1988.

COMPANY
HISTORY

Customer base is primarily women, median age 38; 65 percent work outside home, average household income is $44,600.

MARKETS

LILLIAN VERNON (continued)

FACILITIES	Headquarters are located in Mount Vernon, NY. Operations, outlet stores are in New Rochelle, NY and Virginia Beach, VA.
PRODUCTS, BRAND NAMES, PRICE RANGE	Product mix includes gift and children's items, personal and home accessories, housewares and gardening items. Products are sourced from 300 manufacturers; some items manufactured by company. Free personalization provided. Price range: $3 to $895.

FINANCIAL INFORMATION

	SALES	NET INCOME	PROFIT MARGIN
1988	$126,088,000	$ 7,100,000	5.6%
1989	$140,647,000	$ 8,148,000	5.8%
1990	$154,690,000	$10,810,000	7.0%

TYPE OF ADVERTISING, PROMOTION

Lillian Vernon produces full-color main catalogs averaging 104 pages, featuring 750 items. LV also offers a 64 page Special Sale catalog and Lillian Vernon at Home. The company mailed 11 editions in 1989.

LIST INFORMATION

Quantity Mailed:	102,000,000
Average Order:	$37
Active Buyers:	4,900,000
Total List:	11,000,000
List Source:	direct mail, rental.

COMMENTS

Sales data above is for the fiscal year ended February 24, 1990. Despite a brief setback in 1988 with the move to Virginia Beach, revenues increased 10 percent and net income rose 32.6 percent in what management called the "best year in Lillian Vernon's history." The company mailed 118 million catalogs in 14 editions: nine regular catalogs, three sale catalogs, and two editions of Lillian Vernon at Home. LV plans to launch a children's book in Fall 1990. LV reportedly offers 2,500 different products annually; 550 new products are added annually.

THE LIMITED

The Limited, Inc. Two Limited Parkway P.O. Box 16000 Columbus, OH 43216 Telephone: (614) 479-7000	ADDRESS, PHONE
The Limited is publicly held; its stock is traded on the NYSE, TSE, and LSE.	OWNERSHIP
Leslie H. Wexner, Chairman; Bella Wexner, Secretary; Kenneth G. Gilman, Executive Vice President and CFO; Thomas G. Hopkins, Executive Vice President; Wade H. Buff, Alfred S. Dietzel, William K. Gerber, Timothy B. Lyons, and Margaret T. Monaco, Vice Presidents.	MANAGEMENT
Specialty retail and mail order sales.	TYPE OF MARKETER
The Limited Inc., is one of the leading specialty apparel store and mail order retailers in the world. The majority of the company's sales are through its 3,200 retail stores. Catalogs are published by its Brylane mail order division, as well as by their subsidiary, Victoria's Secret Catalogue, which focuses on intimate apparel. The Limited and all of its mail order and retail divisions employ approximately 56,000 people.	BUSINESS
Leslie H. Wexner started The Limited in 1963, seeing an opportunity in limiting merchandise to fashionable sportswear. At first he opened stores in the Columbus, Ohio area and later expanded in the Midwest. Since it went public in 1969, the company has grown to over 3,200 stores. The Limited's most recent acquisitions are Henri Bendel, Lerner and Abercrombie & Fitch.	COMPANY HISTORY
The Limited, Inc. is in every major United States market.	MARKETS

THE LIMITED (continued)

FACILITIES	The Limited, Inc.'s headquarters are located in Columbus, OH.
PRODUCTS, BRAND NAMES, PRICE RANGE	The Limited markets house and name brand fashions including women's lines for special size needs. About half of the merchandise is supplied through its subsidiary, Mast Industries. Prices range from discount to upscale.

FINANCIAL INFORMATION

	SALES	NET INCOME	PROFIT MARGIN
1987	$3,527,941,000	$235,188,000	6.7%
1988	$4,070,777,000	$245,136,000	6.0%
1989	$4,648,000,000	$346,900,000	7.5%

TYPE OF ADVERTISING, PROMOTION	The Limited utilizes extensive space advertising for its retail operations. Mail order sales are promoted through three Brylane catalogs and its Victoria's Secret Catalogue subsidiary, which mails four catalogs annually.

LIST INFORMATION

Quantity Mailed: 60,000,000*
Average Order: $25-60*
Active Buyers: 3,000,000*
Total List: 10,000,000*
List Source: direct mail, space

COMMENTS

According to <u>Forbes Magazine</u>, The Limited is ranked first in growth among specialty apparel retailers, having an average 40 percent annual growth basis for the past five years. Its Brylane division publishes three catalogs: "Lane Bryant" and "Roaman's" for the size 14 and up market, and "Lerner" for its junior and misses sizes. Victoria's Secret Catalogue which was acquired in 1982, focuses on intimate apparel. It recently added toiletries, fragrances, bath products and accessories, as well as several men's items to its catalog. "Victoria's Secret" is mailed four times a year, with a total circulation of 60 million and responds to two million calls on its toll free number annually.

154

L.L. BEAN

L.L. Bean
Casco Street
Freeport, ME   04033
Telephone: (207) 865-4761

L.L. Bean is privately held. The Bean family owns 100 percent of
capital stock.

Leon Gorman, President; William End, Executive Vice President,
Marketing; John Findlay, Senior Vice President, Operations; Bill
Booth, Vice President Advertising and Direct Marketing; Chris
McCormick, Director Advertising and Direct Marketing; Robert
Felle, Vice President, Catalog Art and Production; Stu McGeorge,
Director Product Development/Merchandise Planning.

Mail order, retail.

L.L. Bean is primarily a mail order marketer of casual and outdoor
sporting apparel and footwear. Bean manufactures hunting boots,
moccasins, sailing footwear and tote bags. The company operates
one retail store in Freeport, ME, as well as an outlet store in
North Conway, NH. Retail sales generated an estimated 12
percent of annual sales volume; the remainder is generated by mail
through Bean's main catalog and a host of specialty books.

Retailer Leon Leonwood Bean started the business in 1912 as a
sporting goods manufacturer. He invented the rubber-soled Maine
Hunting Shoe. The company was incorporated in Maine in 1934.
An extended period of major growth began in 1967. In 1980, Bean
expanded its facilities, but sales began to level off by 1983. Recent
changes reportedly have resulted in significant upturn.

Customer base consists of outdoor enthusiasts and sportsmen
throughout the U.S.; 50 percent are men.

L.L. BEAN (continued)

FACILITIES

Headquarters and distribution facilities are located in Freeport, ME. Manufacturing is in Brunswick, ME.

PRODUCTS, BRAND NAMES, PRICE RANGE

Product line consists of men's and women's casual and outdoor apparel, footwear, luggage sports gear, and gifts. The Maine Hunting Shoe and the L.L. Bean chamois shirt have been standard best-selling items since the 1920s. Prices range from $10 to $500.

FINANCIAL INFORMATION

	SALES	NET INCOME	PROFIT MARGIN
1987	$303,750,000	N/A	N/A
1988	$368,518,000	N/A	N/A
1989	$493,417,000	N/A	N/A

TYPE OF ADVERTISING, PROMOTION

Promotional emphasis is on catalogs. L.L. Bean mails seasonal editions of its catalog, plus a growing number of specialty books targeting specific segments. Company also uses package inserts and space ads in magazines.

LIST INFORMATION

Quantity Mailed:	100,000,000
Average Order:	$67
Active Buyers:	N/A
Total List:	N/A
List Source:	direct mail, space, rental

COMMENTS

L.L. Bean enjoyed a period of profound sales growth during the "preppie era" of the late 70s and early 80s. However, sales began to level off in 1983 as fashions began to change. By returning to focus on its basic, standard products, and by broadening its appeal by spinning off a number of specialty catalogs, Bean has achieved a considerable resurgence in the past few years. Bean attributes its continuing success to a long standing reputation for extraordinary customer service, increasingly precise targeting and significantly expanded circulation. In 1988, L.L. Bean mailed 22 catalog editions for a total circulation of 90 million. Both sales and profits reportedly are now growing at a rate of 20 percent annually. Bean filled roughly 9 million orders in 1990, and sales are expected to reach $500,000,000.

OMAHA STEAKS INTERNATIONAL

Omaha Steaks International
4400 South 96th Street
Omaha, NE   68127
Telephone: (402) 331-1010

ADDRESS, PHONE

Omaha Steaks is privately held; the Simon family owns all of the company's capital stock.

OWNERSHIP

Alan Simon, President and Chairman; Frederick Simon, Executive Vice President Corporate Marketing; Stephen Simon, Vice President and General Manager Foodservice; Vickie Hagen, Vice President and General Manager, Gourmet Foods division.

MANAGEMENT

Mail order, retail, wholesale.

TYPE OF MARKETER

Omaha Steaks markets its products through two separate divisions: the Gourmet Foods division markets to consumers by mail; the Foodservice division markets to restaurants and institutions in quantity. The company also operates Omaha Steakshops retail stores in Omaha, Dallas and Houston. Omaha Steaks publishes its 32-page, standard size, full color catalog in August. Business is reportedly year-round, with only a slight increase during the Christmas season. Omaha Steaks reports 450 employees.

BUSINESS

The business was founded as Table Supply Meat Company in Omaha in 1917. J.J. Simon and son B.A. Simon started out by supplying meats to local restaurants. This was the continuation of a family business started by Lazar Simon in 1850 in Riga, Latvia. Mail order marketing operations were launched in 1952. In 1966, the company name was changed to Omaha Steaks International. Additional plant and storage facilities were completed in 1985.

COMPANY HISTORY

The customer base is 65 percent men; consumer and commercial accounts throughout the U.S. and abroad.

MARKETS

OMAHA STEAKS INTERNATIONAL (continued)

FACILITIES	Headquarters, meat processing and mail order operations are located in Omaha, NE.
PRODUCTS, BRAND NAMES, PRICE RANGE	The company's product line includes choice steaks, prime ribs, tenderloin tips, gourmet burgers, pork, veal, and lamb. A variety of seafoods, dessert items, hors d'oeuvre, and gourmet items have been added to the line. Prices range from $15 to $500.

FINANCIAL INFORMATION

	SALES	NET INCOME	PROFIT MARGIN
1987	$68,000,000	N/A	N/A
1988	$75,000,000	N/A	N/A
1989	$85,650,000*	N/A	N/A

TYPE OF ADVERTISING, PROMOTION	The majority of promotion is accomplished through Omaha Steaks' catalog. Space advertising accounts for 15 percent of the company's advertising budget (10 percent magazines and 5 percent newspapers).

LIST INFORMATION

Quantity Mailed:	N/A
Average Order:	$75
Active Buyers:	300,000
Total List:	390,000
List Source:	direct mail, space.

COMMENTS

1987 and 1988 sales statistics were confirmed by Omaha Steaks management for the company overall. The company reportedly plans for annual sales growth of approximately 10 percent. It is estimated that the Gourmet Foods mail order division generates roughly half of Omaha Steak's total revenues, a ratio which has evolved over the years and is expected to remain steady in the near future. In addition to mailing its 28-page catalog under 3 different covers in August, September and October, Omaha Steaks sends follow-up mailings to customers throughout the year. It also begins business-to-business promotions of its holiday gift incentive programs in spring. Omaha Steaks International gives high priority to product quality, customer service and satisfaction.

READER'S DIGEST

Reader's Digest Association
Pleasantville, NY   10570
Telephone: (914) 238-1000

ADDRESS, PHONE

Reader's Digest went public on February 15, 1990 and is traded on the NYSE under symbol RDA.

OWNERSHIP

George V. Grune, Chairman and CEO; Richard F. McLoughlin, President and COO; Kenneth O. Gilmore, Vice President and Editor-in-Chief, Reader's Digest magazine; Kenneth A. Gordon, M. John Bohane, and Thomas M. Kenney, Presidents.

MANAGEMENT

Mail order.

TYPE OF MARKETER

Reader's Digest publishes a variety of magazines and books, including Reader's Digest magazine (39 editions published in 15 languages monthly). RD also markets its special interest magazines, records, tapes, and compact discs. Books and home entertainment products supply 50 percent of revenues. Management reports approximately 90 percent of business is mail order, over half of revenues are from sales in the international market. Reader's Digest employs 7,400 people in 54 locations worldwide.

BUSINESS

DeWitt and Lila Wallace started Reader's Digest in 1922. They published Reader's Digest magazine and marketed it by mail. The first UK edition appeared in 1938. Condensed books were added in 1950; LPs and how-to books followed shortly. In 1986 RD created its special interest magazine group by acquiring Travel Holiday; Family Handyman and 50 Plus (subsequently renamed New Choices for the Best Years) followed in 1988.

COMPANY HISTORY

Reader's Digest's mail operations focus primarily in Europe, the Far East, and all of the Americas.

MARKETS

READER'S DIGEST (continued)

FACILITIES

World headquarters are in Pleasantville, NY; regional offices are located throughout the U.S. and the world.

PRODUCTS, BRAND NAMES, PRICE RANGE

Products include Reader's Digest magazine, RD book series (Today's Best Non-Fiction, Great Biographies, and The World's Best Reading), how-to books, dictionaries, LPs, cassettes, compact discs, and video tapes. Reader's Digest currently offers 4 special interest magazines.

FINANCIAL INFORMATION

	SALES	NET INCOME	PROFIT MARGIN
1987	$1,420,120,000	$ 94,737,000	6.7%
1988	$1,712,037,000	$142,263,000	8.3%
1989	$1,832,013,000	$151,548,000	8.3%

TYPE OF ADVERTISING, PROMOTION

Direct mail packages with sweepstakes entries combined with optional order forms market a variety of RD products; some catalogs are used for books and home entertainment sales. Some promotions include free gift items.

LIST INFORMATION

Quantity Mailed:	N/A
Average Order:	varies
Active Buyers:	25,000,000
Total List:	50,000,000
List Source:	direct mail, space, inserts

COMMENTS

The once privately-held company offered 28,650,000 shares of class A non-voting stock on February 15, 1990. RD underwent this change of ownership by requirements set forth in Lila Wallace's will and to create liquidity for stockholders' assets. The company's sales rose approximately $120 million in 1989, which management attributes to the increased prices in magazine subscriptions and books, as well as a larger average purchase in the home entertainment segment. RD acquired American Health on February 5, 1990, its fourth special interest magazine. The company's list of 50 million is one of the largest in the world; half of its names are reported as active buyers during the past two years. To maintain list profitability, RD invested $17 million in a new data processing system, which will be operational by 1992.

SEARS, ROEBUCK AND COMPANY

Sears, Roebuck and Co. Sears Tower Chicago, Illinois 60684 Telephone: (312) 875-2500	**ADDRESS, PHONE**
Sears is publicly held; its stock is traded on the NYSE.	**OWNERSHIP**
Edward Brennan, Chairman, President and CEO; Michael Bozic, Chairman, President and CEO, Sears Merchandise Group; James M. Denney, Senior Vice President and CFO; Charles F. Moran, Senior Vice President, Administration; David Shute, Senior Vice President, Corporate General Council and Secretary; Jane J. Thompson, Vice President, Corporate Planning.	**MANAGEMENT**
Retail, mail order.	**TYPE OF MARKETER**
Sears Merchandise Group is the nation's largest retailer of general merchandise, selling through a nationwide chain of 824 stores. In 1988, Sears restructured its merchandise group to establish the catalog and direct mail business as a separate organization, independent of the retail management structure. The company favors vertical business accountability to make managers more responsive and more accountable for their performance.	**BUSINESS**
The business was founded in 1886 by Richard W. Sears in Minneapolis, MN as R.W. Sears Watch Company. Sears moved his business to Chicago in 1887, advertised for a watchmaker, and hired Alvah C. Roebuck from Hammond, IN. By 1895, the 532-page catalog contained numerous additional items and sales exceeded $750,000. The company went public in 1906. As President of Sears, General Robert E. Wood opened the first retail store in 1925.	**COMPANY HISTORY**
The firm's customers reside throughout the United States, Canada, Puerto Rico, and Mexico.	**MARKETS**

SEARS, ROEBUCK AND COMPANY (continued)

FACILITIES

Headquarters in Sears Tower, downtown Chicago, IL; warehouses are located at various regional sites.

PRODUCTS, BRAND NAMES, PRICE RANGE

Sears divides its merchandise into five product areas: home appliance and electronics, home fashions, apparel, home improvements and automotive, and recreation. Recently, Sears has added branded merchandise in all areas and instituted an "everyday low-pricing" structure.

FINANCIAL INFORMATION

	SALES	NET INCOME	PROFIT MARGIN
1987	$31,599,200,000	$646,900,000	2.0%
1988	$30,256,000,000	$524,400,000	1.7%
1989	$28,085,500,000	$787,400,000	2.8%

TYPE OF ADVERTISING, PROMOTION

Sears publishes one annual home catalog and six Style catalogs, featuring fashion and seasonal merchandise. Smaller specialty books cover ten other product areas. Space advertising is done through newspaper inserts.

LIST INFORMATION

Sears does not market its lists or make available any information on its buyer file.

COMMENTS

Financial information is for Sears Merchandising Group only. Sears is making major changes in corporate structure. Sears Tower, the company headquarters, is up for sale, and employees will be relocated to suburban Chicago. In a cost saving move, Sears Merchandise Group is cutting staff from 6,000 to 4,500, expecting to realize savings of $75 million. Sales have been lackluster and earnings even less impressive. In 1988 the Sears Merchandise Group lost $312 million, yet wound up in the black due to earnings of $518 from credit operations and $128 million in international business.

THE SHARPER IMAGE

The Sharper Image, Inc.
650 Davis Street
San Francisco, CA   94111
Telephone: (415) 445-6000

ADDRESS, PHONE

The Sharper Image is publicly held, stock traded on NASDAQ.

OWNERSHIP

Richard Thalheimer, President and CEO; Craig Womack, Executive Vice President and COO; Robert Schultz, Senior Vice President, CFO; Jennifer Grellman, Vice President, Marketing; Vincent Barriero, Vice President, MIS.

MANAGEMENT

Mail order, retail.

TYPE OF MARKETER

The Sharper Image is a specialty retailer of unique and innovative products, characterized by diversity and originality. The company's collection of items available through mail order are presented in a colorful, monthly, award winning catalog and in retail stores throughout the country. The catalog provides advertising for the 66 stores in the US. Retail has been the fastest growing segment of business in recent years; it accounts for 75 percent of total revenues.

BUSINESS

The business was launched in 1978 by attorney Richard Thalheimer. An ad in Runners World magazine offering digital stopwatches for $29 produced $400 in sales. The initial catalog was mailed in 1979, offering an expanded line of exercise-related items, electronics and gifts. Gross sales that year were reported at $500,000. The first retail store opened in 1983; the catalog went monthly in 1985. The Sharper Image went public in April, 1987.

COMPANY HISTORY

Most customers are college-educated professional males. Average household income exceeds $76,000.

MARKETS

THE SHARPER IMAGE (continued)

FACILITIES	Headquarters in San Francisco, CA; warehouses in Emeryville and Berkeley, CA; and Little Rock, AR to open in 1990.
PRODUCTS, BRAND NAMES, PRICE RANGE	Merchandise mix includes Precor Fitness Climbers and Treadmills, Sony Video Walkman, Casio Digital Diaries, and a variety of unique and innovative novelty items. Prices range from $25 to $65,000.

FINANCIAL INFORMATION

	SALES	NET INCOME	PROFIT MARGIN
1987	$160,885,000	$5,607,000	3.5%
1988	$191,341,000	$4,794,000	2.5%
1989	$208,647,000	$4,174,000	2.0%

TYPE OF ADVERTISING, PROMOTION	The company produces monthly catalogs of approximately 68 pages, offering 150-175 products. The catalog is the primary advertising vehicle for retail operations. Television exposure, national news inserts and magazine space ads generate inquiries.

LIST INFORMATION

Quantity Mailed:	39,000,000
Average Order:	$134
Active Buyers:	2,000,000
Total List:	5,000,000
List Source:	rented lists, TV, space ads, and inserts

COMMENTS

The Sharper Image's traditional best sellers are electronic gadgets, such as Sharp's "Electronic Wizard" and various pocket computers. Mail order sales for 1989 were up as the company continued to focus on retail expansion. Increased exposure through media, as well as the appearance of celebrity Danny DeVito on the cover of the 1989 Holiday catalog boosted overall sales this year. The Holiday catalog had a circulation of 6.3 million and contained 112 pages, making it the largest and most widely circulated monthly Sharper Image catalog to date. For Fathers Day 1990, The Sharper Image will feature Bill Cosby on the cover of the June catalog.

SHOPSMITH, INC.

Shopsmith, Inc.
3931 Image Drive
Dayton, OH   45414
Telephone: (513) 898-6070

ADDRESS, PHONE

Shopsmith is publicly held, stock traded over the counter under the symbol "SHOP".

OWNERSHIP

John Folkerth, Chairman and CEO; William Becker, Vice President, Finance and Administration; Barry Hile, Vice President Sales and Marketing; Larry Jones, Vice President Operations.

MANAGEMENT

Mail order, retail.

TYPE OF MARKETER

Shopsmith manufactures and markets power and manual woodworking tools designed primarily for home use. Company also offers a full line of accessories. Shopsmith sells through mail order and its own stores. Direct sales reps conduct demonstrations in shopping malls throughout the country. At the end of 1989, Shopsmith operated 39 stores in the U.S. and three in Canada. The firm employs approximately 400.

BUSINESS

The Shopsmith trademark dates back to 1946. In 1972, John Folkerth, current President, purchased the tooling, machinery, and inventory of the Shopsmith line from Magna America for $250,000. Magna acquired Shopsmith in 1958, but production of the basic Shopsmith unit, the Mark V, had ceased. Present Shopsmith reorganized in 1987, shifting top management and turning focus from heavy dependence on mail order toward greater retail activity.

COMPANY HISTORY

Shopsmith's customers are mostly middle income men with home workshops in the U.S. and Canada.

MARKETS

SHOPSMITH, INC. (continued)

FACILITIES	Administrative, manufacturing, warehouse, and fulfillment operations are located in Dayton, OH.
PRODUCTS, BRAND NAMES, PRICE RANGE	Company's principal product is Shopsmith Mark V, a multi-purpose power woodworking tool. A complete line of accessories is also available. The Mark V, along with some standard accessories, sells for $1,899.

FINANCIAL INFORMATION

	SALES	NET INCOME	PROFIT MARGIN
1987	$39,205,596	-$ 660,775	-1.7%
1988	$38,737,065	$ 451,807	1.2%
1989	$43,223,382	$1,469,634	3.4%

TYPE OF ADVERTISING, PROMOTION	Shopsmith markets the Mark V and its accessories through 100-page, full-color catalogs and direct mail brochures.

LIST INFORMATION

Quantity Mailed:	6,000,000
Average Order:	$150
Active Buyers:	175,000
Total List:	3,500,000
List Source:	direct mail, space, retail

COMMENTS

For fiscal 1989, net sales were up 12 percent from 1988. In spite of past losses due to poor planning, Shopsmith expects significant future growth. Since 1987, the company has focused on retail stores, since growth in mail order and direct sales has been flat. Retail stores account for 55 percent of company's sales; the company expects that figure to grow to 71 percent over the next three years. Mail order and direct sales operations will be maintained to serve customers outside of retail shopping areas. The company's newest product is the Power Station, a lower-priced power stand which can be used with a number of accessories sold by Shopsmith.

SPIEGEL

Spiegel, Inc.
Regency Towers
1515 West 22nd Street
Oak Brook, IL   60522
Telephone: (708) 986-8800

ADDRESS,
PHONE

Publicly held stock represents 10 percent of company; remaining stock largely owned by Spiegel Holdings, Inc.

OWNERSHIP

Michael Otto, Chairman; John J. Shea, President, Vice Chairman and CEO; Kenneth A. Bochenski, Senior Vice President, Operations and Information Services; Alton M. Withers, Senior Vice President and CFO; David Moon and Robert Conradi, Vice President Merchandising; Richard W. Wagner, Senior Vice President, Marketing and Advertising.

MANAGEMENT

Mail order, retail.

TYPE OF
MARKETER

Spiegel is the third largest mail order marketer in the U.S. and has established itself as "the specialty department store in print." Spiegel markets through general semi-annual catalog and smaller seasonal and specialty catalogs. Company also operates nine Chicago-area outlet stores and three "For You" large-sized women's apparel stores. Eddie Bauer and Honeybee subsidiaries operate independently.

BUSINESS

Spiegel was founded by the Spiegel family in 1865. Beneficial Corp. acquired all capital stock in 1965. Since 1977, Spiegel has implemented a "mass to class" strategy, upgrading product line to appeal to up-scale working women. Germany-based catalog giant Otto Versand acquired Spiegel in 1982. Company went public with six million shares of non-voting stock in October 1987. In 1988, Spiegel acquired Honeybee and Eddie Bauer.

COMPANY
HISTORY

Most customers are upscale, professional women from two-income families. Median yearly income is $50,000.

MARKETS

SPIEGEL (continued)

FACILITIES	Headquarters in Oak Brook, IL, outlet stores in Chicago area. Telephone order centers in GA, PA, NV.
PRODUCTS, BRAND NAMES, PRICE RANGE	Spiegel markets women's career and casual apparel by such designers as Calvin Klein, Liz Claiborne, Norma Kamali, and Pierre Cardin. Other products include furniture, cookware, home entertainment, toys, and cameras. Pricing is mid to high end.

FINANCIAL INFORMATION

	SALES	NET INCOME	PROFIT MARGIN
1987	$1,067,345,000	$41,111,000	3.9%
1988	$1,404,419,000	$56,962,000	4.1%
1989	$1,695,806,000	$73,282,000	4.3%

TYPE OF ADVERTISING, PROMOTION	Promotion is primarily through specialty catalogs. Spiegel also runs inquiry-generating television spot advertisements and places space ads in publications such as Vogue, Harper's Bazaar, and The New York Times.

LIST INFORMATION

Quantity Mailed:	190,000,000
Average Order:	$115
Active Buyers:	5,400,000
Total List:	11,000,000*
List Source:	direct mail, space

COMMENTS

Sales for Spiegel reflect gross sales consolidated to include its subsidiaries. Net income for 1987 excludes an $8 million one-time tax benefit. List information reflects only Spiegel, not Eddie Bauer or Honeybee operations. Spiegel launched its prospecting catalog with the caption, "This is Not The Spiegel Catalog" in early 1989. The company's private label "Ready To Wind Down" (RTW) was introduced in Spring 1989 with hopes for future expansion of the apparel line. 1989 "Holiday Thrills" catalog promoted Spiegel's ongoing charitable donation program by making a contribution for every order placed, estimated at $100,000. The two benefitting charities were Covenant House and NAPARE, which aids children endangered by drug abuse.

TALBOTS

Talbots
175 Beal Street
Hingham, MA   02043
Telephone: (617) 749-7600

ADDRESS, PHONE

Talbots is an autonomously operating division of AEON/JUSCO Co., Ltd., Japan's fourth largest retailer.

OWNERSHIP

Arnold B. Zetcher, President and CEO; Clark Hinkley, Executive Vice President and General Merchandise Manager; Mary Pasciucco, Senior Vice President, Catalog Development.

MANAGEMENT

Retail and mail order.

TYPE OF MARKETER

Talbots is a leading specialty retailer selling updated classic apparel to women through direct marketing and retail. Its collection includes updated classic apparel, shoes, and accessories for career, casual, and special occasion dressing. (Talbots' own label provides 60 percent of its merchandise line.) In July 1989, Talbots introduced "Talbots Kids," a catalog which features exclusively children's updated classic apparel, 40 percent of which is marketed under the Talbots Kids label. Talbots' catalogs are theme oriented, and range from "Resume" (career apparel) to "Escape" (resort wear). The company's focus is on marketing complete, coordinated outfits rather than individual pieces.

BUSINESS

Rudolf and Nancy Talbot established Talbots in 1947 with the first retail store in Hingham, Massachusetts; the direct marketing business was added in 1948. General Mills acquired Talbots in 1973. In June of 1988, Talbots was sold to Tokyo-based JUSCO Co., Ltd., (AEON Group).

COMPANY HISTORY

Customers are 90 percent female, well-educated, 70 percent employed. Median annual income is $56,000, average age is 40.

MARKETS

TALBOTS (continued)

FACILITIES

Headquarters are in Hingham, MA. Other locations in Lakeville, MA; Knoxville, TN; Tampa, FL; New York, NY; and Hong Kong; retail stores are located throughout the U.S. and Japan.

PRODUCTS,
BRAND NAMES,
PRICE RANGE

Product mix includes sportswear, dresses, suits, coats, accessories, shoes, and children's outfits. Sleepwear is made available during the Christmas holiday season. 60 percent of Talbots' adult products and 40 percent of the children's wear are marketed under its own label. Prices concentrate in the $50 to $130 range.

FINANCIAL
INFORMATION

	SALES	NET INCOME	PROFIT MARGIN
1987	$331,800,000	N/A	N/A
1988	$391,800,000	N/A	N/A
1989	$453,000,000	N/A	N/A

TYPE OF
ADVERTISING,
PROMOTION

Talbots mails 78 million copies of its 23 catalog editions to consumers in the U.S. and 120 countries worldwide. Talbots releases "theme" spin-off catalogs periodically. Space ads act to support retail and generate catalog inquiries.

LIST
INFORMATION

Quantity Mailed: 78,000,000
Average Order: $120
Active Buyers: 850,000
Total List: 5,000,000 (2,400,000 past buyers)
List Source: direct mail, space

COMMENTS

Above sales figures have all been restated to be comparable since acquisition by JUSCO. Direct marketing operation originates approximately one third of total sales at Talbots. Talbots' aggressive expansion plans call for opening of 25-30 new retail stores through 1994. Talbots opened its first Japanese retail store in Tokyo's Jiyugaoka suburb on February 21, 1990, with a Japanese catalog to follow as early as 1991. An European retail outlet is planned for 1992, a Canadian unit to open mid-1991. Talbots mailed 2.5 million copies of its first children's catalog in summer of 1989. This catalog offered merchandised for boys and girls, aged 4 to 14. Plans are to follow up in Talbots' "theme" manner, with such titles as "Back to School" and "Summer Camp." Talbots recently added jewelry to its merchandise, by including a six-page insert in its Holiday/Fall 1989 catalog; items were priced from $30 to $3,000. Talbots reported a good holiday season 1989, with sales up 20 percent from the previous year. Talbots Kids retail stores to open in summer 1990; plans call for 50 to open nationwide by 1994.

TIFFANY

Tiffany & Company
727 Fifth Avenue
New York, NY   10022
Telephone: (212) 755-8000

ADDRESS, PHONE

Tiffany & Co. is publicly held, stock traded on the NYSE under symbol TIF.

OWNERSHIP

William Chaney, Chairman and CEO; T. Andruskevich, Senior Vice President, International and Trade; J. Loring, Senior Vice President, Design; B. Ohl, Senior Vice President, Retail; B. Dodson, Vice President, Corporate Sales; M. Kowalsk and P. Schneirla, Vice President, Merchandising; S. McMillan, Vice President Marketing; D. Strohl, Vice President Operations; J. Fernandez, Vice President, Finance and CFO; P. Dorsey, Vice President, General Counsel.

MANAGEMENT

Retail, mail order, corporate sales, wholesale.

TYPE OF MARKETER

Tiffany is a retailer, designer, manufacturer, and distributor of fine jewelry and gift items. Products sold through three main channels of distribution: U.S. retail sales occur through nine Tiffany stores and select independent jewelers and specialty retailers; direct marketing programs include U.S. direct sales of business gifts and corporate incentives, as well as consumer mail order and catalogs; international retail sales occur in the Far East and Europe.

BUSINESS

Tiffany celebrated its 150th anniversary in Fall 1987. Its catalog was launched in 1845, and the company knows of no retail catalog that precedes it. The company's flagship New York store was opened in 1937 under the direction of Charles Lewis Tiffany. 1963 saw a second store open in San Francisco and the company expanded into 7 more branch stores in various major U.S. cities. The company was owned by Avon from 1979 until management-led leverage buy-out occurred in 1984. Tiffany went public in 1987.

COMPANY HISTORY

U.S. market comprised primarily of women with household incomes of more than $75,000 and corporate customers.

MARKETS

TIFFANY (continued)

FACILITIES	Headquarters in New York, NY, branch stores in major U.S. and international cities. Distribution center is located in Parsippany, NJ.
PRODUCTS, BRAND NAMES, PRICE RANGE	Tiffany's merchandise mix ranges from moderately-priced gift items to fine jewelry. Other products include sterling silver, china, crystal, timepieces, fragrances, leather goods, scarves, and stationery. Most products priced from under $100 to several thousand dollars.

FINANCIAL INFORMATION

	SALES	NET INCOME	PROFIT MARGIN
1988	$230,488,000	$16,176,000	7.0%
1989	$290,344,000	$24,901,000	8.6%
1990	$383,960,000	$33,310,000	8.7%

TYPE OF ADVERTISING, PROMOTION	Products are promoted through space ads in up-scale magazines, newspapers, and business publications. Tiffany mails quarterly "Selections" catalog and annual "Blue Book." Its annual ad budget exceeds $10 million worldwide.

LIST INFORMATION

Quantity Mailed:	7,500,000
Average Order:	$130
Active Buyers:	86,000
Total List:	248,000
List Source:	direct mail, space, rental

COMMENTS	Financial information above reflects combined distribution channels: U.S. retail, direct marketing, and international retail sales. In fiscal 1989, ending January 31, direct marketing revenues (corporate sales and consumer mail order) rose 8.9 percent to $59.4 million, representing 20.5 percent of total sales. Catalog circulation posted a 15 percent increase, to more than 8 million catalogs mailed in fiscal 1990. International retail has been Tiffany's fastest growing segment in recent years, with primary emphasis on Europe and the Far East. In addition to offering its products through two Japanese distributors, Mitsukoshi department stores and Heiwado and Co., Tiffany has two retail stores in Hong Kong. Tiffany also operates stores in London, Munich and Zurich.

WILLIAMS-SONOMA, INC.

Williams-Sonoma, Inc. 100 North Point Street San Francisco, CA 94133 Telephone: (415) 421-7900	**ADDRESS, PHONE**
Williams-Sonoma is a publicly held company; stock traded on NASDAQ.	**OWNERSHIP**
Howard Lester, Chairman and CEO; Charles Williams, Founder and Vice Chairman; Kent Larson, President; James Riley, CFO; Tom O'Higgins, Vice President W-S Catalog Merchandise Buying; Randy Dirth, Vice President W-S retail Store Merchandising; Patrick Connolly, Vice President, Marketing; John Moore, Vice President Catalog Development.	**MANAGEMENT**
Retail, mail order.	**TYPE OF MARKETER**
Williams-Sonoma markets unique gourmet and professional cookware, plus serving accessories through "Catalog for Cooks." Williams-Sonoma specialty catalogs include: "Hold Everything", organizational household items; "Gardener's Eden", garden and patio equipment; "Pottery Barn", contemporary home furnishings and accessories; and "Chambers", bed and bath accessories. Slightly less than half of sales are generated by mail; remainder of business is retail.	**BUSINESS**
During 1956, Chuck Williams founded the company in Sonoma, CA as a retail business; the main store later moved to San Francisco. Mail order began in 1972 with two brochures. Promotional campaign launched in 1979 resulted in mail order sales doubling each year until 1983. In 1982, Williams-Sonoma acquired Gardener's Eden and began publishing the "Hold Everything" catalog. Williams-Sonoma went public in July, 1983. The Pottery Barn was acquired in fall of 1986. "Chambers" was introduced in spring, 1989.	**COMPANY HISTORY**
Customers are located throughout the U.S.; approximately 85 percent are women in late 20 to 40 age range.	**MARKETS**

WILLIAMS-SONOMA (continued)

FACILITIES

Headquarters are in San Francisco, CA. Company's 400,000 sq. ft. distribution center is in Memphis, TN.

PRODUCTS, BRAND NAMES, PRICE RANGE

"Williams-Sonoma" sells variety of gourmet cookware and accessories under house and national brand names priced from $10 to $600. "Hold Everything" and "Pottery Barn" are medium-priced. "Gardener's Eden" prices range from $6 to $1,900. "Chambers" ranges moderate to high end.

FINANCIAL INFORMATION

	SALES	NET INCOME	PROFIT MARGIN
1987	$136,814,000	$3,346,000	2.4%
1988	$174,179,000	$5,205,000	3.0%
1989	$218,170,000	$8,970,000	4.1%

TYPE OF ADVERTISING, PROMOTION

Catalogs are mailed quarterly, except "The Pottery Barn" and "Chambers," scheduled for 3 times per year. The company does limited amount of advertising in women's and gardening magazines to generate leads, sales.

LIST INFORMATION

Quantity Mailed:	95,000,000
Average Order:	varies, Chambers is $150.
Active Buyers:	2,000,000
Total List:	4,800,000*
List Source:	direct mail, rental, space,

COMMENTS

Management reports Williams-Sonoma has maintained average annual growth rate of 30 percent over the past five years and that trend is expected to continue. Through 1987, mail order business generated more than half of sales. In 1988, that changed, as company pursued retail expansion. By September 1989, the company operated 82 Williams-Sonoma stores (including 3 in Japan), 16 Hold Everything stores, and 30 Pottery Barn units.

Net earnings reported for 1989 were at a 72 percent increase over 1988. Sales increased 25 percent, retail producing 56 percent of 1989 revenues. Mail order sales gains attributed to the success of the new "Chambers" catalog and continued profitability of Williams-Sonoma's other four catalogs.

Chapter 11

Business Profiles

of 25

Business-to-Business

Mail Order

Companies

BLACK BOX

Black Box Corporation
P.O. Box 12800
Pittsburgh, PA 15241
Telephone: (412) 746-5500

ADDRESS,
PHONE

Black Box is a privately held corporation headquartered in
Pittsburgh, PA.

OWNERSHIP

Gene Yost, President and CEO; Jeff Boetticher, Senior Vice
President and COO; Tim Crowe, Vice President Finance and
CFO; Doug Goodall, Vice President Business Development; Bill
Bradley, Vice President Customer Satisfaction; Ken Shaw, Vice
President Manufacturing and Engineering.

MANAGEMENT

Mail order.

TYPE OF
MARKETER

Black Box markets full line of data communications products
through six Black Box, LAN, System 3X, EAZY, WIDGET World,
Special Products catalogs and outbound telemarketing programs
which focus on Fortune 1000 companies through user and resell
programs. The company participates in joint ventures and
subsidiary operations in 14 countries with distributors in 41 more.
Black Box reports 600 headquarter employees.

BUSINESS

Black Box was founded in 1977 by Gene Yost and Dick Raub in
Pittsburgh, PA. In 1982, Micom Systems acquired the company
and in 1988 Black Box Incorporated was formed, taking the
corporation private. First catalog published was 16 pages and was
mailed to 1000 names. Current Black Box catalog is over 200
pages and over 2 million copies are mailed each year.

COMPANY
HISTORY

Black Box markets to Fortune 500 Industrial/Service companies,
local area network users, computer and value-added resells.

MARKETS

BLACK BOX (continued)

FACILITIES

Black Box headquarters and distribution facilities are located in Pittsburgh, PA.

PRODUCTS, BRAND NAMES, PRICE RANGE

Black Box markets unique, higher-end data communications hardware and add-on upgrades which enhance and extend the capabilities of existing computer systems.

FINANCIAL INFORMATION

	SALES	NET INCOME	PROFIT
1987	$64,000,000	N/A	N/A
1988	$78,500,000	N/A	N/A
1989	$88,000,000	N/A	N/A

TYPE OF ADVERTISING, PROMOTION

Black Box publishes and distributes separate catalogs covering a broad range of segments among the computer user base. The company also uses card decks, package inserts, telemarketing and in-house promotions.

LIST INFORMATION

Quantity Mailed: 4,000,000
Average Order: N/A
Active Buyers: N/A
Total List: 750,000
List Source: direct mail

COMMENTS

Black Box expects sales for fiscal year 1990 at around $103,800,000. Total mailings of all business units exceed 4 million copies per year. The company offers free telephone technical support before and after purchases to its customers; in addition, a minimum of a one year warranty is offered with a lifetime warranty standard on cable and switch products. Black Box maintains its own database marketing system.

BUSINESSLAND

Businessland, Inc.
1001 Ridder Park Drive
San Jose, CA   95131
Telephone: (408) 437-0400

ADDRESS, PHONE

Businessland is publicly held, stock is traded on NYSE under the symbol BLI.

OWNERSHIP

David A. Norman, Chairman, President and CEO; Leo Korman, CFO, Senior Vice President of Finance; Douglas C. Johnson, Senior Vice President, Product Operations; Paul M. Schuman, Vice President, Direct Division.

MANAGEMENT

Direct sales, retail, and mail order.

TYPE OF MARKETER

Businessland, Inc. is an international leader in the distribution, integration and support of microcomputer and workstation systems for business by integrating products from selected manufacturers to create systems tailored to specific customer needs. Products are sold primarily through the direct sales force operating from 120 company-owned centers and branch offices worldwide. Businessland Direct sells a complete line of software, after-market computing products, supplies and accessories through catalogs. The company also offers a wide range of end-user training and after-sales support and service.

BUSINESS

Businessland was founded in 1982 by David Norman and Enzo Torresi. Initial public offering was completed in December 1983. IBM personal computers were the first items sold; mix has expanded to include Compaq, Macintosh, etc., as well as networking equipment and software. The company established national presence in a short time and began international expansion in 1987 with acquisition in the U.K. The company now operates offices in the U.S., Canada, France, Japan, U.K. and West Germany.

COMPANY HISTORY

Businessland markets to large and medium-sized corporations, as well as small businesses, professional people and government agencies.

MARKETS

BUSINESSLAND, INC. (continued)

FACILITIES	Headquarters are located in San Jose, CA; distribution centers are located in Hayward, CA and Erlanger, KY.
PRODUCTS, BRAND NAMES, PRICE RANGE	Products from leading manufacturers include Apple Computer, Compaq Computer, Hewlett-Packard, IBM, Lotus Development, Microsoft, NCR, NEC, NetFRAME, NeXT, Novell, 3Com and Wyse. The Direct division provides fast delivery and 800 telephone number ordering of nearly 10,000 products including software, peripherals, supplies and accessories.

FINANCIAL INFORMATION

	SALES	NET INCOME	PROFIT MARGIN
1987	$ 600,039,000	$ 8,370,000	1.4%
1988	$ 871,552,000	$18,833,000	2.2%
1989	$1,188,741,000	$32,876,000	2.7%

TYPE OF ADVERTISING, PROMOTION

Direct marketing emphasis is on the 134-page catalog. Businessland mails approximately 1,800,000 catalogs during the year. Other direct mail promotions are conducted on a frequent basis. The catalog is used as a sales tool by Businessland marketing representatives.

LIST INFORMATION

Quantity Mailed:	1,800,000
Average Order:	$450
Active Buyers:	100,000
Total List:	300,000
List Source:	direct mail, rental

COMMENTS

Financial information provided above refers to total Businessland sales for fiscal years ending June 30. While catalog sales remain a small portion of the overall business (less than 10 percent), direct marketing operation is growing faster than the company's overall growth. The company commitment to mail order reportedly continues to increase due to the success of the program. Total orders processed were in excess of 175,000 per year. The average order size increased by 10 percent in fiscal 1989. Management does not break out mail order sales separately.

180

CAREERTRACK

CareerTrack
3080 Center Green Drive
Boulder, CO   80301
Telephone: (303) 447-2323

ADDRESS, PHONE

CareerTrack is privately held. Founders Jimmy Calano and
Jeff Salzman own 100 percent of capital stock.

OWNERSHIP

Jimmy Calano, President and CEO; Jeff Salzman, Vice President,
Creative Director and Director of Program Development; Joe
Jaltuck, Director of Finance; Steve Juedes, Director of Market
Strategy; Penny Sinclair, Director of Operations.

MANAGEMENT

Mail order, retail.

TYPE OF MARKETER

CareerTrack claims to be the nation's number-one producer of
business seminars. The company promotes business
communications and productivity seminars by mail through catalogs
and supplemental brochures. CareerTrack Publications produces
the company's live seminars on audio and video cassettes. Tapes
and books are marketed through the catalog, at seminars and at
retail. CareerTrack operates a single retail store in Boulder, CO.
Company reports close to 400 employees.

BUSINESS

In 1982, Calano, a consultant, and Salzman, an advertising man,
put up $10,000 to launch CareerTrack. Their initial strategy was to
undercut the industry by offering seminars at $95 (going rate was
roughly $150) through low-budget, newsletter-style brochures.
Later, prices were slashed even further to $45 per seminar and
enrollment soared. In 1989, CareerTrack trained more than
750,000 people; sales on combination public/private seminars
topped $62 million.

COMPANY HISTORY

CareerTrack customers are business men and women throughout
the U.S. and foreign countries.

MARKETS

CAREERTRACK (continued)

| FACILITIES | CareerTrack's headquarters and single retail outlet are located in Boulder, CO. |

PRODUCTS, BRAND NAMES, PRICE RANGE

Seminars include "Image and Self-Projection", "In Search of Excellence", "Power Presentation Skills" and "One Minute Manager". The product line also includes 45 audio tape programs and videos, as well as several books. One-day seminars are priced at $48 and $98.

FINANCIAL INFORMATION

	SALES	NET INCOME	PROFIT MARGIN
1987	$38,000,000	N/A	N/A
1988	$52,000,000	N/A	N/A
1989	$62,000,000	N/A	N/A

TYPE OF ADVERTISING, PROMOTION

All CareerTrack products, including seminars, books and tapes, are sold through the company's three annual 52 page catalogs. The company also mails supplemental brochures throughout the year to promote individual seminars.

LIST INFORMATION

Quantity Mailed:	70,000,000* (US 47,500,000*)
Average Order:	$69
Active Buyers:	131,600*
Total List:	2,000,000
List Source:	direct mail

COMMENTS

In eight years, CareerTrack reportedly has grown from start-up sales of $220,000 to more than $62 million annually. Management expects sales to reach $70 million in 1990. The publishing division alone reportedly generates $15 million. In 1987, CareerTrack crossed over into the consumer sector with seminars such as "How To Find and Keep a Mate" and "How to Raise Happy and Confident Kids". It has also gained exclusive rights to present seminars based on leading business books, including Tom Peter's "In Search of Excellence". In recent years, CareerTrack has expanded into foreign markets. It claims to be the largest seminar producer in Canada, and it also offers seminars in Great Britain, continental Europe, Australia and Southeast Asia.

COMPUADD

CompuAdd Corporation
1203 Technology Boulevard
Austin, TX   78727
Telephone: (512) 250-1489

ADDRESS, PHONE

CompuAdd is privately owned by Bill H. Hayden.

OWNERSHIP

Bill H. Hayden, CEO; Edward Thomas, President and COO; Richard McLemore, Director of Sales and Marketing.

MANAGEMENT

Retail, direct mail and direct sales.

TYPE OF MARKETER

CompuAdd designs, manufactures and markets its own line of personal computers and is a major marketer of add-on products, peripherals, office products and hundreds of popular software products. In just over one year, CompuAdd has grown from 15 to 89 retail outlets, making the company the largest privately held computer retailer. Its present ratio of revenue source is 60 percent retail, 40 percent direct marketing. CompuAdd employs 1,385 people.

BUSINESS

CompuAdd was founded in 1982 by Texas Instruments engineer, Bill H. Hayden. His initial efforts were through ads for IBM compatible add-on equipment in personal computer trade publications. In 1984, the first retail unit was added and the company expanded to sell the CompuAdd computer systems. The "CompuAdd" catalog was added in 1987. "MacAvenue" catalog was launched in March, 1990.

COMPANY HISTORY

The customer base is 75 percent individuals and small to medium sized businesses, and 25 percent Fortune 1000 clientele.

MARKETS

COMPUADD (continued)

FACILITIES	Headquarters are located in Austin, TX. CompuAdd has one overseas distribution center in Bristol, England. 88 retail stores are located throughout the U.S., and one Canadian outlet.
PRODUCTS, BRAND NAMES, PRICE RANGE	The product line includes approximately 450 Macintosh and 2,000 IBM PC-compatible items. 50 percent of sales result from CompuAdd's private label computer systems. Prices range from $4.74 for 10 floppy disks to $595 and up for PC systems.

FINANCIAL INFORMATION

	SALES	NET INCOME	PROFIT MARGIN
1987	$100,000,000	N/A	N/A
1988	$241,000,000	N/A	N/A
1989	$400,000,000	N/A	N/A

TYPE OF ADVERTISING, PROMOTION	Primary promotional emphasis is on catalogs; "CompuAdd", mailed 4 times per year, and "MacAvenue", planned 2-4 times annually. The company advertises regularly in <u>PC Magazine</u> and <u>MacWorld</u>. Regional promotions are conducted through newspaper inserts.

LIST INFORMATION

Quantity Mailed:	5,500,000*
Average Order:	$350
Active Buyers:	425,000
Total List:	1,000,000
List Source:	direct mail, space ads, rental

COMMENTS	The company reports 50 percent average annual sales growth since 1985. CompuAdd also reports high profitability, attributed to their successful catalog venture launched in 1987. 1990 sales are predicted at $612 million, a 35 percent increase from 1989. CompuAdd plans expansion in Europe, Central and South America and the Pacific Rim. The company owns and operates its distribution channels and strives for a personal relationship with its customers. CompuAdd also serves the government and educational segments, including over 500 colleges and universities nationwide. CompuAdd recently entered into an exclusive agreement to provide IBM PC-compatibles to several state-funded schools.

184

DAK INDUSTRIES

DAK Industries, Inc.
8200 Remmet Avenue
Canoga Park, CA   91304
Telephone: (818) 888-8220

ADDRESS,
PHONE

DAK Industries is privately held; founder Drew Kaplan owns the majority of capital stock.

OWNERSHIP

Drew Kaplan, President and Owner.

MANAGEMENT

Mail order.

TYPE OF
MARKETER

DAK is a mail order marketer of a wide assortment of electronic gadgetry ranging from stereo equipment, home security devices, to computers and computer software. The company markets discounted merchandise from major manufacturers and offers many products at close-out prices.

BUSINESS

Drew Alan Kaplan, who considers himself the "ultimate electronic gadget freak," started the business in 1965. Throughout its history, DAK has offered high-tech electronic products at discounted prices. Kaplan has always maintained control over the merchandise selection and presentation. He reportedly tests all merchandise, photographs products and writes all catalog copy. The firm has grown steadily throughout its history and serves more than 500,000 customers.

COMPANY
HISTORY

DAK's buyers purchase high-tech electronic equipment and are mid- to upscale in education and income; 95 percent are men.

MARKETS

DAK INDUSTRIES (continued)

FACILITIES

The firm's headquarters and mail order fulfillment center are in Canoga Park, CA.

PRODUCTS, BRAND NAMES, PRICE RANGE

DAK's product line includes portable phones, security devices, stereo equipment, pollution shields and computer hardware and software. Brand names include Emerson, BSR, Sharp, Hitachi, and DAK. Price ranges from $5 to $1,500.

FINANCIAL INFORMATION

	SALES	NET INCOME	PROFIT MARGIN
1987	$21,600,000	N/A	N/A
1988	$25,920,000	N/A	N/A
1989	$31,104,000	N/A	N/A

TYPE OF ADVERTISING, PROMOTION

About 50 percent of the company's customers are generated by direct mail. The rest come from space ads in The Wall Street Journal, Stereo Review, Popular Science, Popular Mechanics, and OMNI. DAK mails 4 catalog editions per year.

LIST INFORMATION

Quantity Mailed:	15,000,000
Average Order:	$120
Active Buyers:	259,200
Total List:	850,000
List Source:	direct mail, space

COMMENTS

DAK markets electronic gifts and gadgetry exclusively by mail. The merchandise is heavily discounted and copy in catalogs and space ads explains in detail each product, how it was acquired, its utility, and any limitations the product might have. Its main catalog is published seasonally and is 8 1/2" by 11", full color, with 68 pages. Full page ads in such publications as Popular Science features specially discounted products, with copy blocks often emphasizing DAK's quantity buying abilities. Both catalogs and space ads include extensive copy and rely primarily on informing customers to sell products.

DATA GENERAL DIRECT

Data General Direct
4400 Computer Drive, MS1-D
Westboro, MA   01580
Telephone: (508) 366-8911

ADDRESS, PHONE

Data General Direct is the mail order channel of Data General Corporation's Customer Service Division.

OWNERSHIP

Herb Fox, Director DG/DIRECT; John Poldoian, Marketing Manager DG/DIRECT; Gwynne Jamieson, Marketing Communications Manager; Jay Gauthier, Catalog Publisher; Linda Rothstein, Catalog Editor.

MANAGEMENT

Mail order.

TYPE OF MARKETER

DG/DIRECT markets a broad range of consumable computer products to installed-base DG customers and value added resellers. DG/DIRECT employs direct response vehicles and complimentary marketing programs along with catalogs; direct mail campaigns are supported by the group's outbound telemarketing efforts, a field marketing organization and a direct sales force. DG/DIRECT reports 200 employees worldwide.

BUSINESS

Established in 1983, DG/DIRECT grew out of Data General's Field Engineering division. Initial direct marketing efforts centered around its catalog which promoted supplies and accessories. Current computer users and computer products catalogs offer products and accessories; a sales tracking and reporting system monitors progress while providing divisional management with marketing data.

COMPANY HISTORY

Data General markets to end-user customers and to various vertical markets.

MARKETS

DATA GENERAL DIRECT (continued)

FACILITIES

The company's divisional headquarters and 20,000 square foot distribution facility are located in Westboro, MA.

PRODUCTS, BRAND NAMES, PRICE RANGE

DG/DIRECT products range from $.75 diskettes to $75,000 Uninterruptible Power Supplies (UPS). The group also offers terminals, printers, peripherals, add-ons, low-end systems, and software.

FINANCIAL INFORMATION

	SALES	NET INCOME	PROFIT MARGIN
1987	N/A	N/A	N/A
1988	N/A	N/A	N/A
1989	$17,631,000*	N/A	N/A

TYPE OF ADVERTISING, PROMOTION

Along with catalogs, the company uses space ads, video, outbound telemarketing, direct mail, continuity campaigns and prospecting tools for promotional efforts. Catalog creative focus is on customer testimonials.

LIST INFORMATION

Quantity Mailed:	1,000,000
Average Order:	$775
Active Buyers:	13,000
Total List:	33,000
List Source:	direct mail, telemarketing

COMMENTS

Although 1987 and 1988 sales figures were not released by DG/DIRECT, sales are reported to have grown continuously during the company's brief history. The current full-line Computer Users' Catalog contains more than 1,600 items on 136 pages. In addition to being primarily a direct marketing vehicle, catalogs are used as sales tools by DG's sales force. Catalog production value is very high; DG/DIRECT is at the forefront of selective binding and ink-jet messages. In telephone response, the company employs a two-level strategy that includes technical sales reps for product information and consultation, and telemarketing sales representatives to handle incoming orders and inquiries.

DAY-TIMERS

Day-Timers, Inc.
P.O. Box 2368
Allentown, PA 18001-9967
Telephone: (215) 398-1151

ADDRESS, PHONE

Day-Timers is a subsidiary of American Brands, Inc.,
Old Greenwich, CT.

OWNERSHIP

Steve Rowley, President; William Dorney, Vice President,
Manufacturing; Herb Brown, Vice President, Operations;
Mark La Douceur, Vice President, Marketing; Glenn Large,
Vice President, Information Systems.

MANAGEMENT

Mail order.

TYPE OF MARKETER

Day-Timers manufactures, prints, and sells supplies geared toward
achieving efficient business operations through effective time
management systems. Products include planning books, calendars,
compartment wallets, binders, and briefcases. The company also
markets business-related items sourced from other manufacturers.
Management reports approximately 1,200 employees.

BUSINESS

The Dorney family's printing firm began marketing a Lawyer's Day
Diary created by attorney Morris Perkin in the 1930s. By 1951,
they were marketing other business diaries and time-management
tools by mail and printing material for Day-Timers, a similar
business founded in 1947. The two firms merged in the early
1960s. The new company was acquired by Beatrice foods in 1972,
and American Brands acquired it in February 1988.

COMPANY HISTORY

Sales are primarily to major U.S. corporations; 60 percent of
customers are men with upscale incomes.

MARKETS

DAY-TIMERS (continued)

FACILITIES	Headquarters, manufacturing and fulfillment are located in East Texas, PA.
PRODUCTS, BRAND NAMES, PRICE RANGE	Day-Timers sells desk and wallet-size planning books, calendars, memo pads, binders, diaries and appointment books. Prices range from $15 to $50; most customers take advantage of quantity discounts offered.

LIST INFORMATION

	SALES	NET INCOME	PROFIT MARGIN
1987	$122,640,000*	N/A	N/A
1988	$141,125,000*	N/A	N/A
1989	$162,400,000*	N/A	N/A

TYPE OF ADVERTISING, PROMOTION	Day-Timers publishes several catalogs with guaranteed prices annually, mailing them throughout the year. It markets single products through periodic solo mailings containing a letter, brochure, and order form.

LIST INFORMATION

Quantity Mailed:	8,000,000*
Average Order:	$58
Active Buyers:	1,792,000
Total List:	4,600,000
List Source:	direct mail, space.

COMMENTS	Although Day-Timers is a subsidiary of a mega-million dollar corporation, it prides itself on being a family business, with relatives and long-term employees all taking personal responsibility for "product quality ... and a commitment to excellence." Management attributes the company's success to the "continuing need for products that will help business people be more productive at work," and to a continuous influx of new Day-Timers products which help them to achieve that goal. Catalogs are full-color, standard size; main book is printed only once a year to help contain costs. There are also two smaller seasonal editions.

DELL COMPUTER

Dell Computer Corporation
9505 Arboretum Blvd
Austin, TX 78759-7299
Telephone: (512) 338-4400

ADDRESS, PHONE

Dell Computer is publicly held. Stock traded on NASDAQ.

OWNERSHIP

Michael S. Dell, Chairman and CEO; E. Lee Walker, President; Joel J. Kocher, Senior Vice President, Sales; G. Glenn Henry, Senior Vice President, Product Marketing; Andrew R. Harris, Senior Vice President, Marketing; Donald D. Collis, Vice President, Finance and CFO; Jim Handmarch, Vice President of Manufacturing.

MANAGEMENT

Direct marketing and sales.

TYPE OF MARKETER

Dell Computer is involved in the design, manufacture and distribution of a range of personal computers, software, supplies and accessories. Primary products are personal computers compatible with IBM PC/AT, as well as 386 processors. Sales occur by mail, in response to space ads and direct mail, through network of value added re-sellers, and directly through a team of 100 sales representatives. Corporate sales account for a substantial portion of the business.

BUSINESS

Michael Dell started PC's Limited in May 1984 at age 19. A college student, Dell began selling PCs from his apartment. He patterned products after IBM PCs and sold them at 30 to 50 percent below name-brand products. First computers were sold in 1985 through space ads in PC magazines. In 1987, the company changed its name to Dell Computer and later went public. 1987 also marked Dell's catalog debut and the beginning of expansion abroad.

COMPANY HISTORY

Customer base includes small to medium-sized businesses; corporate accounts; educational and governmental markets.

MARKETS

DELL COMPUTER (continued)

FACILITIES	Administrative offices, manufacturing and fulfillment facilities are located in Austin, TX.
PRODUCTS, BRAND NAMES, PRICE RANGE	AT-compatible systems range in price from $1,700 to $9,000. Company sells and services internal processor boards, modems, monitors, printers, drives, software, and accessories; 286 and 386 computers were introduced in 1988.

FINANCIAL INFORMATION

	SALES	NET INCOME	PROFIT MARGIN
1987	$ 69,500,000	$ 2,200,000	3.2%
1988	$257,800,000	$14,400,000	5.6%
1989	$388,600,000	$ 5,100,000	1.3%

TYPE OF ADVERTISING, PROMOTION	Products are promoted through multi-page ads in PC industry magazines and range of direct mail promotions. Full-line catalog mailed to rented lists and in response to requests.
LIST INFORMATION	Dell Computer does not release numerical information regarding its list.
COMMENTS	Dell Computer virtually exploded into being, reporting sales of $6 million in first year of business and close to doubling sales in each succeeding year through fiscal 1989. Growth continues to be strong. Marketing operations expanded significantly in '87 when Dell launched catalog effort. Current advertising strategy pits Dell's direct marketing approach against retail, emphasizing service advantages. Dell reportedly employs twice as many customer service reps as sales people and resolves more than 90 percent of customer questions over the phone. On-site technical requests are handled through nation-wide next-day service program. Dell signed Xerox on as its service contractor early in 1989. Dell recently ranked number one in PC Week's "Corporate Satisfaction" poll. International sales are expected to generate 25 percent of revenues in 1990, as opposed to 15 percent in 1989.

DELUXE CORPORATION

Deluxe Corporation
P.O. Box 64399
St. Paul, MN   55164
Telephone: (612) 483-7111

Deluxe is publicly held; stock is traded on the NYSE under symbol DLX.

Harold Haverty, President and CEO; Jerry Twogood, Executive Vice President; Arnold Angeloni, Senior Vice President; Charles Osborne, Senior Vice President and CFO; William Phillips, Jr., Senior Vice President.

Direct sales, mail order.

Deluxe's Payment Systems Division produces and distributes business and personal checks, electronic funds transfer (EFT) software and processing services. The Business Systems Division supplies short-run computer forms, business forms, and forms for small businesses and professional practices. The Consumer Specialty Products Division markets greeting cards, stationery, and related products. Deluxe Corporation reports 16,628 employees.

W.R. Hotchkiss founded Deluxe in 1915, incorporating it in 1920. The original business was checks and banking forms; the company has since diversified to expand sales. The company went public in 1965 and began trading on NYSE in 1980. Business Systems was launched in 1981. The company acquired Chex Systems in 1984, Colwell Systems in 1985, Deluxe Data Systems in 1986 and Current, Inc. in 1987.

Customer base includes financial institutions and small to medium-sized businesses; some consumer accounts (Current).

DELUXE CORPORATION (continued)

FACILITIES	Headquarters are located in St. Paul, MN. The company also operates 80 production/service facilities in 34 states.
PRODUCTS, BRAND NAMES, PRICE RANGE	Deluxe's business-to-business units offer a wide range of checks and specialty forms for banking and general office operation; stationery, greeting cards, and related items are marketed to consumers through Current.

FINANCIAL INFORMATION

	SALES	NET INCOME	PROFIT MARGIN
1987	$ 948,010,000	$148,512,000	15.7%
1988	$1,195,971,000	$143,354,000	12.0%
1989	$1,315,828,000	$152,631,000	11.6%

TYPE OF ADVERTISING, PROMOTION	The primary marketing channel is financial institutions for Deluxe's core business; Business/Consumer Divisions sell by direct response methods, including catalogs, telemarketing, packages and inserts.
LIST INFORMATION	Deluxe does not release information regarding its list.
COMMENTS	Overall, Deluxe serves approximately 50 percent of the U.S. check business. Deluxe's Business Systems Division grew more than 20 percent in 1988, a rate significantly faster than that of the core business. The Business Systems Division is viewed as a means for its vertically integrated parent to expand into additional product lines -- business, computer forms, and general office products -- and to penetrate new markets -- non-financial businesses, medical, and professional offices. The Consumer Specialty Products Division accounted for 14 percent of Deluxe's 1988 revenues. The company anticipates continued growth and expansion, both through internal development and acquisition. 1987 income reflects a non-recurring $17 million sale of Data Care Corp. stock, and the comparatively low bottom-line for 1988 is attributed to Deluxe's expenditures in acquiring Current, Inc. that year.

INMAC

Inmac
2465 Augustine Dr.
Santa Clara, CA   95054-3099.
Telephone: (408) 727-1970

ADDRESS,
PHONE

Inmac is publicly held, stock is traded NASDAQ under the symbol INMC.

OWNERSHIP

Ken Eldred, President and CEO; Ed Schooler, Executive Vice President; Michael J. Waide, Vice President and CFO; Al Cotton, Vice President Human Resources; John Ayer Senior Vice President Marketing.

MANAGEMENT

Mail order, direct sales.

TYPE OF
MARKETER

Inmac markets data communications products and computer accessories, supplies, storage media and furniture in the U.S., Europe, and Japan. Sales occur primarily through the targeted monthly catalog. Inmac reportedly mailed 35 million catalogs in eight languages during fiscal 89. Mailings are supplemented with direct sales force focused on selected large accounts. Roughly 25 percent of revenues are from products manufactured by Inmac; 90 percent of products are sold under Inmac label. Inmac employs 670 in U.S. and 650 abroad.

BUSINESS

Current President, Ken Eldred, along with Jim Willenborg, John Emrick and John Mumford, formed International Minicomputer Accessories Corp., as a partnership in the fall of 1975. They mailed the first catalog in April 1976. The company has grown rapidly; expanded to England in 1980, Germany in '82, France and Sweden in '83, and has recently added Japan late in '89. Inmac went public in 1986.

COMPANY
HISTORY

Inmac markets to mini and microcomputer users in business and governmental organizations in the U.S., Europe and Japan.

MARKETS

INMAC (continued)

FACILITIES	Executive offices are located in Santa Clara, CA; manufacturing in CA, Europe and Japan.
PRODUCTS, BRAND NAMES, PRICE RANGE	Inmac's line of 3,700 products focuses on magnetic media, computer supplies, furnishings, modems, multiplexers, accessories, power conditioners and network systems. Only 10 percent of merchandise carries label of outside brands. Prices range from $4 to $2,000.

FINANCIAL INFORMATION

	SALES	NET INCOME	PROFIT MARGIN
1987	$165,436,000	$7,736,000	4.7%
1988	$222,827,000	$9,712,000	4.3%
1989	$249,515,000	-$6,414,000	-2.5%

TYPE OF ADVERTISING, PROMOTION	Promotion is through monthly full-line catalogs supplemented with smaller specialty formats. Inmac produces 8 language versions of its catalogs and introduced a Macintosh and a LAN catalog in 1989.

LIST INFORMATION

Quantity Mailed:	35,000,000
Average Order:	$200
Active Buyers:	500,000
Total List:	2,000,000
List Source:	direct mail

COMMENTS

Sales growth in 1986 and 1987 is attributed to better targeted catalogs, successful new product introductions and Inmac's "just-in-time" delivery (85 percent of orders shipped same day; 90 percent within 24 hours). The drop in profit in 1989 corresponds to a new marketing strategy which slashed prices 40 to 70 percent on many products in the competitive U.S. market and a restructuring of the distribution network. Stressing long-term profitability, Inmac continues to expand; adding Italy early in fiscal 1989 and Japan early in fiscal 1990 to its international markets. In 1990 first quarter, Inmac showed a gain in profits.

MISCO

MISCO, Inc.
One MISCO Plaza
Holmdel, NJ   07733
Telephone: (201) 264-8200

ADDRESS, PHONE

MISCO is a wholly-owned subsidiary of Electrocomponents, P.L.C., Great Britain.

OWNERSHIP

Steve Purcell, President, Rick Puckett, Controller; Keith Grabow, Vice President of Marketing; Deidre Gaffney, Catalog Manager; Paul Hess, Director of Operations; Betty Hermann, Director of Personnel.

MANAGEMENT

Mail order.

TYPE OF MARKETER

MISCO is a mail order marketer of word and data processing supplies for computer systems. The company manufactures some of the cables it markets, but most of its merchandise is sourced from outside manufacturers. MISCO sells exclusively by direct mail and employs no direct salespeople. Telemarketing to improve ordering convenience and a toll-free number for technical support reportedly have been factors in the rapid growth of MISCO's customer base.

BUSINESS

The company was founded in 1978 by Joseph Popolo. It was established to market supplies and accessories directly to computer and word processor operators. Telemarketing operations were tested in 1982 and were implemented fully in 1983. The Gillette Company, which had owned 40 percent of MISCO, acquired the remaining 60 percent in early 1984. In November 1987, Gillette sold MISCO to Electrocomponents, P.L.C.

COMPANY HISTORY

The customer base is primarily business accounts; 93 percent are four-line business addresses.

MARKETS

MISCO (continued):

FACILITIES	U.S. headquarters and shipping are in Holmdel, NJ; distribution center is located in La Marada, CA.
PRODUCTS, BRAND NAMES, PRICE RANGE	MISCO sells a wide range of computer supplies and accessories, including magnetic media, CRT accessories, cables, workstation furniture, storage products, diskettes and ribbons. Brand names include Verbatim, IBM, BASF, 3M, and MISCO. Prices range from $5.95 to over $2,000.

FINANCIAL INFORMATION

	SALES	NET INCOME	PROFIT MARGIN
1987	$26,300,000*	N/A	N/A
1988	$30,300,000*	N/A	N/A
1989	$36,000,000*	N/A	N/A

TYPE OF ADVERTISING, PROMOTION	Full-line catalog is published four times annually. In addition, MISCO publishes specialty catalogs, including one featuring data communications equipment (published every quarter, two editions having been mailed).

LIST INFORMATION

Quantity Mailed:	8,000,000
Average Order:	$200
Active Buyers:	110,000
Total List:	540,000
List Source:	direct mail

COMMENTS

MISCO has grown at an estimated annual rate of roughly 15 percent since 1986. The company has experimented with a variety of marketing vehicles in the past including mini catalogs, card deck inserts, space advertising and others, but management reports that catalogs have proven to be the most cost-effective. In November 1987, Gillette sold MISCO to Electrocomponents, P.L.C., a UK holding company consisting of a number of distributing firms in Britain and the eastern U.S. Electrocomponents, Inc., a U.S. subsidiary, acquired MISCO's U.S. operations, while parent P.L.C. acquired its international concerns in Britain, Germany, and Italy; operations in Spain were recently added.

MOORE BUSINESS PRODUCTS

Moore Business Products
701 Woodlands Parkway
Vernon Hills, IL   60061
Telephone: (708) 913-3200

ADDRESS, PHONE

Moore Business Products is a division of Moore Business Forms, Inc., Glenview, IL; a subsidiary of Moore Corporation Ltd., Toronto, Canada.

OWNERSHIP

Jack Heist, President, Moore Business Products & Services division; Brandt Morrell, Vice President and General Manager, Moore Business Products; Deb Kobak, Director of Marketing.

MANAGEMENT

Mail order.

TYPE OF MARKETER

Moore Business Products Division is one of the nation's largest mail order marketers of continuous computer forms and paper products, computer supplies and accessories, and forms handling equipment. Products are sold by mail primarily to business end users through catalogs, direct mail, outbound telemarketing and space advertising. Moore offers product support and direct entry ordering via toll-free ordering and customer service.

BUSINESS

Moore Corporation has been in the forms business for more than 100 years, designing, manufacturing and marketing custom and multi-purpose forms and systems for businesses and industry. The company markets its products primarily through its network of 2,200 direct sales representatives. The first edition of its computer supplies catalog was mailed in 1982.

COMPANY HISTORY

Moore markets to small businesses throughout the U.S.

MARKETS

MOORE BUSINESS PRODUCTS (continued)

FACILITIES	Divisional headquarters are located in Vernon Hills, IL, with 5 distribution centers and 1 imprinting facility nationwide.
PRODUCTS, BRAND NAMES, PRICE RANGE	The product line includes forms and form handling equipment, computer supplies and accessories, and workstation and office furniture. Unit prices range from $7 to $1,200.

FINANCIAL INFORMATION

	SALES	NET INCOME	PROFIT MARGIN
1987	$53,900,000*	N/A	N/A
1988	$72,226,000*	N/A	N/A
1989	$96,783,000*	N/A	N/A

TYPE OF ADVERTISING, PROMOTION

The division's primary emphasis is on its full-line catalog. The catalog is 88 pages, full-color and contains 1,200 items. Space ads are also used in 15-20 computer related publications to generate inquiries. Telemarketing uses the catalog as a support tool and offers a complete line of forms not currently pictured in the catalog.

LIST INFORMATION

Quantity Mailed:	7,000,000
Average Order:	$150
Active Buyers:	200,000
Total List:	425,000
List Source:	direct mail, telemarketing, space ads

COMMENTS

The above sales information is for the direct response and telemarketing channels only. The Moore catalog entered the market at the height of the boom in mail order computer supplies and had the additional benefits of Moore's vast corporate resources to back it. The combination of strong catalog sales, telemarketing, and Moore's large nationwide direct sales forces has reportedly proven a successful one. Moore Business Products employs a staff of 50 operators to handle inbound toll-free orders and customer service as well as conducting a telemarketing effort through 130 outbound representatives. The catalog has been expanded beyond forms products with a line of computer supplies and accessories.

NATIONAL LIBERTY CORPORATION

National Liberty Corp.
Liberty Park
Valley Forge, PA   19413
Telephone: (215) 648-5000

ADDRESS, PHONE

National Liberty Corp. is a wholly-owned subsidiary of Capital Holding Corp. Stock is traded on the NYSE.

OWNERSHIP

Norman L. Phelps, President, Chairman, CEO; Geoffrey R. Banta, Senior Vice President, Strategic Planning; Kenneth R. Clolery, Senior Vice President, Acquisitions & New Business Development; Timothy J. Alford, Senior Vice President, Marketing; R. Lee Delp, Senior Vice President, Marketing; John E. Hoey, Senior Vice President, Marketing; Pete Cole, Vice President Information Systems; Don Kennedy, Senior Vice President General Counsel; Richard H. Smith, Senior Vice President & CFO.

MANAGEMENT

Mail order.

TYPE OF MARKETER

Company markets life and health insurance by mail. Company heavily involved in affinity group sales. Subsidiaries include National Liberty Marketing, Inc., National Home Life Assurance Co., Veterans Life Insurance Co., and National Home Life Assurance Co. of New York. National Liberty Marketing is the primary mail order marketing arm.

BUSINESS

National Liberty was organized as a holding company in 1967 for insurance and marketing subsidiaries. Capital Holding acquired National Liberty in 1981 for a reported $358.7 million in cash debentures. National Liberty acquired ACI Financial Corp. in September 1987. In January 1987, Capital Holding acquired Worldwide Insurance Group from the employees of Wausau, forming the Direct Response Group.

COMPANY HISTORY

The company markets to specialty groups include bank and saving & loan customers, veterans and seniors.

MARKETS

NATIONAL LIBERTY (continued)

FACILITIES	National Liberty marketing headquarters and direct mail operations are located in Valley Forge, PA.
PRODUCTS, BRAND NAMES, PRICE RANGE	The company offers term and whole life insurance. Health products include accident and sickness hospital insurance as well as medicare supplements. Prices vary by product.

FINANCIAL INFORMATION

	SALES	NET INCOME	PROFIT MARGIN
1987	$436,670,000	N/A	N/A
1988	$415,339,000	N/A	N/A
1989	$439,844,000*	N/A	N/A

TYPE OF ADVERTISING, PROMOTION	National Liberty Marketing promotes products through direct mail packages, inserts and television spots. TV advertising represents 15 percent of promotional effort. Telemarketing is used extensively on back end.

LIST INFORMATION

Quantity Mailed:	125,000,000
Average Order:	varies by product
Active Buyers:	2,500,000
Total List:	5,000,000
List Source:	direct mail, broadcast

COMMENTS	The financial information above refers to National Liberty's overall revenues. In 1986, mail order revenues were $463 million, nearly 50 percent of total. While the company's product mix has changed substantially in recent years, mail order growth has remained steady; increasing by more than 50 percent since 1982. The bulk of National Liberty's business was once health insurance, but life products have grown to become a major factor in recent years. In addition, the company has made a firm commitment to third party affinity group marketing, evidenced by September 1987 acquisition of ACI Financial Corporation. ACI markets insurance and financial services through alumni and professional association group sponsored programs.

NEW ENGLAND BUSINESS SERVICE

New England Business Service, Inc.
500 Main Street
Groton, MA   01450
Telephone: (508) 448-6111

ADDRESS, PHONE

NEBS is publicly held, its stock traded NASDAQ.

OWNERSHIP

Richard Rhoads, Chairman and CEO; Bart Calder, President and COO; Christopher Corbett, Vice President, Operations; Russel Corsini, Jr., Vice President, Finance; L. Kent Lineback, Vice President, Marketing.

MANAGEMENT

Mail order.

TYPE OF MARKETER

NEBS Business Forms, company's flagship of its 6 divisions, designs, produces and markets by mail a line of business forms, printed products, computer supplies and related office equipment. Sycom markets business forms and systems to small professional offices. All divisions cater to the specialized needs of small businesses. The U.K. operation extends selling capabilities beyond the established U.S. and Canadian small business markets.

BUSINESS

NEBS founder, Albert E. Anderson, started the company in the rear of a Townsend, MA barbershop in 1952 and incorporated in 1955. For over 35 years, NEBS has been researching and servicing the needs of small businesses. Consolidated sales have grown at an average annual rate of 16 percent over last 10 years. The company divested its Devoke subsidiary in March 1989. The May 1987 acquisition of Sycom (Madison, WI) is proving to be a good synergistic match.

COMPANY HISTORY

The primary customer base is comprised of small businesses (20 or less employees), in the U.S., U.K. and Canada.

MARKETS

NEW ENGLAND BUSINESS SERVICES, INC. (continued)

FACILITIES

Headquarters are located in Groton, MA; production/distribution facilities at 6 U.S., Canada and U.K. locations.

PRODUCTS, BRAND NAMES, PRICE RANGE

NEBS markets standardized and highly targeted business forms, printed products, general office products, computer forms, software and related products to small businesses. Prices vary with order size and the amount of imprinting/personalization required.

FINANCIAL INFORMATION

	SALES	NET INCOME	PROFIT
1987	$172,574,000	$19,130,000	11.1%
1988	$202,423,000	$22,431,000	11.1%
1989	$225,931,000	$22,189,000	9.8%

TYPE OF ADVERTISING, PROMOTION

Direct mailings of catalogs and promotional material are created by the company's in-house advertising department. NEBS' mail order programs are directed primarily to its house list, although rented lists are used as well.

LIST INFORMATION

Quantity Mailed:	60,000,000
Average Order:	$75
Active Buyers:	1,097,000
Total List:	N/A
List Source:	direct mail, rental

COMMENTS

For the fiscal year ending June 30, 1989, NEBS' consolidated sales rose 11.6 percent to $225,931,000, while costs of discontinued operations reduced net earnings from the prior year. In 1989, NEBS and its subsidiaries served over one million small businesses and professional offices in the U.S., Canada and the U.K. Its Canadian subsidiary completed a 42,000 sq. ft. expansion to a Midland, Ontario facility, while the Sycom acquisition is beginning to have impact on NEBS' marketplace. Devoke's large business focus was deemed incompatible and NEBS subsequently divested the company in late March. Management reorganized to focus on the small business market. The company is currently looking to capitalize on worldwide outreach.

NIGHTINGALE-CONANT

Nightingale-Conant Corporation
7300 Lehigh Avenue
Niles, IL 60648
Telephone: (708) 647-0300

ADDRESS, PHONE

Nightingale-Conant Corporation is privately held; the officers own 1 million shares of common stock valued at $1 each.

OWNERSHIP

Victor Conant, President and CEO; Kevin McNeely Vice President and COO; Michael Kelly, CFO; David Nightingale, Vice President, New Products.

MANAGEMENT

Mail order.

TYPE OF MARKETER

Nightingale-Conant produces, manufactures and markets a variety of business training and self-help programs sold in audio and video cassette formats. The company claims to be the world's largest producer of business and motivational cassette programs. Series featuring well known authors, seminar leaders and other public figures are produced in company studios and marketed through catalogs and brochures. The company employs 200.

BUSINESS

The company was founded in 1956 by principals Lloyd Conant and Earl Nightingale. Nightingale had been a national radio and television personality and a well known speaker and author. Conant had been involved with several businesses, including Specialty Mail Services (Chicago, IL). Nightingale-Conant was incorporated in Delaware on February 2, 1960.

COMPANY HISTORY

Markets include businesses, groups and consumers throughout the U.S. and Canada.

MARKETS

NIGHTINGALE-CONANT (continued)

FACILITIES	Headquarters and all operations are housed in a 62,000 square foot facility located in Niles, IL.
PRODUCTS, BRAND NAMES, PRICE RANGE	Prices for audio cassette programs on business skills and personal motivation range from $14 to $110. Video cassette titles encompass sports, weight loss, psychology, stop smoking programs and others.

FINANCIAL INFORMATION

	SALES	NET INCOME	PROFIT MARGIN
1987	$36,555,000*	N/A	N/A
1988	$47,100,000*	N/A	N/A
1989	$60,712,000*	N/A	N/A

TYPE OF ADVERTISING, PROMOTION	Products are sold through catalogs, direct mail packages, card/package inserts, syndication, telemarketing and regional distributors (to retailers and end users).

LIST INFORMATION

Quantity Mailed:	2,500,000
Average Order:	$40.00
Active Buyers:	N/A
Total List:	510,000
List Source:	direct mail, telemarketing, card/package inserts

COMMENTS

Nightingale-Conant has maintained strong sales growth through its history as the self-help industry expands. Consumers are individually and corporately looking to improve and supplement income through better education. Corporations are turning to management training and mental "good health" programs to increase efficiency and productivity. Out-of-house training is increasing in popularity and legitimacy.

QUILL

Quill Corporation 100 Schelter Road Lincolnshire, IL 60069-3621 Telephone: (708) 634-4850	**ADDRESS, PHONE**
Quill is privately held; brothers Jack, Harvey L. and Arnold Miller own 100 percent of the capital stock.	**OWNERSHIP**
Jack Miller, President; Harvey L. Miller, Secretary; Arnold Miller, Treasurer.	**MANAGEMENT**
Mail order.	**TYPE OF MARKETER**
Quill Corporation is a mail order marketer of a full line of office supplies and equipment; including paper products, business machines, microcomputers, furniture and data and word processing supplies. Products are marketed by mail through catalogs, principally to business end users. The company buys its merchandise from a number of manufacturers and suppliers and does none of its own manufacturing. Sales reportedly are consistent throughout the year. Quill currently employs 1,000.	**BUSINESS**
Jack Miller started as a direct seller of office products in 1956. Later that year he mailed 156 postcards promoting five sales specials; the company then evolved into a mail order business. In 1957, brother Harvey L. joined as a partner and the two converted a coal bin into their first office; Arnold Miller joined in 1974. Quill was incorporated in Illinois in 1962. Headquarters moved from Northbrook to Lincolnshire in 1980.	**COMPANY HISTORY**
Quill sells nationally to all types of businesses, organizations and institutions.	**MARKETS**

QUILL (continued)

FACILITIES	Quill owns 442,000 sq.ft. of warehouse and office space in IL, 183,000 sq.ft. in CA, and 30,000 sq.ft. in Ontario, Canada.

PRODUCTS, BRAND NAMES, PRICE RANGE

Quill catalogs offer a full range of office supplies, equipment and furniture. National brands include Scotch, Pendaflex and the Quill label. Unit prices range from $.88 to over $1,500.

FINANCIAL INFORMATION

	SALES	NET INCOME	PROFIT MARGIN
1987	$200,000,000	N/A	N/A
1988	$240,000,000	N/A	N/A
1989	$270,000,000	N/A	N/A

TYPE OF ADVERTISING, PROMOTION

Promotion is primarily through direct mail catalogs and flyers. Quill mails two major catalogs annually and follows up with sales flyers and other literature throughout the year, including magazine ads and card decks.

LIST INFORMATION

Quantity Mailed:	50,000,000
Average Order:	$100
Active Buyers:	790,000
Total List:	2,000,000
List Source:	direct mail, rental.

COMMENTS

Quill's revenues grew rapidly in the early 1980s, particularly in 1981 and 1982 when sales jumped 40 percent to roughly $70 million. Typically conservative, management purposely slowed sales in 1986 when it was expanding its facilities. The company is now reportedly maintaining a steady growth rate of 15 to 20 percent annually. Company sources report that operations have been profitable and that earnings have been improving steadily. Quill's semi-annual main catalog is supplemented with monthly sales flyers. Mailing strategy reportedly has remained the same throughout the '80s. While Quill does not rent its list, it is expanding its customer base by mailing to rented commercial and industrial lists. Significant repeat business reportedly has contributed to the company's steady growth.

RED LINE

Red Line 8121 10th Avenue North Golden Valley, MN 55427 Telephone: (612) 545-5757	**ADDRESS, PHONE**
Red Line is a division of Prudent Supply.	**OWNERSHIP**
Herb Goldenberg, Chairman of the Board and CEO; Mark A. Pulido, President and COO; Dale Kratchen, Vice President Sales and Marketing; Carl Brady, Vice President Operations; Bill Brown, CFO.	**MANAGEMENT**
Wholesale, direct sales, mail order, and telemarketing.	**TYPE OF MARKETER**
A supplier of medical and surgical supplies for long-term health care institutions since 1961, Red Line markets its products primarily by direct sales, but also by mail through a 500-page, full line catalog. Red Line services the entire country through a network of 22 distribution facilities. America's Medical Market Place division provides health care and medical supplies to the end user through a 92-page catalog. The heaviest sales reportedly occur in May/June and October through December.	**BUSINESS**
Red Line was founded in Minneapolis in 1961, by Herb Goldenberg. It began as a spin-off of a local pharmacy which supplied subscriptions to an area nursing home. The first products sold were basic medical and surgical supplies for use in nursing homes, and the line has expanded to include linen, clothing, furniture, and equipment. America's Medical Market Place division was added in 1975. The company has expanded substantially over the past five years as stepped up direct sales efforts broadened its institutional base.	**COMPANY HISTORY**
Nursing homes throughout the U.S. and elderly and disabled individuals.	**MARKETS**

RED LINE (continued)

FACILITIES	Headquarters in Minneapolis, MN with 9 service centers nationwide.
PRODUCTS, BRAND NAMES, PRICE RANGE	Red Line's product line includes medical and surgical supplies, food supplements, furniture, clothing, bedding, and equipment for nursing homes. Products are sourced outside. AMMP catalog mix consists of health care supplies and aides to daily living, including arthritic and diabetic aids, diagnostic equipment, braces and supports, exercise equipment, food supplements, and wheelchairs. AMMP prices range from $1.50 to $2,500.

FINANCIAL INFORMATION

	SALES	NET INCOME	PROFIT MARGIN
1987	$3,425,000*	N/A	N/A
1988	$4,700,000*	N/A	N/A
1989	$6,439,000*	N/A	N/A

TYPE OF ADVERTISING, PROMOTION

Red Line promotes its products through a full line institutional catalog and sales force of over 100. In addition, the company mails 10 direct flyers/brochures per year. The company runs an estimated 250,000 catalogs per year and the AMMP catalog is mailed once per year. Some space ads are used to promote selected items in trade publications.

LIST INFORMATION

Quantity Mailed:	250,000*
Average Order:	$65* (AMM); $250 (Redline)
Active Buyers:	2,750* (AMM); 11,000 (Redline)
Total List:	6,750* (AMM); 19,000 (Redline)
List Source:	direct mail, space ads

COMMENTS

Red Line is reportedly the largest wholesale distributor to long term institutions in the U.S. The company has grown at an annual rate of 40 percent over the past eight years. On the home care side, AMMP services over 4,000 home care clients through the mail. Management expects the rate of growth to continue.

RELIABLE

The Reliable Corporation
1001 West Van Buren Street
Chicago, IL   60607
Telephone: (312) 666-1800

ADDRESS, PHONE

Merrill Zenner owns 100 percent of The Reliable Corporation's capital stock.

OWNERSHIP

Merrill Zenner, Chairman; Gary Rovansek, President; James P. Jones, CFO; Duane Rataj, Executive Vice President; Kathy Armknecht, Vice President, Quality Assurance; Art Hanover, Vice President, Corporate Development and Planning.

MANAGEMENT

Mail order.

TYPE OF MARKETER

The Reliable Corp. is a mail order marketer of a wide range of general office supplies, computer and word processing supplies, office equipment and furnishings. The company places heavy promotional emphasis on serving small business, through discount pricing, sales and limited-time offers on brand name products. Products are sold through a combination of full-line catalogs, supplemental sale books, "HomeOffice" and "Computer Supplies & Accessories" specialty books. Reliable reports 600 employees.

BUSINESS

Originally Reliable Stationery Co., the business was founded in 1917 by William and Morris Sokolec. Sol Zenner purchased it in 1938, renaming it The Reliable Corp. In the 1960s, the company evolved from a direct sales base to mail order focusing on small businesses. Merrill Zenner became president in 1978. In 1983, Reliable sold its 8,000 sales accounts. HomeOffice catalog started in 1986.

COMPANY HISTORY

Reliable sells its products primarily to small and home-based businesses throughout the U.S.

MARKETS

RELIABLE (continued)

FACILITIES	Headquarters in Chicago; fulfillment facilities in Chicago, IL; New Castle, DE and Stone Mountain, GA.
PRODUCTS, BRAND NAMES, PRICE RANGE	Reliable offers wide range of general office supplies including office furnishings, computer supplies, forms and paper products, and office machines. Reliable places heavy emphasis on sale pricing, up to 70 percent off retail. Prices range from 25 cents to $1,200.

FINANCIAL INFORMATION

	SALES	NET INCOME	PROFIT MARGIN
1987	$100,000,000	N/A	N/A
1988	$125,000,000	N/A	N/A
1989	$150,000,000	N/A	N/A

TYPE OF ADVERTISING, PROMOTION	Reliable publishes full-line catalog yearly and the "HomeOffice" specialty book nine times annually. The full-line catalog is supported with sale catalogs, tabloids, and other media. The "Business Furniture" catalog is published four times per year.

LIST INFORMATION

Quantity Mailed:	40,000,000
Average Order:	$100
Active Buyers:	625,000
Total List:	1,000,000*
List Source:	direct mail

COMMENTS	Reliable management's 1983 decision to spin off the company's direct sales accounts and concentrate on serving its small business market solely by mail has resulted in an outstanding record of growth. Since 1983, Reliable has grown from 88 employees to 600, and sales volume, growing at a rate of about 30 percent annually, has increased from roughly $28 million to $150 million. Reliable prides itself on good customer service, with 90 percent of its orders shipped within one day and delivered free. In order to maintain that level of service, Reliable has had to expand its fulfillment capability; it added a third facility in Delaware, and plans to add additional distribution facilities within the next year.

SPORTIME

Sportime
2905-E Amwiler Road
Atlanta, GA   30360
Telephone: (404) 449-5700

ADDRESS, PHONE

Sportime is a division of Select Service and Supply Co.,
Atlanta, GA.

OWNERSHIP

Larry Joseph, President; Peter Savitz, Vice President; Barry Traub,
Vice President Marketing (Merchandising and Advertising).

MANAGEMENT

Mail order.

TYPE OF MARKETER

BUSINESS

Sportime markets physical education, athletic, recreation, and
movement equipment, via direct mail catalogs, directly to schools
and institutions and at wholesale to other dealers. Their customer
base includes 70% of all U.S. public school districts, as well as
private schools, preschools, colleges, recreation departments,
summer camps, youth clubs, adult programs, armed services,
prisons, etc. Through partnerships, Sportime is moving into other
countries, including Canada and a test run in England. Sportime
also markets its own brand to other catalogs and is a leading
innovator of sports equipment. Sales follow a school ordering
cycle, peaking in July and September. Sportime employs 38.

COMPANY HISTORY

Sportime was established in Atlanta in 1967 by Larry Joseph. The
company was first a food equipment contractor for summer camps
in the Northeast and quickly expanded its product line to include
sporting goods. As the product line expanded, the customer base
grew to include a variety of institutions.

MARKETS

All fifty states, Puerto Rico, Canada, England, Germany, Italy,
and Israel.

SPORTIME (continued)

FACILITIES

Headquarters and mail order facilities are in Atlanta, GA.
A new 60,000 sq. ft. facility is under construction in Atlanta.

PRODUCTS,
BRAND NAMES,
PRICE RANGE

The catalog contains a full range of equipment (covering all
areas of movement, development and competition) for all ages,
pre-school through adult. Emphasis focused on continually
expanding Sportime branded products (Sportime, Dur-O-Sport,
Yeller, Gradeballs, etc.) The products cover a large cross-section
of manufacturers. Prices range from under $1 to over $7,000.

FINANCIAL
INFORMATION

	SALES	NET INCOME	PROFIT MARGIN
1987	$5,626,000	N/A	N/A
1988	$6,144,700	N/A	N/A
1989	$8,000,000*	N/A	N/A

TYPE OF
ADVERTISING,
PROMOTION

Approximately 10% of sales is spent on the Sportime catalog,
which remains the primary source of sales. Sportime is printed
semi-annually (mid August and late December) and broken into
three major mailings (December printing is multi cover). Space
advertising has been expanded as have trade show exhibitions.

LIST
INFORMATION

Quantity Mailed:	866,000
Average Order:	$240
Active Buyers:	27,000
Total List:	35,000
List Source:	direct mail, rental.

COMMENTS

Sportime continues its rapid growth rate which, in 1989 accelerated
further. This growth is directly attributable to the company's
ability to carve out a unique place in its market via product
development and presentation (more consumer than business to
business). Management reports that sales are expected to be
strong in 1990 with projections targeting $9,400,000. Plans for the
introduction of two new catalogs are in the developmental stages.

20TH CENTURY PLASTICS

20th Century Plastics 3628 Crenshaw Blvd. Los Angeles, CA 90016 Telephone: (213) 731-0900	**ADDRESS, PHONE**
20th Century Plastics is privately held by investment partnership Comann, Howard and Flamen.	**OWNERSHIP**
John Kidwell, President; Ted Alpert, Vice President, Finance.	**MANAGEMENT**
Mail order.	**TYPE OF MARKETER**
20th Century Plastics manufactures and markets products geared to organize, protect and display paperwork, photographic and hobby supplies. 80 percent of the company's products are manufactured in-house. 20th Century Plastics markets through catalogs, flyers and telemarketing to businesses and consumers.	**BUSINESS**
The company was founded in 1947 by Mr. and Mrs. Morris Shipp as a manufacturer of vinyl products. In 1973, their son joined 20th Century Plastics initiating the firm's mail order operations. In 1984, Avery International acquired 20th Century Plastics and focussed exclusively on direct mail. The company was purchased by Comann, Howard, and Flamen in August 1988.	**COMPANY HISTORY**
20th Century Plastics sells to businesses and individuals throughout the U.S.	**MARKETS**

20TH CENTURY PLASTICS (continued)

FACILITIES

Headquarters, manufacturing and fulfillment facilities are located in Los Angeles, CA.

PRODUCTS, BRAND NAMES, PRICE RANGE

The product line includes sheet protectors, photo pages, binders, albums and similar items for protecting, organizing and displaying documents and photography. Price ranges from $.25 to $100.

FINANCIAL INFORMATION

	SALES	NET INCOME	PROFIT MARGIN
1987	$20,500,000*	N/A	N/A
1988	$22,600,000	N/A	N/A
1989	$24,600,000	N/A	N/A

TYPE OF ADVERTISING, PROMOTION

Promotional emphasis is on the company's four-color, 48-page catalog. Solo mailers and brochures are utilized to highlight individual products. Telemarketing makes up the remainder of marketing practices through a highly trained inbound service team and an outbound sales force which makes periodic contact with "high potential" customers.

LIST INFORMATION

Quantity Mailed:	10,000,000*
Average Order:	$85/business, $40/individual
Active Buyers:	250,000 at business address
	240,000 at private address
Total List:	1.3 million
List Source:	direct mail

COMMENTS

20th Century Plastic's catalog is printed in five annual editions. Mailings vary from 4 to 22 times per year, depending on the customer's previous purchasing practices. A 16-page catalog featuring photo albums is mailed four times per year.

UARCO

Uarco, Inc. 121 North Ninth Street De Kalb, IL 60115 Telephone: (815) 756-9581	**ADDRESS, PHONE**
Uarco is privately owned by Settsu of Osaka, Japan.	**OWNERSHIP**
Herbert Koelling, Chairman and CEO; Bruce Moses, President and COO; Matt Dorfman, General Manager; Jack K. Marshall, Senior Vice President, Secretary and Treasurer.	**MANAGEMENT**
Mail order, telemarketer, manufacturer.	**TYPE OF MARKETER**
Uarco is a supplier of business forms and computer supplies, and markets more than 2,000 different computer and word processing products and other specialized items. Sales are by mail through Uarco Computer Supplies catalogs and through 750 sales representatives. Uarco has 30 manufacturing plants and distribution centers in the United States and Canada, and is licensed to do business in several European countries. Business and computer forms are primarily custom-designed.	**BUSINESS**
The business which later became Uarco, Inc. was established as a business supply company more than 100 years ago. Publicly held City Investors Company acquired Uarco in 1979 and the catalog was developed as a new channel of distribution. In 1984, privately owned Pace, Inc. purchased Uarco, and in 1988, Settsu bought Uarco.	**COMPANY HISTORY**
Uarco markets to businesses in the U.S. and several foreign countries.	**MARKETS**

UARCO (continued)

FACILITIES	Headquarters are located in De Kalb, IL and warehouse and distribution facilities are located in Sycamore, IL.
PRODUCTS, BRAND NAMES, PRICE RANGE	Products include office supplies and computer-related merchandise, emphasizing continuous forms, diskette storage units, and workstation furniture. Most continuous forms are manufactured and printed by Uarco. More than 5,000 items are priced from under $1 to over $3,000.

FINANCIAL INFORMATION

	SALES	NET INCOME	PROFIT MARGIN
1987	$23,136,000*	N/A	N/A
1988	$27,821,000*	N/A	N/A
1989	$33,456,000*	N/A	N/A

TYPE OF ADVERTISING, PROMOTION	Uarco direct marketing division's emphasis has been on its 84 page, full-color catalogs that are updated every three months. The company offers incentives and free gifts.

LIST INFORMATION

Quantity Mailed:	2,600,000*
Average Order:	$215*
Active Buyers:	120,000*
Total List:	400,000*
List Source:	direct mail

COMMENTS

Sales estimates are for the company's mail order marketing operations only. Uarco reports a high repeat buying factor; catalog customers are offered incentives, free gift offers, and quantity discounts. Uarco offers full line service to respond to the need for fast, problem free deliveries; an on-line ordering system is linked to all its distribution facilities. Management attributes the company's healthy growth to state-of-the-art products, prompt and dependable service, and competitive pricing.

VIKING

Viking Office Products
13809 S. Figueroa Street
Los Angeles, CA   90061
Telephone: (213) 321-4493

A little over half of the stock is owned by Dillion Reed, an investment banking firm; Viking President Irwin Helford owns approximately 11 percent; the remainder is publicly held and traded OTC under the symbol VKNG.

Irwin Helford, President, Chairman and CEO: William Dankers, Senior Vice President, Operations; John Maxwell, Vice President, Operations; Stephen R. Kroll, Vice President, CFO and Secretary; Mark Brown, Vice President, Information Systems.

Mail order.

Viking markets a wide range of office supplies, equipment, machines, and furniture. All products are obtained from outside manufacturers and sold through direct marketing catalogs and packages.   Management considers Quill and Reliable Corporations at its primary competitors in mail order. Viking employs over 500 people.

Viking was founded by Rolf Ostern in January 1960. Operations and sales grew steadily through the early 1980s when management made a commitment to expand the company rapidly. On March 14, 1990, Viking went public by offering 2.465 million shares of stock. Additional regional facilities have been opened to improve fulfillment and localize service to customers and to handle the increased sales volume associated with the aggressive growth plan.

Merchandises with promotional prices and offers directed to small and medium-sized businesses.

VIKING (continued)

FACILITIES	Corporate headquarters are located in Los Angeles, CA; warehouse and fulfillment centers in TX, OH, CT and FL.
PRODUCTS, BRAND NAMES, PRICE RANGE	Prices for items in Viking's catalogs range from $.10 to over $1,500 for copiers. Through catalogs, Viking maintains a discount/sale price position in all its direct mail media.

FINANCIAL INFORMATION

	SALES	NET INCOME	PROFIT MARGIN
1987	$ 80,993,000	$3,690,000	4.6%
1988	$105,139,000	$7,195,000	6.8%
1989	$131,187,000	$4,302,000	3.3%

TYPE OF ADVERTISING, PROMOTION

Viking generates sales through catalogs published monthly, plus a large sixth month catalog goes to its main customer base.

LIST INFORMATION

Quantity Mailed:	30,000,000*
Average Order:	$98
Active Buyers:	400,000*
Total List:	700,000*
List Source:	direct mail

COMMENTS

Viking reports its sales growth as being substantial, averaging in excess of 30 percent per year. Major expansion occurred in early 1984 under the direction of Irwin Helford, who became President in January 1984. Mr. Helford previously served with office products cataloger, Reliable Corporation, for 23 years. Net income for fiscal year 1989 is comparatively low due to a $5.7 million interest expense on the leveraged buyout. Viking's aggressive catalog mailings continue in increased quantities together with the development of specialty catalogs for office furniture. The company's latest expansion includes an U.K. facility, expected to open in September 1990. Viking sees this as an entry into the European market; if successful, West Germany will be the next target market.

VISIBLE COMPUTER SUPPLY

Visible Computer Supply Corp.
3626 Stern Avenue
St. Charles, IL   60174
Telephone: (312) 377-2586

ADDRESS, PHONE

Visible is a division of publicly held Wallace Computer Services; stock traded on the NYSE.

OWNERSHIP

Wallace Computer Services: Ted Dimitriou, Chairman and CEO; John Turner, President. Visible Computer Supply: Jim Kersten, General Manager; Mike Duffield, Vice President of Distribution.

MANAGEMENT

Mail order.

TYPE OF MARKETER

Visible is a division of parent company Wallace Computer Services, a manufacturer and marketer of business forms. Wallace is also involved in commercial printing and mail order. Visible is the primary mail order division and markets a broad range of computer supplies and accessories and other office products through catalogs. Visible's inventory is reportedly in excess of 10,000 items.

BUSINESS

The company was started in the 1930s as the Visible Record Equipment Company, specializing in prepunched accounting forms. Computer supplies and accessories were added to the line when the company was purchased in the 1950s by David Malbrough, a former UARCO salesman. Malbrough designed the first pressboard printout binder which company sources claim launched the computer supplies industry in the 1940s. Malbrough's first catalogs offered between 300 and 500 forms. Wallace acquired Visible in 1971.

COMPANY HISTORY

Fortune 1,000 companies comprise main customer base; some small-to-medium businesses, consumers.

MARKETS

VISIBLE COMPUTER SUPPLY (continued)

FACILITIES	Headquarters are located in St. Charles, IL; distribution facilities in IL, NC, and CA.
PRODUCTS, BRAND NAMES, PRICE RANGE	Products range from pens and pencils to a fireproof safe that lists for $3,000. The majority of the catalog's products are computer and office supplies with a high percentage of forms and paper products.

FINANCIAL INFORMATION

	SALES	NET INCOME	PROFIT MARGIN
1987	$23,136,000*	N/A	N/A
1988	$27,821,000*	N/A	N/A
1989	$33,456,000*	N/A	N/A

TYPE OF ADVERTISING, PROMOTION	Visible publishes a catalog twice a year, mails flyers every four weeks, makes heavy use of package inserts, and uses alternate mailing packages to sell merchandise and to promote the main catalogs.

LIST INFORMATION

Quantity Mailed:	6,000,000
Average Order:	$175
Active Buyers:	250,000
Total List:	575,000
List Source:	direct mail

COMMENTS	Visible's management attributes its healthy growth to the innovative aspects of its customer service department and the breadth of the product line. Technical support is provided by the merchandise managers. The company has a toll-free number, direct-entry ordering system, and a 30-day return policy. More than 90 percent of its orders are shipped within 48 hours. Visible reaches its buyers through direct response catalogs and through Wallace's 600-person nationwide direct sales force. Its current marketing thrust is to be the complete source for products needed to run today's automated office.

WANG EXPRESS

Wang Express M/S 017-040 800 Chelsford Street Lowell, MA 01851 Telephone: (508) 656-8000	**ADDRESS, PHONE**
Wang Express in division of publicly held Wang Laboratories, whose stock is traded on the AMSE.	**OWNERSHIP**
Noel Greiner, Vice President and General Manager of Wang Express; Philip Campaigne, Director of Merchandising; Charles V. Laing, Director of Business Development.	**MANAGEMENT**
Mail order.	**TYPE OF MARKETER**
Wang Express sells a full line of supplies and accessories designed specifically to be compatible with Wang data and word processing systems, desktop computer systems, hardware upgrades and add-ons through direct mail and telemarketing to the installed Wang user-base.	**BUSINESS**
Wang mail order operations originally consisted of a Supplies Division (selling consumable supplies and software) and Wang Direct (selling hardware components). All products were offered through one "Wang Direct" catalog (four editions per year). The company reorganized its Supplies Division in 1984 to create a separate "Express 800" catalog. International editions of both primary catalogs were first distributed in January 1985. In 1989 the Wang Supplies Division was merged with Wang Direct to create a sincere direct marketing operation called Wang Express.	**COMPANY HISTORY**
Wang Express targets operating supervisors, supplies and system buyers in the U.S. and abroad.	**MARKETS**

WANG EXPRESS (continued)

FACILITIES	Headquarters and all operations are located in Lowell, MA.
PRODUCTS, BRAND NAMES, PRICE RANGE	The division markets a full line of supplies and accessories designed specifically to be compatible with Wang data and word processing systems. Prices range from $2 function strips to full systems that can sell for more than $200,000.

FINANCIAL INFORMATION

	SALES	NET INCOME	PROFIT MARGIN
1987	$315,000,000*	N/A	N/A
1988	$385,000,000*	N/A	N/A
1989	$483,175,000*	N/A	N/A

TYPE OF ADVERTISING, PROMOTION	Wang Express publishes accessories and supplies, software and literature, and systems catalogs. Direct mail is used to market special product offers to market segments.

LIST INFORMATION

Quantity Mailed:	1,500,000
Average Order:	$250
Active Buyers:	450,000
Total List:	1,000,000
List Source:	direct mail, internal lists

COMMENTS

Management reports that only 2.5 percent of sales is spent on advertising and marketing because most of their mailing lists are generated by other divisions of the company. The Wang Express catalogs are updated and mailed three times annually and are currently distributed in French, Oxford English, German, Dutch, and Spanish. More than 70 percent of Wang Express customers are large corporate entities. The division's catalogs contain more than 5,500 items.

WEARGUARD

WearGuard
141 Longwater Drive
Assinippi Park
Norwell, MA   02061
Telephone: (617) 871-4100

ADDRESS, PHONE

WearGuard is a privately held corporation owned by the Salem family.

OWNERSHIP

Richard Salem, President; Bruce Humphrey, Executive Vice President; Joel Hughes, Executive Vice President; George MacNaughton, Senior Vice President; Jessie Bourneuf, Senior Vice President; Thomas Fay, III, Senior Vice President; Ken Lubar, Vice President of Direct Response.

MANAGEMENT

Mail order, retail.

TYPE OF MARKETER

WearGuard claims to be the largest U.S. mail order marketer of customized business uniforms and work clothes. It sells primarily to businesses concentrated in the service, construction and manufacturing industries. Two catalog editions are published annually, although mailings are year-round with periodic updates. Direct salespeople use the catalogs as a follow-up sales tool. The firm owns and operates 72 retail outlets. WearGuard employs approximately 1,300 people full time.

BUSINESS

Eastern Uniform Company, which later became WearGuard, was founded in 1952. E. L. Salem, then a gas station owner, started selling uniforms out of a milk truck. The business grew rapidly so Salem sold his gas station and opened a retail store in Cambridge, MA. The company remained a small retailing business until Richard Salem joined the firm in 1978 and started catalog operations as part of an expansion program.

COMPANY HISTORY

The firm's customers are throughout the U.S.; 85 percent are men. WearGuard has limited international sales.

MARKETS

WEARGUARD (continued)

FACILITIES	WearGuard's main offices and one of its 72 retail outlets are in Assinippi Park, Norwell, MA.
PRODUCTS, BRAND NAMES, PRICE RANGE	Merchandise consists primarily of work clothing and uniforms. Accessories include sunglasses, hats, emblems, and flashlights; even bullet-proof vests are available. Brand names include WearGuard, Timberland and others. Unit prices range from $1.50 to $150.

FINANCIAL INFORMATION

	SALES	NET INCOME	PROFIT MARGIN
1987	$115,000,000*	N/A	N/A
1988	$130,000,000*	N/A	N/A
1989	$146,000,000*	N/A	N/A

TYPE OF ADVERTISING, PROMOTION	Advertising is primarily through direct mail catalogs with some space ads. "Spring/Summer" and "Fall/Winter" catalogs are published annually.

LIST INFORMATION

Quantity Mailed:	50,000,000*
Average Order:	$105
Active Buyers:	N/A
Total List:	over 2 million
List Source:	direct mail

COMMENTS

In 1984, WearGuard launched a 64-page sportswear catalog, Weekend Editions, offering boots, pants, shirts, and foul weather gear. In 1985 two specialty catalogs were added. Corporate Image Maker contains exclusive direct embroidery and silk screened apparel for corporations that utilize premiums, incentives, employee awards and corporate gift programs. WearGuard Identity Apparel is geared toward the service industry, offering personalized aprons, smocks and work-wear cover-ups. Both catalogs reportedly far surpassed management's expectations. Catalog operations have grown faster than other divisions, but WearGuard sees mail order growth and direct sales stabilizing. Retail expansion is planned. The company is exploring new opportunities in cross-marketing with other firms, and seeking acquisitions.

MAXWELL SROGE PUBLISHING, INC.
228 North Cascade Avenue, Suite 307
Colorado Springs, CO 80903-1325
(719) 633-5556
FAX: (719) 633-5585

NEWSLETTERS

Non-Store Marketing Report, bi-weekly newsletter, monitors the entire non-store market for management executives. Vital, expert analysis of up-to-the-minute news, facts and developments. A must for inside information and predictions on this challenging industry. Includes two Company Profiles in each issue, quarterly Trendwatch report and Special Report to analyze significant areas in-depth.

The Catalog Marketer, the "how-to" newsletter on creating and producing catalogs. Industry experts share proven ideas and advice on every area of cataloging: design, art, copy, lists, printing, merchandise, telephone, cost controls, analysis, etc. Quarterly supplement, Business-To-Business Direct Marketer, focuses on areas of special interest to business-to-business and industrial marketers. Published bi-weekly.

INDUSTRY DATA REPORTS

Comprehensive business analyses of Food, Apparel, Sporting Goods and Computer Supplies and Accessories By Mail. Detailed, in-depth look at each industry analyzing the major catalogs down to the square inch, dissecting financial statements, studying the leaders and interviewing key executives. With this information you'll be able to intelligently position your company for maximum profits . . . and with the minimum risk of major mistakes.

MARKE/SROGE COMMUNICATIONS, INC.
233 East Wacker Drive, Suite 3611
Chicago, Illinois   60601
(312) 819-1890
FAX: (312) 819-0411

CATALOG CREATIVE/PRODUCTION

Marke/Sroge Communications is the Chicago based subsidiary of Marke Communications, New York. The company specializes in catalog creative and production work. It is the leading catalog design company and the largest independent contractor of catalog printing in the country. Clients include business-to-business and consumer catalog firms.

OTHER BUSINESS ONE IRW

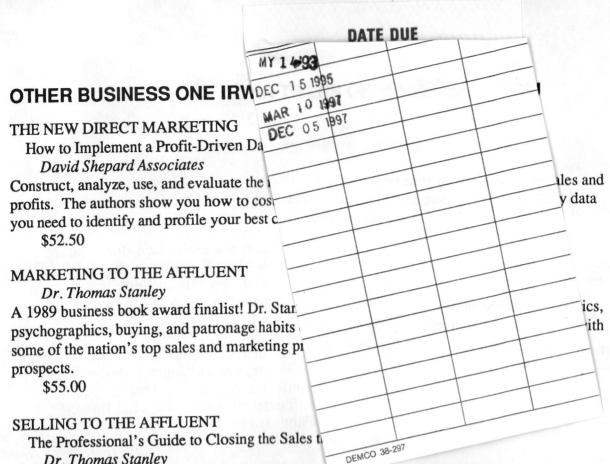

THE NEW DIRECT MARKETING

How to Implement a Profit-Driven Da...
David Shepard Associates

Construct, analyze, use, and evaluate the .... ales and
profits. The authors show you how to cos............ y data
you need to identify and profile your best c...

$52.50

MARKETING TO THE AFFLUENT

Dr. Thomas Stanley

A 1989 business book award finalist! Dr. Star............ ics,
psychographics, buying, and patronage habits .... ith
some of the nation's top sales and marketing pr...
prospects.

$55.00

SELLING TO THE AFFLUENT

The Professional's Guide to Closing the Sales t...
Dr. Thomas Stanley

Improve your closing percentage . . . and income. Dr. Stanley shows you how to approach
wealthy prospects at the moment they are most likely to buy. In Marketing to the Affluent,
Stanley told you how to find them. Now he tells you how to sell to them.
$55.00

PLAYING IN TRAFFIC ON MADISON AVENUE

Tales of Advertising's Glory Years
David J. Herzbrun

After an award-winning 40-year career in the ad business, David Herzbrun chronicles his
adventures and paints a picture of the many characters with whom he worked closely, and who
shaped the "Creative Revolution." Bill Bernbach, David Olgivy, Lou Dorfsman, Bob Levenson,
Helmut Krone, George Lois, and others. Herzbrun shows how they rebelled against the
commonplace, the boring, and the mediocre to create truly memorable advertising.

$24.95

ADVERTISING AGENCY MANAGEMENT

Jay McNamara, former president McCann-Erickson Worldwide

"Jay McNamara has concisely and comprehensively compiled in one volume what every
aspiring agency manager should be learning on the way up and what no advertising manager
should ever forget after he or she gets there."

Allen Rosenshine, Chairman and CEO
BBDO Worldwide Inc.
$29.95

Prices Subject to Change without Notice
Available in fine bookstores and libraries everywhere.